Know Your
Superpowers
Know Your
Future

Using NUMEROLOGY to
unlock your full potential

Suzan Owens

LUMINOUS MOON PRESS
BOULDER, COLORADO

Published by Luminous Moon Press, LLC, Boulder, CO

Cover and interior layout and design by Carolyn J. Oakley, Luminous Moon Design + Press | luminousmoon.com

Cover photo of Antelope Canyon by Suzan Owens | suzanowens.com
Author photo by Rachel Jordan | racheljordanphotography.com

First Edition
First Printing: June 11, 2025

Publication Data
Suzan Owens
Know Your Superpowers, Know Your Future: Using Numerology to Unlock Your Full Potential

ISBN-13: 979-8-9916548-4-5

BODY, MIND & SPIRIT / Numerology — BODY, MIND & SPIRIT / Inspiration & Personal Growth — SELF-HELP TECHNIQUES

Printed and bound in the United States of America

For my grandchildren who have brought so much love into my life:
Brady, Layton, Marcus and Rebekah.

▲

A heartfelt thank you to Carolyn J. Oakley and Luminous Moon Design for believing in me and my writing capability. I am blessed to work with you. Your guidance and enthusiasm has made this a better book. My editor, Valerie Costa deserves special mention for her ability to zero in on my missing punctuation. To my dear, life-long friend, Susan Marra for her insightful feedback and suggestions that shaped this manuscript. Finally, to all the podcasters who invited me to speak on their shows. Their interviews were the impetus for writing this book.

Contents

Introduction

My journey with numerology began with the first book I ever read on Numerology. It captivated me instantly; the information seemed to seep into my soul. I had never encountered something so naturally intuitive and engaging. I was enthralled, quickly discovering books eager to guide me deeper into the mysteries of numerology.

Understanding the vibrations of numbers has transformed my life in countless ways.

I know what my specific gifts—superpowers—are from my life path number. When I add the numbers in my birthdate together and keep adding them together until I have one digit, I get a 3. My life path number, my "superpower," is 3. Those of us with 3 Superpowers are exceptional communicators, thriving through expression. Whether through song, dance, painting, or art, we find our voice. At my core, I am a writer. Discovering this earlier in life would have been invaluable. Identifying our gifts early allows us to harness them, achieving our fullest potential. Our superpowers remain consistent and grow deeper over time, guiding our journey throughout life.

In the first part of this book, I discuss Life Paths or Superpowers 1 through 9 and then explore Master Numbers 11, 22, and 33. Those with a 1 Life Path, are leaders and entrepreneurs. 2s are supportive and intuitive. 3s are the communicators. 4s are diligent and stable. 5s search for freedom and adventure. 6s love home, family and relationships are paramount. 7s are the intellectuals who ask big life questions. 8s love business and learn about the energy of money. 9s are the humanitarians who work for the greater good. All master numbers are numbers with repeating digits and carry a higher vibration of their single-digit counterpart. In any calculation, if a reduced number ends in a repeated digit, do not reduce it any further. 11s' energy is higher than the number 2s and are spiritual messengers. 22s have a legacy to build. 33s are exemplary caregivers and healers.

Knowing my superpower has given me the courage to strive to reach my full potential as a writer and communicator. As a numerologist, I read the numbers. Clients are amazed at how much their numbers reveal about themselves. The guidance they receive is generated from the numbers in their charts and resonates with them on a deep level.

In the second part of this work, we delve into a more dynamic number: the Universal Year number, which transforms with the calendar. 2025 is a 9 year (2+0+2+5=9), indicating the culmination of the numerological cycle. We calculate our Personal Year number by combining our birth month and day with the year's sum, revealing the energy we'll navigate throughout. Each year, starting in January, a new cycle commences. The year 2026, for example, ushers in the freshness of a 1 year.

Numerology functions on a nine-year cycle, with every number reducible to the first nine digits. In a 1 year, I anticipate new beginnings and carefully document my aspirations for the next nine years. A 2 year brings a slower pace, emphasizing cooperation and new partnerships. The 3 year sparks creativity and a zest for life. Meanwhile, a 4 year calls for discipline and structure. The 5 year is about freedom, expansion, and reaching new heights. During a 6 year, home and family take center stage, placing relationships in the limelight. The 7 year beckons for introspection, prompting self-assessment and path alignment. My online business was launched in an 8 year, a period of investment and growth. Finally, a 9 year signifies completion, resolution, and letting go of the past cycle.

INTRODUCTION

Since embracing numerology, I've learned to harness the energy of the numbers, moving in harmony rather than opposition. A 7 year, for instance, is deeply introspective—no time for large ventures. I once struggled against the current, but a profound shift occurred when I aligned with the energy's natural flow instead of resisting it.

Numerology elegantly weaves life's milestones through two fundamental elements: our birthdate and the name inscribed on our birth certificate. From birth, our birthday reveals our life path, a unique collection of talents and gifts, our natural "superpowers." This book only focuses on some of the information we get from the birthdate. My first book, Wisdom of Numerology, is a more comprehensive study of Numerology.

Finally, we further explore personal monthly and daily numbers, providing guidance on the vibrations each day brings. Discover which days are best for productivity, creativity, or financial focus. For example, a 4 day encourages diligent work, whereas a 3 day invites joy and imagination.

In summary, the initial section of this book reveals your innate superpowers from 1 through Master Number 33, while the latter part delves into daily numerical energies, offering a foundation to guide you to work the vibrations of numbers upon which to design your life. As days continuously evolve, so too does numerology, following a 9-year cycle.

Inspired by countless interviews, this book crystallizes the essence of numerology. People are eager to uncover their inherent gifts and strengths, and numerology graciously illuminates this path through the wisdom embedded in our birthdate. So, join me in an exploration of your greatest gifts and how to most effectively use them in this deep dive into your personal numerology.

PART 1
KNOW YOUR
SUPERPOWERS

Life Paths or Superpowers

Your life path number is calculated from your birth date and serves as a constant guide throughout your life. It reflects the unique talents and abilities you were born with, which you will utilize to fulfill your life's purpose. This number also highlights challenges that you are meant to overcome and important lessons to learn during your journey. It is the most significant number among your core numbers, shaping your experiences and personal growth.

To calculate your life path, add all the digits in your birthday. For example:

March 16, 2002

3 + 1 + 6 + 2 + 0 + 0 + 2 = 14   1 + 4 = 5

Or reduce each segment of numbers and add across:

3 + 7 (1+6) + 4 (2+2) = 14   3 + 7 + 4 = 14   1+4 = 5

Life Path 1 Superpowers

A Superpower 1 embodies the essence of leadership and independence, presenting a wealth of benefits paired with unique challenges. Individuals on this path are original and authentic leaders whose success springs from the courage to follow their own ideas and carve out new avenues in life. With a natural flair for initiating and developing projects, you possess the remarkable ability to attract the people and circumstances necessary to bring your visions to fruition. You thrive on adventure, favoring the dynamic over the routine, and your high standards apply equally to yourself and to others. Your diverse array of talents equips you to navigate the complexities of life with creativity and confidence.

Your journey revolves around the pursuit of self-discovery, enhanced self-awareness, and the celebration of your individuality. You are called to stand firm in your leadership role, drawing upon your rebellious nature to learn valuable lessons in true forgiveness.

Achievement and a desire for success provide the foundation of your character, empowering you to overcome obstacles with extraordinary resilience. Your inventive spirit ignites when you fix your sights on a goal, leading you to explore original ideas that set you apart.

You are the center of your Universe, and your conviction in your own path is unwavering. While you possess remarkable managerial capabilities, it is crucial to guard against the pitfalls of micromanagement, which can undermine your effectiveness.

Life offers a grand adventure for those who wisely wield their talents, attracting followers with your visionary perspective and positive outlook. However, it is essential to temper any tendencies toward domination and control; keeping your ego in check will enhance your journey. Remember, patience is a virtue, and you are not an island; you thrive in connection with others.

Moments of surrendering your ego will cultivate profound lessons, helping you appreciate the value of diverse perspectives. Resist the urge to become self-absorbed, and remain mindful of the impact of your strong opinions. By fostering compassion and understanding, you will gather a community of supporters who resonate with your vision. With a strong spiritual connection, you have the capacity to illuminate others and contribute to a collective shift in consciousness.

As a natural-born leader and trailblazer, you are here to master your own abilities while honing your keen intuition. Your unwavering integrity and high standards propel you forward, while your quick mental agility enhances your entrepreneurial acumen. With a magnetic personality that draws people in, they turn to you for guidance and direction. Yet, be aware that the solitary nature of the number 1 may lead to feelings of loneliness at times. Regardless of gender, you embody masculine qualities of strength and assertiveness.

Gather your courage, for challenges will arise on your journey, presenting opportunities for growth and self-improvement. While your fierce independence may lead you to work alone, you excel at contemplating your next great adventure. Embrace challenges wholeheartedly, for it is through these experiences that you learn to believe in yourself and stand tall in your truth. Your competitive nature can drive you to success, yet it requires balance. The greatest achievement lies in understanding our interconnectedness and serving humanity for the greater good.

The characteristics of the number 1 embody those of a leader, inventor, entrepreneur, achiever, and CEO. Being marked by the energy of 1, you are destined to stand confidently on your own. You are called to be assertive yet not aggressive, embodying ambition and self-sufficiency without tipping into arrogance or domineering behavior. Courage and innovation are your hallmarks as you pave your own path of individuality and independence. The energy of 1 is inherently masculine, characterized by focus and rationality; however, it can also manifest as stubbornness, willfulness, and impulsiveness, with a distinct aversion to being overlooked. Through these attributes, your essence as a number 1 shines as a beacon of leadership and pioneering spirit.

Embrace your individuality, cultivate self-awareness, and believe in yourself wholeheartedly. Harness your creative power to pursue those dreams that ignite your spirit. Strive to be a diplomatic leader, mastering your assertiveness while honoring your strength, individuality, and independence throughout your remarkable journey.

Life Path 2 Superpowers

A world rich with emotion and connection unfolds in the journey of those who embody the essence of 2 Superpower. You are the gentle souls who navigate life with kindness and understanding, your hearts attuned to the rhythms of those around you. Deeply emotional, you possess an innate ability to delve into your feelings, feeling them profoundly and reflecting this emotional depth back into your relationships. This profound empathy is a superpower that enables you to forge bonds that are both meaningful and lasting.

On this path, you find joy in companionship and truly thrive in the presence of others. Being a supportive partner, friend, or collaborator is not just a role; it's a natural expression of your loving nature. Your ability to understand and validate others' feelings makes you an excellent listener and confidant. You have a special gift for making people feel valued and cherished, using your gentle demeanor to create supportive environments where open communication flourishes. In this capacity, your patience and understanding become vital, transforming them into the cornerstones of your relationships.

While the 2 has many strengths, one of its most notable is the incredible intuition that guides you through life's complexities. This intuitive sense often expands into deeper realms, transcending the ordinary to tap into psychic and mediumistic abilities. When connected to your divine guidance, you become a fountain of wisdom and inspiration, capable of offering invaluable insights to others. Drawing from this wellspring of intuitive knowledge is

KNOW YOUR SUPERPOWERS, KNOW YOUR FUTURE

pivotal, especially when supporting friends, family, or colleagues. Maintaining your inner balance and equilibrium becomes essential, as it enables you to provide care without becoming overwhelmed by those you support.

Harmony is the essence of life path number 2. You may find yourself continuously striving for balance, seeking cooperation and collaboration over the often-chaotic nature of competition. Your innate diplomacy allows you to navigate through conflict with grace, making you an exemplary peacemaker. You have a unique ability to analyze situations and discern the best approach, often acting as a mediator to restore equilibrium when tensions arise. The calm energy that emanates from you serves to soothe distressed hearts and minds, drawing people toward your magnetic and gentle presence.

This path thrives in partnerships, whether personal or professional. Working with others amplifies your capabilities, and you shine brightest when contributing to shared goals and visions. Your detail-oriented nature helps you pick up on the nuances that others may overlook, leading to a comprehensive understanding of the dynamics at play within any collaboration. However, despite your strengths, you must remember that surrendering too much of yourself can lead to burnout. You must honor your own needs and establish boundaries to ensure your own well-being.

Learning to trust your intuition is a fundamental lesson for those on the life path of 2. Each time you listen to your inner voice, you empower it to grow stronger. This enhances your ability to advise and support others, because you are not just speaking from personal experience but from a place of divine wisdom. The power of your intuitive insights allows you to foretell the potential outcomes of situations, providing essential guidance.

However, it is important for you sensitive souls to remain cautious of becoming overly critical or absorbed in others' emotions. You need to set limits and boundaries, learning to say no when you start to feel your energies being depleted or when someone's demands overshadow your own needs. This balance of caring for yourself while supporting others is crucial for your happiness and effectiveness as a partner and friend.

Feminine energy flows through the life path 2, emphasizing receptivity and adaptability. You embody these qualities naturally, making you skilled at navigating life's complexities, supporting and uplifting those around you. Your superpowers lie not only in your ability to connect emotionally but also in your capacity to help others realize their visions and dreams.

Ultimately, life path number 2 teaches the significance of cooperation, patience, and compassion. As you journey through life, you embrace your role as nurturer, diplomat, and mediator while continually learning the vital lesson of self-care.

The characteristics of the number 2 are those of a diplomat, moderator, peacekeeper, counselor, artist, and healer. As a person infused with the energy of 2, you excel as a partner, embodying support, understanding, and tact. You are called to be nurturing and diplomatic, avoiding criticism and co-dependence.

The energy of 2 is inherently feminine, characterized by its receptivity, intuition, and captivating attention to detail. However, it may also manifest as self-consciousness, oversensitivity, or meddlesomeness. Trust your intuitive nature, but remember to set clear boundaries and maintain balance in all aspects of your life.

You are guided to establish reciprocal relationships, ensuring mutual security and trust. Your sensitivity enables you to perceive the nuances in human interactions, fostering connections that are both meaningful and enduring. Let your intuitive sense lead the way, and strive to bring harmony and peace to those you touch. Through these traits, you resonate as a beacon of harmony and empathy, inspiring others with your compassionate and balanced approach to life.

By embracing your sensitivity and intuition, you illuminate the lives of others and, in doing so, create a harmonious world that reflects your loving essence. The more you honor your own needs alongside those of others, the more profound your connections become, leading to a life rich with meaningful relationships and fulfilled dreams. With each step you take, you create a ripple effect of harmony that nurtures not only yourself but the Universe around you.

Life Path 3 Superpowers

Cheerful, optimistic, and brimming with enthusiasm for life, a Superpower 3 embodies the essence of inspiration and serves as a catalyst for change, encouraging others to savor the beauty of existence. Your adaptability shines through as you consistently generate new ideas, driven by a desire to be loved and a capacity to feel a wide array of emotions. With a keen and clever mind, you prefer the freedom of exploration over the confines of rigid structure, allowing your versatile and energetic self-expression to form the foundation of your identity.

Yet, as vibrant as you are, there exists a penchant for self-criticism, impatience, and occasional intolerance. Typically a visual thinker, you possess an open heart and a preference for an easygoing life, and this carefree attitude can sometimes lead to procrastination and neglect of responsibilities. Insightful and perceptive, you occasionally indulge in drama and gossip, adding a layer of complexity to your multifaceted nature. The harmonious integration of the pioneering spirit of number 1 and the nurturing qualities of number 2 enables you to manifest your ideas into the tangible realm, effortlessly shifting concepts without losing your rhythm.

Your purpose is deeply rooted in living joyfully and uplifting those around you. Creative, spontaneous, and eager to embrace life's adventures, you approach every moment with a vivid imagination and infectious enthusiasm that inspires everyone you encounter. Utilize your magnetic personality and optimistic outlook to motivate others, sharing your boundless artistry as a vibrant expression of your joy. Recognized as the quintessential communicator, you are destined to articulate your thoughts and feelings with clarity and passion. Embrace this gift by learning to wield your words thoughtfully and authentically.

Your visual talents allow you to express your emotions through various artistic mediums, illuminating your surroundings with your creations. You understand the healing power of laughter, and through your vibrant happiness, you bring joy to countless lives. Innately optimistic and resilient, you navigate obstacles with grace, and when you share your heartfelt creative ideas, you fulfill your life's purpose. Make every endeavor an expression of your joy, and allow that energy to guide you, as success will inevitably follow through dedication and commitment.

While the natural charm of number 3 often invites financial opportunities, it's essential to remain grounded and avoid letting fortune slip through your fingers. Embrace a light-hearted approach to life and guard against allowing sensitivity to criticism or sarcasm to overshadow your spirit. Be mindful of negativity, which can lead to feelings of lethargy and discouragement. Remember, your words hold immense power; gossip, exaggeration, and complaints can divert you from your true path.

The characteristics of the number 3 are those of an artist, musician, speaker, teacher, salesperson, and visionary. As someone graced with the energy of 3, you embody creativity, spontaneity, and versatility, lifting others with your optimism and artistic flair. Let your creative spirit soar, and approach life with a sense of adventure.

The number 3 is the harmonious unification of the originating 1 energy with the nurturing 2 energy, embodying the very essence of creation. You are called to be imaginative and adaptable, channeling your enthusiasm into meaningful pursuits rather than allowing it to become dissipated or unfocused.

While your exuberance can sometimes lead to drama or criticism, embrace your ability to entertain and inspire. You thrive on life's adventures and eschew routine and the mundane. Cultivate a joyful, creative lifestyle rooted in discipline, allowing your visionary nature to flourish. With this dynamic energy, you shine as a beacon of creativity and joy, inspiring those around you with your zest for life and innovative spirit.

However, you possess a resilient spirit capable of recovering from setbacks, and when you channel your endless talents to uplift humanity, the rewards will be both joyful and abundant. Embrace your authentic self, find delight in creativity, and let your unwavering light inspire those around you to join you on this beautiful journey of life.

Life Path 4 Superpowers

As a 4 Superpower, you embody the essence of the builder and creator, transforming ideas into tangible realities. Honest, dependable, and practical, you approach life with a serious-minded and pragmatic outlook. Your innate desire is to construct a solid foundation that supports your visions, ensuring that everything you create is both useful and meaningful. Unlike those who thrive on the abstract, you prefer to hold and mold your creations, making them real and accessible.

Industrious and capable, you continuously seek solutions, embodying a conscientious spirit that values order and structure. With a deep-rooted appreciation for the laws of the Universe and science, you prefer to follow rules and regulations precisely. Your foresight enables you to see plans through to fruition, cultivating substantial relationships built on loyalty and honesty. Persistent and dedicated, you approach tasks with steadfast commitment, albeit with an aversion to change and inconsistency. While your dedication is commendable, there are moments when you might come across as stubborn or rigid, reluctant to be rushed or pushed into decisions.

Your thoughtful nature leads you to visualize the entire plan before diving in, allowing you to navigate complexities with patient persistence and a strong moral compass. You firmly believe that "you get what you pay for," which informs your practical approach to projects. Solution-oriented and dignified, you prioritize building lasting endeavors, valuing the mechanics of how things work over impulsivity or gamble.

Your path as a diligent worker is marked by stability. You comprehend the significance of adhering to rules and fostering loyalty, laying the groundwork for a robust career built on reliability and responsibility. Organized and efficient, punctuality is paramount in all your ventures. Every accomplishment you achieve is founded on the strong pillars you erect, so clarity of intention is critical to your success.

In many ways, you exemplify the qualities of the tortoise: steady and unwavering, unfazed by the quick pace of others. Dedication is your hallmark, and you thrive on the challenge of bringing order to chaos, making you an exceptional manager and leader. A life path 4 teaches the invaluable lesson of establishing a secure foundation upon which to build your dreams. As you align with your life path, you actively create the aspirations you hold in your heart.

You recognize the profound importance of perseverance, organization, and commitment. Known as the worker bees, those on this path excel at transforming ideas into reality, investing time and effort to honor their successes. You embody the "nose to the grindstone" ethos, enjoying the harmony that comes with loyalty and patience. However, it is essential to remain open to new perspectives, as your tendency toward rigidity can sometimes cloud your vision.

The characteristics of the number 4 are those of a business manager, lawyer, accountant, administrator, builder, scientist, and worker-bee. As someone infused with the energy of 4, you are goal-oriented, diligent, and focused on achievement. Your determination and productivity are unmatched, driving you to success, yet it's essential to remain adaptable and open-minded.

Embrace your natural ability to be focused and organized but avoid becoming rigid or unyielding. Occasionally, it's beneficial to lighten up and consider perspectives outside the box. Your dedicated and dependable nature makes you exceptionally skilled in handling practical and mundane tasks. You take great care in ensuring that every detail is attended to with precision and thoughtfulness.

While you thrive on stability and structure, be mindful of avoiding argumentativeness or becoming tedious. Embrace change as an opportunity rather than a disruption. Your practical spirit is invaluable; it allows you to excel in achieving objectives and building solid foundations.

The 4 energy equips you to manage and administer with skill and precision. You are a master at navigating life's challenges, and as you cultivate this balance between diligence and adaptability, you will continue to inspire with your steadfast, reliable approach to life's adventures.

At times, you may find yourself overly serious, lacking sensitivity, or leaning into workaholism. It is vital to take time to celebrate your accomplishments and recognize your achievements, for self-acknowledgement fosters growth. The vibration of the number 4 can also indicate a need for health awareness; thus, taking special care of your body is crucial. By balancing your dedication with moments of celebration and flexibility, you will unlock the full potential of your remarkable journey on Life Path 4.

Life Path 5 Superpowers

As a bearer of the 5 Superpower, you possess an insatiable curiosity about life and are driven by a yearning to break free from restrictions and embrace a realm of complete freedom. Unconventional and fiercely independent, you march to the beat of your own drum, thriving on the exhilaration of constant change. Routine and the mundane are not your allies; rather, you are adaptable and drawn to anything new and different. Your passion for life's experiences, particularly those that bring joy, fuels your adventurous spirit, though you may occasionally indulge impulsively.

You harness a magnetic personality that naturally attracts followers, yet you often struggle to remain committed to any one endeavor for too long. This path is defined by progress and offers immense potential for growth. As a gifted promoter, you find great fulfillment in sharing life lessons and enlightening others. Your charm and keen wit position you as a natural entertainer, captivating those around you with your vibrant energy. However, the continuous fluctuation of your lifestyle can lead to ups and downs, often resulting in transient relationships.

To navigate this dynamic existence, patience, tolerance, and a degree of moderation will serve you well. You are a great explorer, eager to experience every facet of life, and others often find themselves living vicariously through your adventures. Your competitive nature, bold spirit, and desire for autonomy allow you to embrace life on your own terms, making you a master of opportunity in public endeavors.

While your versatility and vibrant disposition are commendable, they can sometimes lead to inconsistency, thoughtlessness, and a lack of reliability. Your lightheartedness, optimism, and intriguing persona make you endlessly interesting to those around you, allowing you to adapt quickly to any situation and find your rhythm without missing a beat.

You are the quintessential freedom-seeker and adventurer, with expansion as the foundation of your life. A lover of experiences, you yearn to explore everything life has to offer. Born an explorer, you want to immerse yourself in each new venture, embracing a life filled with lessons learned through firsthand experience rather than following the path laid out by others. Careers in travel or those that keep you in the public eye align beautifully with your skill set, and your ability to absorb a myriad of experiences renders you a quick and versatile learner.

Embrace the surprises that sudden changes may bring, for they present remarkable opportunities for growth. Flexibility and adaptability are your steadfast companions as you navigate the vast array of experiences that life unfolds before you. As a sensual being, you desire to explore through all five senses, fully immersing yourself in the richness of existence.

Inconsistency and change are the only constants in your life, so approach each day as a new adventure, free from judgment. You are a trailblazer, breaking old conventions and carving out new paths. A talented communicator and gifted motivator, you make an exceptional teacher or speaker. To attain mastery, however, focus and commitment are essential. Moderation and discipline will provide the stability and success you seek.

The characteristics of the number 5 are those of an adventurer, promoter, actor, public figure, and salesperson. As someone graced with the energy of 5, you are a freedom seeker with an insatiable desire to live life to its fullest. Embrace adaptability and the rich tapestry of diversity, yet it is vital to discern when to remain steadfast rather than changing merely for change's sake.

With the rapid energy of expansive growth, you are naturally drawn to adventure and competition. Your spirit thrives on the unconventional and you often eschew routine and the mundane. However, it's important to stay centered, grounded, and disciplined amidst this whirlwind of possibilities.

The 5 vibration is characterized by your sensuality, charisma, and influence, but be mindful of tendencies toward procrastination or addiction. Continue to channel your vibrant energy into meaningful pursuits, crafting a life filled with vibrant stories and impactful experiences. By balancing spontaneity with stability, you will navigate life's journey with grace and leave an indelible mark on the world around you.

Live fully in the moment, resisting the temptation to dwell on the past or fret about the future. Be mindful of your impulses, ensuring that you do not scatter your energies or succumb to distractions. Cultivate an idea to fruition and experience the fulfillment of completion rather than allowing unfinished projects to linger. Your possibilities are boundless; the true reward in your journey lies in sharing the wisdom gleaned from your life experiences with others. The number 5 symbolizes expansion, change, and freedom; embrace these truths, and allow your adventurous spirit to thrive as you dance through life with exuberance and authenticity.

Life Path 6 Superpowers

As a Superpower 6, you embody the essence of responsibility and a service-oriented heart, making you the consummate caretaker. Fueled by a profound sense of duty to humanity, you find joy in serving others, yet it is crucial for you to establish boundaries; without them, you risk being taken advantage of by those who may not recognize your precious emotional depth. Your love for home and family is paramount, with your greatest desire being to both love and be loved in return.

The principles of truth and justice serve as the bedrock of your values, and you tend to gravitate toward calmness and comfort rather than the allure of high fashion. Your appreciation for the beauty of nature in all its forms enriches your spirit and enhances your emotional well-being. While you enjoy order and a structured schedule, you also recognize the importance of progress and change; these elements of life energize you.

As a sensitive and emotionally aware individual, you derive inspiration and strength from peaceful environments. You have a keen appreciation for art and the beauty that surrounds you, and your ability to listen makes you an excellent counselor. Your happiness blossoms most profoundly when you are surrounded by loved ones, and you take pride in being the cornerstone of your family.

Possessing a strong sense of justice, you advocate for the vulnerable and needy, truly embodying the spirit of a humanitarian.

However, there may be times when your caring nature veers into the territory of being a busybody or excessively stubborn. Your idealism can lead to judgmental tendencies, and as a perfectionist, you may set standards that are difficult to meet. Yet, you excel as an advisor and supporter, providing stability and care to those in your circle.

The number 6 is inherently linked to love; romantic, caring, and benevolent. Your generosity and kindness shine through as you dedicate your life to meaningful relationships founded on love and beauty. True success emerges when you assist others, and your desire to contribute to the greater good solidifies your role as a compassionate humanitarian. Home and family hold profound significance for you, making it vital to strike a balance between your needs and those of others.

As a nurturing parent and understanding partner, you epitomize the ideals of support and care. It's essential to remember to prioritize your own well-being; by caring for yourself with the same devotion you offer others, your life will be enriched. A relationship that ends in divorce is not a failure, but a valuable opportunity to learn more about love and connection. Every relationship comes with its own set of challenges and growth opportunities.

You appreciate luxury in your surroundings, expressing your artistic talents to create a beautiful home that reflects your aesthetic sensibilities. Your strong character is admirable, yet it's important to avoid wasting energy on controlling tendencies or a burdensome sense of pride. Martyrdom does not suit your spirit; it's impossible to please everyone all the time. Quiet the critical voice within and embrace the reality that not everything needs to be perfect.

The characteristics of the number 6 are those of a caregiver, service-oriented individual, responsible counselor, and healer. As someone imbued with the energy of 6, you are a stable and nurturing soul who finds fulfillment in being of service to others. Embrace your strength in creating a loving and harmonious environment, though it is crucial to avoid the pitfalls of codependency or becoming a martyr.

Your heart yearns for a safe and harmonious home where the bonds of family and love are cherished and nurtured. While you thrive in stability and security, you may find discomfort in instability and unfamiliarity. To flourish, establish healthy and harmonious relationships both in your personal and professional life.

Balance your desire to care for others with your own needs; it is important not to overextend yourself. By maintaining this equilibrium, you will continue to shine as a gentle and stable force, inspiring others with your compassion and devotion. In doing so, you fulfill your role as a caretaker who brings balance and warmth to the world around you.

Respecting your own boundaries is essential. While your core desire to assist others is commendable, understanding the difference between genuine help and interference is crucial. Every individual, including yourself, has their own life lessons to learn. Ultimately, your journey is about cultivating a deep relationship with yourself, taking responsibility for your own happiness and well-being. Love, appreciate, and respect yourself and you will find the fulfillment you seek on your remarkable path.

Life Path 7 Superpowers

As a bearer of the 7 Superpower, you possess a unique ability to bridge the material world with the unseen, delving into the depths of existence with an investigator's keen eye. Your analytical prowess forms the very foundation of your superpowers, driving you to continually seek deeper meanings in life. The pursuit of wisdom is your ultimate goal, and you hold both yourself and others to high standards as a perfectionist. While your inclination is to work best in solitude, free from distractions, you are a nonconformist who trusts your own decisions and value systems above all.

You find solace in a select few personal and intimate relationships, appreciating the depth they bring rather than seeking broad social connections. Your affinity for the finer things in life drives your desire for quality over quantity. You prefer to approach projects in your own unique way, adhering steadfastly to your own set of rules and values. Your psychic and intuitive abilities are latent superpowers waiting to be developed. Immersing yourself in nature rejuvenates your spirit and strengthens your connection to your intuitive side.

A lifelong learner, you are intrigued by the mysteries of existence and are guided by your intuition. Faith in the divine enhances your journey, as does access to a good education and a well-stocked library, essential tools for your quest. Skepticism is not your ally; rather, you do your best work in isolation, allowing your creative mind and understanding of universal wisdom to flourish.

You thrive on uncovering hidden truths, feeling a profound sense of achievement when you gain new insights into the deeper meanings of life. Adept at quickly assessing situations, you are not particularly sentimental or romantic; your focus leans more toward exploration and understanding.

You are a consummate seeker, fueled by an unquenchable thirst for wisdom and clarity regarding life's fundamental questions: Who am I? Why am I here? With strong analytical skills and a sharp intellect, you reject superficial explanations and strive for truth in all things. Because 7 is the number associated with metaphysics, you embody the essence of inquiry as an observer, researcher, and skeptic who shuns the crowded noise of the world. Your philosophical approach to life often finds you engaged in quiet contemplation.

Technology is a realm where you excel, resonating with the innovative and the intellectual, while metaphysical pursuits guide you on a spiritual odyssey to unravel the mysteries of life. Your life lesson revolves around connecting to your spiritual guidance and having the faith to follow it. Although you may appreciate moments in the spotlight, it is solitude that restores your balance. As a private individual, intimacy can occasionally pose a challenge, leaving you feeling isolated.

It is important to be mindful of tendencies toward excessive criticism or skepticism, as well as the potential to become overly absorbed in detail. Sarcasm and cynicism may emerge as aspects of your character to guard against. While you may not always be forthcoming, it's essential to communicate openly and avoid omitting valuable insights. Your time for rejuvenation is best spent engaging with nature, where introspective walks can revitalize your spirit.

The characteristics of the number 7 are those of a seeker, researcher, spiritualist, analyst, philosopher, and consultant. As someone enriched with the energy of 7, you are a truth seeker, constantly on a quest to uncover life's meaning and forge a spiritual path. Embrace your private and philosophical nature without becoming overly reclusive or critical.

Your analytical and meditative inclinations allow you to dive deep into reflection, yet it is essential to remain approachable and guard against pessimism or cynicism. You are drawn to profound spiritual connections and often require solitude to nurture your inner world. While you may shy away from the limelight and avoid demanding social interactions or relationships, you thrive in moments of quiet introspection.

Being among the most metaphysical of numbers, you are encouraged to find solace in nature, allowing its tranquility to deepen your meditative practice. By balancing your need for solitude with openness to the world around you, you can illuminate the depths of existence with your insightful and spiritual wisdom.

As you navigate your path, remember not to retreat too far into your own world, as this can inadvertently push others away and hinder your ability to form genuine friendships and connections. This journey offers profound lessons as you ponder the deeper significance of life, and the ultimate reward lies in sharing your insights and wisdom with humanity. Embrace your gifts and allow your superpowers to illuminate the lives of those around you.

Life Path 8 Superpowers

As a bearer of the Superpower 8, you excel at transforming the intangible into the tangible, wielding the unique ability to manifest ideas into reality. Born into this life with an innate desire for wisdom and knowledge, your journey is shaped by the intention to share these insights with others in the future. You embody the principle of "you reap what you sow," stepping confidently into the realm of mastery and influence. Typically extroverted, you understand that following established rules is essential to achieving success.

Your character is marked by good judgment and integrity, establishing you as a powerful force in your endeavors. With a profound desire for achievement across all levels—spiritual, mental, physical, and emotional—you recognize that balance in these areas enhances your potential for greatness. Through deep spiritual understanding, you will achieve remarkable success built on the foundations of strength, courage, stability, and equilibrium.

You possess an innate loyalty and honesty that makes you a true friend, though your perspective often transcends romantic inclinations as you embrace the bigger picture. Enjoy the fruits of your labor, but remember that true success requires a commitment to the greater good. Your life must have a clear destiny and purpose to fuel your achievements. With a keen sense of judgment about people, business, and life's intricacies, you are here to bring balance to all things.

Being driven and achievement-oriented, determination is key to your success. A solid understanding of financial management is essential, as you are a natural executive and promoter. Others perceive you as a leader and authority figure, recognizing your mastery in manifestation.

The characteristics of the number 8 encompass power, authority, ambition, leadership, wealth, prosperity, excellence, success, balance, and harmony. You are a natural manager, attracting abundance through your strong problem-solving skills and business acumen. Fueled by a potential for self-mastery, you expand the visions born from the energy of the number 7, propelling them toward humanitarian service associated with the number 9.

As a natural-born business executive, you exude confidence and command authority in your actions. Your commitment to self-improvement shapes your success, as the tools you acquire throughout your journey support your quest for mastery. The energy of 8 is demanding, inviting you to strive continually for the best version of yourself.

Embrace your visionary spirit, take charge, and exercise your entrepreneurial skills. People look to you as an authority figure, valuing your superior judgment and insight. Understand the true significance of money and the quality of life. You may find that while you possess a natural aptitude for financial matters, there might also be struggles. Life will provide the essential experiences to help you fully grasp the value of financial resources.

If your successes are built on shaky foundations of greed, deception, or negativity, they may be fleeting. Your journey teaches resilience, empowering you to recover from setbacks with grace. The essence of 8 is stability, which is required in all areas of life. Strive to maintain your equilibrium and seek harmony in both your career and family life, even when the allure of the office calls to you more strongly.

This is your lifetime to harmonize the spiritual and material realms, living with integrity and honesty. The rewards for such alignment are profound, and maintaining a positive mindset will enhance your journey. Remember that what you put into the Universe will return to you: "As above, so below." Ultimately, you will reap what you sow, and with your Superpower 8, the possibilities for abundance and fulfillment are boundless.

Life Path 9 Superpowers

As a bearer of the 9 Superpower, you embark on a transformative journey, free from the attachments of material desires, to illuminate a higher vibrational existence for humanity. Your life is a tapestry woven from the lessons learned in previous lifetimes: creation, expansion, creativity, structure, change, responsibility, research, power, and ultimately, service to all. Your paramount goal is to share your profound wisdom and elevate the collective consciousness of humanity. Through experiences of loss and the process of letting go, you master the art of detachment. You exude generosity, often to a fault, and possess an idealistic vision that allows you to perceive the noblest aspects of humanity.

Guided by compassion, unconditional love, and forgiveness, you thrive when you are in the service of others. While your perfectionist tendencies can lead to high expectations, it is essential to learn to release these ideals, especially regarding those around you. Your journey may present emotional roller coasters, but the practice of detachment will help you navigate these transitions with grace. Your talents naturally gravitate toward the spiritual realm, where, through selfless service, you will reap the rewards of your efforts. Staying aligned with a higher moral code and remaining focused will ensure that you remain on your destined path.

You are characterized by a profound understanding of the interconnectedness of all things, reflecting the essence of Universal Love and compassion. The world's challenges weigh heavily on your heart, and you are often convinced that you hold the keys to the solutions. Adhering to a strict moral code and high ideals, you consistently practice the golden rule: Do unto others as you would have them do to you. It is a source of confusion when others fail to follow this edict. The underlying energy in all your endeavors is focused on uplifting humanity, and you embody the spirit of a compassionate humanitarian.

As you navigate your path, it is vital to temper your perfectionism with acceptance. Rise above the melodrama that can sometimes ensnare you, enabling you to devote your energies to making the world a better place. By releasing judgments and embracing forgiveness, you enhance your life journey. Your deep reverence for Universal Love leads you to acknowledge the divine energy present in all things. Your appreciation for beauty in all its forms is profound, and you strive to raise Universal Consciousness to embrace love in all its manifestations.

Forgiveness, compassion, acceptance, and unconditional love are the guiding forces that propel you forward. Recognizing your connection to everything around you is essential, as the number 9 symbolizes completion. This realization may bring about the conclusion of events, relationships, experiences, and various projects in your life. As an old soul, you are finishing tasks from many lifetimes and are committed to the service of all humanity, with a fervent desire to contribute positively to the world.

This journey embodies Universal-God energy, instilling in you a deep quest for understanding. Embrace the practice of forgiveness, unconditional love, and self-acceptance for yourself and others, just as they are. The energies embodied in the numbers 3, 6, and 9 reflect the various aspects of love, creativity, and service within your life.

The characteristics of the number 9 are those of a humanitarian, minister, spiritualist, psychic, community leader, bodyworker, artist, and actor. As someone imbued with the energy of 9, you are a dreamer who yearns for universal harmony and the betterment of humankind. Embrace your idealism, understanding, forgiveness, and tolerance, while being cautious not to become aimless or overly gullible.

You are drawn to the pursuit of a global impact, aspiring to elevate the consciousness of the world around you. Adhering to the Golden Rule, your benevolent, compassionate, and creative spirit guides you, although at times you may find focus elusive. Restrictions and uncontrolled emotions are unwelcome companions on your journey, as you strive to break free and inspire others.

By channeling your creative energies and compassionate nature, you have the potential to enact significant change and leave a lasting mark on the world. Let your ideals illuminate the way as you work towards a grand vision of harmony and collective upliftment.

In essence, the characteristics of the number 9 include universal love, altruism, compassion, benevolence, the creative artist's spirit, and the relentless seeker of Universal Harmony. However, be mindful of the potential for aimlessness, gullibility, and feelings of powerlessness. While your generous nature shines brightly, it can lead you to be overly idealistic or indiscreet. You may find yourself grappling with pessimism, intolerance, unforgiveness, or temperamental behaviors. Through awareness and growth, you can harness your superpowers to foster a legacy of love and healing for humanity.

Master Number Superpowers

In your calculations, if you see a number with a repeated digit, or Master Number, you don't reduce it. It remains the repeated digit and carries a higher vibration than its single-digit counterpart. If you choose to accept this gift from the Divine, your life will include a more universal focus. Should you refuse this opportunity, you will live with the energy of the single digit. For instance, 11 reduces to a 2. The 11 is a spiritual messenger and the 2 carries the energy of cooperation and diplomacy. You have the option of accepting the higher vibration of 11 or accepting the energy of the 2. We all have free will and this is your choice.

Life Path 11 Superpowers

As an embodiment of the 11 Superpower, you are a lightworker destined to elevate and expand consciousness. Harmony and balance are essential in your journey, serving as the cornerstones for fulfilling your profound purpose. You represent the ideal to which others aspire, inspiring admiration and respect from those around you. It is important, however, not to be lost in the minutiae; instead, maintain a focus on the bigger picture as you navigate your life's path. Your career serves as a platform for you to express your wisdom, knowledge, and expertise, allowing you to shine as an inspirational leader capable of guiding others toward enlightenment.

Meditation and prayer are vital practices for connecting with your inner wisdom, intuition, and guidance. While maintaining balance may present its challenges, your journey as a teacher, spiritual advisor, and counselor offers you a chance to be a genuine source of inspiration. With natural psychic and intuitive abilities, you possess the power to uplift and inspire humanity through the sharing of your spiritual insights. Embrace a positive mindset and guard against the distractions of self-criticism, remembering that you possess the free will to navigate your life's purpose. Should you choose, you might opt for a more subdued existence as a number 2, yet the potential for notoriety as a public figure remains within your reach.

As you walk the path of the Spiritual Messenger in search of enlightenment, honor your intuition and follow its guidance for a fulfilling life journey. Your charismatic nature draws seekers who look to you for inspiration and spiritual truths. Embrace a strong moral code, diligently adhering to the Laws of the Universe as you forge ahead on this sacred path. With the soul of a humanitarian, your life finds its greatest rewards in selfless service to others. This isn't a path of egocentrism; true success flourishes when you remain humble, even amidst potential celebrity status.

The energy of the number 11 represents the desire to balance masculine and feminine forces within yourself. You are a beacon of light, striving to illuminate the world with harmony and peace. Your innate intuition guides you as you seek higher consciousness, while your ability to uplift and teach others enriches the lives of those fortunate enough to cross your path. As the Spiritual Messenger, you create a profound impact on the world around you, drawing abundance into your life when you embody a high moral standard.

The characteristics of the Master Number 11/2 are those of an inventor, counselor, minister, celebrity, spiritualist, writer, and teacher. As someone blessed with the energy of 11, you embody both the foundational qualities of 2 and a heightened spiritual vibration brought by the double 1. This is a profound gift bestowed by the Universe, alongside the responsibility to follow this masterful path.

With this master number, you possess the remarkable capability to elevate humanity's consciousness. However, you have the free will to choose whether to embrace this higher vibration; you may instead align with the nurturing energy of 2. The choice to operate with the master number is yours to make. As an intuitive messenger, your purpose is to inspire and uplift humanity with your spiritual insights.

The energy of 11 is highly intuitive, transformative, and philosophical, yet it can also lead to overstimulation and heightened sensitivity. You tend to shy away from anything that imposes limitations or causes distress. Enlightenment is your ultimate goal, which then allows you to step into the role of a spiritual teacher. With Master Number 11, you integrate higher consciousness energy with the harmonious qualities of 2, creating a path of profound purpose and impact.

However, you may also opt for the gentler yet equally significant energy of number 2, should you choose to express yourself in that manner. Ultimately, the journey of an 11 invites you to embrace your gifts fully, illuminating the path for others while enjoying the rewards that come from a life dedicated to service and enlightenment.

Life Path 22 Superpowers

The calling of a 22 Superpower is profound: to establish a solid foundation for the collective. Embrace the surrender to higher influences and follow this guidance with unwavering determination, cooperation, and commitment throughout your lifetime. As a grand visionary, you possess the remarkable ability and endurance to take projects from inception to tangible completion, aiming to construct a new framework for consciousness on our planet. You carry the duty of uniting humanity for a brighter future, meticulously planning and executing your vision with precision.

This journey may lead you down diverse career paths, each offering wisdom and experience that will ultimately serve the greater good. As a beacon of inspiration, you set a fine example for others to emulate. Think on a global scale; by believing in yourself and focusing on the highest good for all, your path to success will unfold.

The energy of 22 embodies a higher vibration of the number 4, endowing you with advanced skills that elevate your presence. You are a Master Builder, an exceptional visionary who seamlessly integrates spiritual wisdom into practical realms for humanitarian pursuits. Methodical, disciplined, and diligent, you showcase masterful organizational abilities. The potent energy of the double 2 amplifies this vibration, enhancing your intuition and fostering harmony in your endeavors.

As a Master Builder, you are dedicated to forging a legacy that resonates with a greater purpose. Your creations are vast and imbued with the desire to reconstruct the world on a foundation grounded in spiritual principles for the well-being of humanity. You bring higher wisdom into practical application, embodying a blend of practicality and mysticism complemented by a deep understanding of sacred geometry.

You are the architect of your own reality, here to serve humanity with grace and purpose. Your diligence and steadfast commitment, combined with your spiritual insights, earn you an extraordinary reputation as an authority in your field. While you may exhibit tendencies toward control or arrogance, you also possess a sensitive and intuitive side, reminding you of the power of empathy.

The characteristics of the Master Number 22/4 are those of a global entrepreneur, world leader, public developer, master builder, producer, and CEO. As someone endowed with the extraordinary energy of 22, you embody the foundational qualities of 4 but with an elevated spiritual vibration from the double 2. This gift from the Universe comes with the profound responsibility to follow the master number path.

With Master Number 22, you possess the unique ability to leave a legacy that can uplift humanity. However, the choice remains yours—to embrace this higher vibration or to align with the steadfast nature of 4. To harness the master number's potential is a decision to integrate higher consciousness with practical missions.

As a 22 individual, you unite visionary thinking with tangible actions, building a lasting legacy. Your energy is committed, tenacious, and enthusiastic, always seeing the big picture. Yet, be mindful of the tendency to become a workaholic or to overextend yourself. Often a forward thinker, you may at times feel misunderstood or underappreciated. Embrace the Master Number 22 as an integration of higher consciousness with the stable energy of 4, leading you toward a path of immense purpose and impact.

However, should you choose to pursue only your own selfish gains, you may find your success limited. Through your exceptional ability to harmonize spiritual insights with the material world, you

46

hold the potential to make the world a better place. Embrace your role with humility and dedication, and you will undoubtedly leave a lasting impact as you

Life Path 33 Superpowers

As a holder of the 33 Superpower, you embody Universal joy and compassion for all living beings, representing the essence of love in its highest form. Your purpose is to elevate humanity's capacity for unconditional love, inspiring others through your profound wisdom and nurturing spirit. You are destined to teach and to uplift those around you, particularly serving as a guiding light for educators and healers. With a remarkable ability to facilitate healing, you are encouraged to surrender to Universal guidance and use your gifts to support others on their journeys.

Your path involves a deep understanding of self-sacrifice, which requires you to work diligently without selfish motives. To genuinely serve those in need, mastering your own emotions is essential. It is only when you have navigated your inner landscape that you can effectively assist others. At your core, you are a seeker of peace and love, aspiring to foster harmony in the world.

As a joyfully compassionate intuitive, you are here to uplift and heal humanity. This elevated spiritual vibration brings forth multiple Divine blessings, enhancing your ability to impart a higher consciousness of love to those you encounter. As a loving caregiver, you possess legendary skills that apply to individuals of all ages, using your nurturing nature to promote well-being. Your driving force is unconditional love, transcending material gain and worldly fame.

You possess an innate ability to recognize the goodness in people, and you hold a deep intolerance for injustice. By adhering to Universal Laws, you bring a heightened spiritual vibration to humanity. However, be mindful not to become ensnared in the struggles of the world, as doing so may dilute your energy. Practice detachment and allow your love to flow freely, embodying the essence of the 33/6 healing vibration.

The characteristics of the Master Number 33/6 encompass those of a world leader, global human services provider, skilled master healer, and universal earth mother. As someone imbued with the magnificent energy of 33, you carry the foundational qualities of 6 along with an exalted spiritual vibration derived from the double 3. This is a divine gift from the Universe, accompanied by the responsibility to pursue the master number path.

With the Master Number 33, you possess the extraordinary capability to elevate humanity's consciousness. Nonetheless, the choice is yours—to embrace this loftier vibration or to align with the nurturing attributes of 6. Opting to harness the master number's potential signifies a commitment to manifesting spiritual truths in the material world.

As a 33 individual, you embody compassion and unconditional love, with a focus on humanity at a global level. Your energy resonates with healing, spiritual enlightenment, and altruism, much like the Christ-like path. You are called to work tirelessly for the greater good and uplift the collective consciousness. However, the journey may demand you to relinquish personal ambitions for the benefit of all. Challenges arise when selfish concerns overshadow your mission. Embrace the Master Number 33 as an opportunity to heal and elevate, enriching both yourself and the world around you.

While it is essential to be a compassionate presence, remember not to follow any path aimlessly or to become overly concerned with pleasing everyone. Each individual has their unique journey and life lessons to learn; therefore, you must reserve some energy for your own path. In doing so, you will maintain the balance necessary to fulfill your extraordinary purpose while continuing to inspire others with your gifts of love and healing.

PART 2
KNOW YOUR
FUTURE

Personal Years
Introduction

There are numbers that transit our charts, and because the dates change, the number energies change as well. Every year is different. 2025 is a 9 year, the last of the numerology 9-year cycle. Numerology gets more detailed when we look at the personal months within the year and even more information when we look at each day. This section details each month and each day of the 9-year cycle.

How to Use This Section

To calculate your personal year, add your birthday and birth month to the current year. (Our birth year is not used in this calculation.) For instance, if you were born on March 16, add these numbers to 2025. The equation looks like this:

$$3 + 1 + 6 + 2 + 0 + 2 + 5 = 19 = 1 + 9 = 10 \text{ or } 1 \text{ year.}$$

Calculate your personal year and then use the tabs to flip to the corresponding section. Read the information about your year ahead and then skip to the current month. Read about your present month and then look for the current day. If you're in a 1 year, and it is January 15th, skip to line #15 and read the advice for the current day. The current day reflects the number energy for that day and suggests how to best utilize that energy.

Personal Year 1

A personal year marked by the number 1 heralds a dawn of new beginnings. It is a year where your actions will chart the course for your future. Approach this time with decisiveness and discernment, nurturing a powerful sense of purpose while embracing fresh perspectives and realities. This is a moment to assert your independence and step confidently into a leadership role. Trust in yourself and your abilities.

I highly suggest you have a manifestation journal. It is important to visualize what you want in your future, but it is equally important to put your ideas into physical form. In your manifestation journal, make three columns. The first column is, "Must Haves." These are things you must have to survive. "Good health," would fit in this column. The second column is entitled, "Would Be Nice, If." These are things that would add to your life. Maybe you want to lose a few pounds or gain some body strength. The third column is, "My Wildest Dreams." This is where you do NOT censor yourself. You let your pen go and write down every thought that comes into your mind. Dream big. Most people don't dream big enough. This is your foundation for what you create in the future.

Thoughtful planning and clearly defined goals will pave the path to success. Seize every opportunity that comes your way, as this year lays the foundation for what the next nine years will hold. Be attentive to your instincts and summon the courage to welcome change and explore new ventures. Both your home and career paths may embark on exciting new directions.

To thrive this year requires ambition and foresight, as you stand at the forefront of new beginnings. The singularity of the number 1 positions you as the central figure in your life's narrative, driven to create and innovate. With your visionary prowess, sow the seeds for the years to come to shape your destiny. Reflect on what you wish to manifest and actively engage in molding your future.

Embrace the courage and determination necessary to become the person you aspire to be, shedding anything that no longer serves you and welcoming a renewal of opportunities. This is not the time for hesitation or retreat. Stand resolute and independent. Nurture your well-being and invest in personal growth, expanding your knowledge across all aspects of life.

The energy is ripe for leadership, with your intuition guiding you forward. This period calls for outward engagement, urging you to step into the limelight and seize the abundance of opportunities. Rest assured that next year will allow you to relax and witness the fruition of the seeds planted now. Focus on positivity, and it will yield positive outcomes. Embrace the dynamic, active energy of this year, and let it propel you into a future of your own making.

January
2 Personal Month

If you find yourself in a 1 personal year, January unfolds as a month touched by the energy of 2. The first year of a 9-year cycle calls for clarifying what you wish to manifest over the coming years. Envision your position at the cycle's culmination, setting the stage for a year brimming with activity and outward focus. You will encounter numerous ideas, opportunities, and directions to explore.

Within the first month, the influence of the 2 guides you to emphasize precision and clarity regarding your aspirations. This period is not about rushing forward, but rather about turning inward to heed your internal guidance. Cultivating a relationship with your own divine wisdom will prove more fruitful than any physical undertaking. The sensitivity of the number 2 may stir your emotions more than usual, so keep your intentions discreet. This is a year of manifestation, yet it is wise to reserve some knowledge within.

Adopt a cooperative and diplomatic stance, centered on what you wish to create in the next nine years. Embrace compromise as the interplay between the energies of 1 and 2 ignites a desire to act. Cultivate calmness and the capacity for compromise.

Direct your attention to details and tend to the small matters. Nurture the seeds sown in the preceding month. Cooperation in relationships becomes essential, following a period of "all about me" energies. This emotionally charged month may call on your diplomacy skills to navigate its nuances effectively.

Personal Day
(January)

1. Create something using your own imaginative skills.
2. Organize and prioritize your life tasks.
3. Let it go and let it flow.
4. Honor your partner with a good meal and conversation.
5. Read a book that expands your mind.
6. Make a sound investment with your resources.
7. Volunteer where your heart sings.
8. Gather the right people and begin a project.
9. Check out real estate for fun or speculation.
10. Use your imagination to create something new.
11. Do your due diligence and ignite a strong work ethic.
12. Be receptive to surprises coming your way.
13. Work on a home improvement project. Think beauty.
14. Spend time in your happy place in nature.
15. Assess your financial portfolio.
16. See the bigger picture to serve humanity.
17. Make a to-do list and check things off.
18. Be the diplomat and moderate a disagreement.
19. Make it an enjoyable day. Do what brings you happiness.
20. Focus on your workload and get shit done.
21. Changes happening regardless of your readiness.
22. Take solace at home and enjoy your nest.
23. A day for internal focus and reflection.
24. Be fearless and step up as an authority.
25. Do a good deed for those in need.
26. Be original and express your individuality.
27. Lend support and compassion to a friend.
28. Express yourself in all possible ways today.
29. Think of a firm foundation underneath you.
30. Be adventurous today and do something brand new.
31. Honor boundaries. Don't give unsolicited advice.

February
3 Personal Month

This year is dedicated to manifesting and shaping the future you envision. What kind of life do you aspire to create? Each month brings its unique energy to your manifestations, and February, with its creative 3 vibrations, invites you to think innovatively and expansively.

This month, let your imagination explore your wildest dreams. Consider what you truly desire for your life and make detailed lists to guide your journey. Be attentive as the Universe presents opportunities aligned with your aspirations. Revel in this joyful month by embracing social activities, whether attending a theater performance or a concert. Allow your senses to luxuriate in creativity, viewing life through a lighthearted lens and steering clear of negativity.

Channel your creative spirit into redecorating, initiating a new project, or writing a story. Manage your emotions as they surge with inspiration. February is your time to create and indulge in joy, laying the groundwork for the efforts you will embark on next month to solidify a new foundation based on these creative endeavors.

The combined energies of 1 year and 3 month inspire a creative flourish. Be mindful of frivolous spending and temper any impulsive tendencies. In this 3 month, creativity flows abundantly. Discover new ideas that can lead to abundance and prosperity. While this period is indeed playful, aim to keep things simple and maintain focus. Engage in activities like redecorating, redesigning projects, writing stories, and dancing, allowing your creative spirit to soar.

Personal Day
(February)

1. Create an agenda and complete it.
2. Be ready for any opportunity coming your way today.
3. Have a heart-to-heart with your partner and genuinely listen.
4. Take some "me" time in a tranquil environment.
5. Audit your bank account and charge cards.
6. Forgiveness and unconditional love bring peace.
7. Start a creative enterprise with others.
8. Allow your intuition to flow freely and follow it.
9. Sing, dance, paint, or write. A day for self-expression.
10. Concentration and focus are required to get the job done.
11. Welcome a distraction. It may lead you down a new path.
12. Make some enhancements to your residence. Redecorate.
13. Take an online self-development course.
14. Balance your accounts, both material and spiritual.
15. Compassion and understanding go a long way.
16. Independence and individuality rule your world today.
17. Sit quiet and listen to your intuition.
18. Attend a social gathering and enjoy yourself.
19. Envision a solid foundation underneath you.
20. Ignite your adventuresome spirit. Follow your heart.
21. Enjoy a family gathering and remember your boundaries.
22. Are you solidly on your spiritual path?
23. Focus on your aspirations and level up.
24. Honor the greater good and bless someone.
25. Invite something new into your life.
26. Maintain balance, harmony, and peace today.
27. Write in your gratitude journal.
28. Complete and check off an item on your docket.
29. Explore the unknown and be open to expansion.

March
4 Personal Month

March ushers in the steadfast energy of a 4 month, marking a period of building a solid foundation for the remainder of the year. It is a time to implement structures that will help transform your aspirations from your manifestation list into reality. March is a month of resets. While January offered a gentle start and February allowed for playful creativity, now it is time to focus and get down to work.

Set yourself up for success by instilling the disciplines necessary to achieve your goals. This is not a month for taking risks; rather, it is a time for diligent labor. Maintain focus and resist the temptation to look outside the box. Keep your nose to the grindstone, ensuring that tasks at both work and home are organized and completed. Finish any projects you began earlier with the support of the focused, centered energy that accompanies this month.

Procrastination is not an option; attention to detail is essential as you channel your energies into productive endeavors. This period of focused determination will pave the way for changes in the forthcoming months. Prioritize your health through mindful diet and exercise, and maintain a positive outlook. Your diligence now will yield rewards.

The combined energies of 1 and 4 foster a strong desire to construct and build. Use this time to initiate a new project and lay the groundwork meticulously. This month is about organization, discipline, and diligence. Bring your creative ideas from February into material form, completing projects and resetting your foundation in preparation for the expansive energy of the upcoming 5 month.

Personal Day
(March)

1. Prepare for a significant shift; leadership requires adaptability.
2. Use your workspace to foster productivity and innovation today.
3. Add exercise in your routine; be well physically and mentally.
4. Balance and manage finances to support your goals.
5. Complete ongoing projects; every accomplishment matters.
6. Make a focused to-do list; streamline your monthly priorities.
7. Address unfinished tasks to maintain clarity and momentum.
8. Enjoy your day; a light heart fuels effective leadership.
9. Diligence is rewarded; consistency leads to progress.
10. Change is coming; see it as a growth opportunity.
11. Focus on relationships; they're vital to your support system.
12. Allow for quiet contemplation; reflection aids decision-making.
13. Stay open to workplace shifts; flexibility leads to innovation.
14. Let go of burdens and constraints; embrace freedom.
15. Reflect on emerging insights; they guide strategic choices.
16. Details are the building blocks of effective leadership.
17. Identify your joy; weave those elements into your leadership.
18. Be stable personally and professionally as challenges arise.
19. Elevate the workload with confidence and rise to the occasion.
20. Make home improvements that enhance your ability to lead.
21. Prioritize fresh, nutritious foods to sustain your energy.
22. Honor your knowledge and use it to guide leadership decisions.
23. Complete your to-do list, celebrating each achievement.
24. Embrace new beginnings with enthusiasm and purpose.
25. Read between the lines; discernment is a key to leadership.
26. Hold yourself accountable; integrity matters.
27. Avoid overthinking; trust your instincts and act decisively.
28. Prepare for a fast-paced month; stay agile and responsive.
29. Bring home flowers to brighten and inspire your space.
30. Focus on improving your skills for continued leadership.
31. Commit to balance and harmony for effective management.

April
5 Personal Month

In your year of fresh beginnings and manifestations, April steps into the spotlight as a month of expansion, brimming with freedom and endless possibilities. This period is marked by surprises, both anticipated and unforeseen, urging you to prepare for imminent change. Your career, home, and relationships are poised to ascend to new heights. Embrace the opportunities that unfold before you, taking bold steps through risks, travel, and adventure. You may discover that your path shifts dramatically, opening doors to new directions.

This is also a prime time for self-promotion. Seize the moment to voice your desires and leverage your communication skills to attain what you seek. Let the energy of this month flow freely, whilst maintaining a semblance of balance amidst the whirlwind of activities. Avoid losing yourself in the midst of transitions or potential chaos.

With new heights to reach and perspectives to explore, this is certainly not a time for introversion. Harness the vibrant energy of the 5, pushing boundaries and striving for greater achievements. The changes that arise this month hold the potential to elevate your life. Cultivate a positive mindset as you embrace this transformative journey.

The combined vibrations of 1 and 5 bring delightful surprises, fostering feelings of independence and empowerment. New relationships may blossom this month, further enriching your personal journey. In April, the energy of 5 brings an unexpected change, inviting travel and adventure. Permit yourself to change directions entirely if needed. Promote yourself, employing your communication talents to their fullest. Step up, take risks, and trust that the transformations of this month are geared toward the betterment of your life. Allow the energy to flow, embracing all that comes your way.

Personal Day
(April)

1. Embrace the opportunities around you; lead responsibly.
2. Read an interesting self-improvement book.
3. Maintain balance even in chaos; find your rhythm.
4. Spread kindness with spontaneous gestures to uplift others.
5. Write your wildest dreams as a first step to manifesting them.
6. Collaborate and connect; teamwork fuels innovation and fun.
7. Dance freely; enjoy the movement.
8. Sometimes a clear path leads to unexpected adventures.
9. Enjoy a day of freewheeling adventure and spontaneity.
10. Plan a date with a friend; laughter and connection are key.
11. Take a day trip somewhere new; explore new horizons.
12. Stay connected with business while thinking outside the box.
13. Trust your inner guidance and follow your instincts.
14. Step out of your comfort zone and try something new.
15. Listen to your intuition for exciting experiences.
16. Live boldly and love fully; break free from constraints.
17. Define and pursue your personal version of success.
18. Let today lead you to new possibilities and horizons.
19. Have a deep conversation with a loved one; share your ideas.
20. Meditate in nature; hug a tree and connect with the earth.
21. Get organized and embrace structure; it enhances freedom.
22. Brighten a stranger's day; small acts make a big difference.
23. Explore new thoughts or experiences that intrigue you.
24. Silence your inner critic; explore without judgment.
25. Let your creativity roam; the world is your canvas.
26. Realign your beliefs to support your adventurous spirit.
27. Take action on something from your wild desires list.
28. Focus your full attention on someone close; connection matters.
29. Go on a vision quest; seek your true aspirations.
30. Show your authority; lead with confidence and authenticity.

May
6 Personal Month

Home and family take center stage this month, drawing attention to your relationships, which are illuminated by special significance. Embrace your responsibilities towards those you love, as they may lean on you more heavily during this time. In your independent year, it is crucial to consider how you want to design your future, particularly in relation to the people closest to you.

If you find yourself single, take this opportunity to articulate the qualities you desire in a partner, ranging from essential attributes to your most audacious dreams. Don't hesitate to jot down everything you envision; now is the time to plant the seeds for what you wish to nurture. Seek harmony across all areas of your life, especially within your relationships and home. Dedicate time to nurture and appreciate the loved ones around you.

Embrace forgiveness and the art of letting go, as these elements are vital to cultivating joy this month. Consider planning a family vacation or embark on home improvement projects to enrich your domestic space. While honoring your responsibilities, it is equally important to carve out moments for self-care. This month serves as an opportunity to realign your priorities.

May unfolds as a 6 month, emphasizing family and domestic pursuits. Address your responsibilities and ensure that your home and relationships receive the care they deserve. Create opportunities to strengthen family bonds by scheduling a vacation or engaging in home enhancement projects. Strive for harmony in both your career and your home life, taking the necessary steps to realign your priorities for greater fulfillment.

Personal Day
(May)

1. Create time in a sacred space to nurture your well-being.
2. Strive for balance in all aspects of life to ensure harmony.
3. Spread warmth and understanding with unconditional love.
4. Fulfill responsibilities with grace, kindness, and compassion.
5. Show gratitude for your family, acknowledging their support.
6. Share joy and happiness, spreading positivity.
7. Set and maintain boundaries, honoring your needs.
8. Explore something new with a loved one on a fun adventure.
9. Have a heartfelt conversation with your beloved.
10. Befriend your inner critic & turn it into constructive guidance.
11. Focus on expanding your career & nurturing professional growth.
12. Make a positive impact through kind and thoughtful deeds.
13. Spend quality time with a loved one to deepen your connection.
14. Use diplomacy to resolve past issues, fostering peace.
15. Enhance your environment with a creative home project.
16. Plan and complete your project with creativity & commitment.
17. Spend a day on activities that nourish your soul.
18. Build lasting connections by creating cherished memories.
19. Meditate and connect with your intuition for clarity.
20. Maintain resilience by finding and keeping your center.
21. Trust life's journey by surrendering to higher wisdom.
22. Set new goals with your partner to foster shared growth.
23. Be willing to yield to maintain balance and harmony.
24. Enjoy a fun evening full of laughter and joy.
25. Embrace structure and discipline to support well-being.
26. Celebrate today's amazing events and relish the moment.
27. Confidently handle responsibilities with care.
28. Retreat with a good book for comfort and inspiration.
29. Honor your wisdom by embracing your authority.
30. Forgive and let go, allowing love to flow freely.
31. Be open to new ideas and welcome fresh perspectives.

June
7 Personal Month

As we transition into June, you find yourself at the culmination of six months filled with new beginnings and the pursuit of your desires. With the influence of the 7 energy now guiding you, it's time to turn inward and establish a deeper connection with your divine guidance. Listen carefully; what does your intuition suggest you add to your manifestation list? The introspective energy of the 7 invites new questions and, when carefully considered by month's end, will yield a refined creation list.

Take this opportunity to rest and rejuvenate after the family-focused nature of May; it is now a period dedicated to you and your quest for inner peace. Center yourself and pay heed to your inner guidance. Spend time in nature, meditate as frequently as possible, and consider enrolling in a weekend course that enhances your knowledge and well-being. A nature retreat could provide the perfect backdrop for reflection and rejuvenation.

This month is ripe for reevaluating your current circumstances and embracing necessary changes. Pay attention to your health and address any legal matters that may arise, for June is your dedicated month for personal growth. Direct your energy towards bettering yourself, paying close attention to your dream state as the subconscious whispers insights into your journey.

June transforms into a 7 month, embodying the essence of rest, relaxation, and rejuvenation. Solitude is essential for inward focus; take the time to reevaluate your past and contemplate the direction in which you wish to travel. Engage in studying metaphysics, embark on a retreat, and immerse yourself in the tranquility of nature. Embrace this sacred time for reflection and spiritual exploration, allowing your intuition to guide you as you navigate this transformative journey.

Personal Day
(June)

1. Opportunities are coming; think it through before you act.
2. Tie up loose ends; complete something and put it away.
3. Use your individuality to express who you truly are.
4. Cooperation is key; play nice with others.
5. Take a moment (many moments) to just enjoy your day.
6. Eat right, exercise, and take care of your health.
7. Spontaneity and synchronicity fill the day.
8. Handle your responsibilities, do your work.
9. Find your sacred space; enjoy your alone time.
10. Abundance, not always currency, is on the way.
11. Work on patience and understanding today.
12. Good day for negotiating business deals.
13. Match one for one, honoring others' contributions.
14. Take a break from the introspective month and be social.
15. Good day for a wellness check.
16. Variety adds spice to your inner work; be extraordinary.
17. Beautify your home; buy flowers or just clean up a mess.
18. Review your life's path; are you where you want to be?
19. Balance your checkbook; manage your credit card(s).
20. Let go of something you cannot control; don't ruminate.
21. Align the highest goals; assess where you are on your path.
22. Defer to others; you are not in charge today
23. Reach out to an old friend; write a letter or call someone.
24. Be practical and find order through chaos.
25. Promote yourself and your work.
26. Keep your boundaries and honor others.
27. Collect your thoughts on a nature walk.
28. Be your own authority; present yourself professionally.
29. Honor humanity; volunteer to help someone.
30. Ambition, success, and achievement support your foundation.

July
8 Personal Month

As you navigate a year of new beginnings and the cultivation of your future manifestations, July emerges as a month dedicated to focusing on finances, management, and asserting your authority. The energy of the number 8 prominently highlights matters of wealth, and you can expect an increased flow of money this month. However, it is essential to monitor your spending closely.

For those who often feel financially constrained, this is the perfect time to initiate transformative changes. Consider establishing a money management program, organizing your finances, and practicing the discipline of saying "no" to unnecessary expenditures. Conversely, if you are accustomed to allowing money to flow freely into your life, explore innovative and creative investment opportunities.

With new beginnings on the horizon, it is crucial to articulate your desires regarding financial abundance. The energy of 8 also embodies authority, and you may find your own authority put to the test this month. Stand firm in your knowledge and trust in your capabilities. This July serves as a pivotal time to organize and manage your finances effectively, planting the seeds for improved financial circumstances, regardless of how you previously related to money.

July represents an 8 month, characterized by an emphasis on power and authority. It is a time for focused business endeavors, requiring you to step into a leadership role. Organize and manage all facets of your life while striving to maintain a balance between your material aspirations and spiritual growth. Embrace your role as an authority in your own life, channeling this energy to create the abundance and stability you desire.

Personal Day
(July)

1. Donate to a worthy cause, either currency or sweat equity.
2. Start a new research project or read a new book.
3. Center yourself, connect, and follow your intuition.
4. Allow your creative juices to flow freely.
5. Order and organization; structure your workday.
6. Variety fuels your day; be ready for surprises.
7. Be ready to aid those in need.
8. Use your imagination to explore an old path in a new way.
9. Advancement on material horizons.
10. Put finishing touches and complete an idea or project.
11. Be your independent self and express your individuality.
12. Details matter, so fill in the blanks.
13. Reach out to an old friend and catch up.
14. Fire up your practical and pragmatic skills.
15. Self-promotion is paramount; burst onto the scene.
16. Shore up your boundaries and stand behind them.
17. Rest and regenerate to fill your reserves.
18. Balance your accounts and invest wisely for a fruitful return.
19. Use your gifts to donate to the greater good.
20. Combine your efforts with others for maximum benefit.
21. Allow your boat to float naturally; don't paddle upstream.
22. A day to play and enjoy yourself; find your joy.
23. Be sure the ground under you is solid and stable.
24. Meet people and make new friends; networking is powerful.
25. Give attention to important relationships.
26. Find your space and allow the energy to flow to you.
27. All financial matters are in play today; think dollar signs.
28. Find a solution to a problem and let it go.
29. Know what you know and share it with others.
30. Use your diplomacy skills to settle a squabble.
31. Communication in any medium benefits you.

August
9 Personal Month

Release and completion are the themes that define this month. As you transition into August, you'll find that what no longer serves you is coming to a close. After seven months of embracing the energy of 1 and manifesting your intentions for the next nine years, life has likely felt both busy and fulfilling. This 9 month presents a unique opportunity to reassess your desires and shed the unnecessary elements that clutter your existence.

If you have engaged in your personal growth, this 9 month can be a smooth and rewarding experience. However, if you have ignored your intuition and allowed procrastination to take root, this time may feel somewhat chaotic. Trust that whatever falls away is ultimately for your greater good, helping you to lighten your load. Expect the potential end of friendships or the dissolution of old habits; embrace these changes and release what needs to dissolve.

In this moment, unconditional love and forgiveness will serve you best on your journey. Carve out time for yourself to connect with your creative energy. Consider volunteering to give back to humanity in some meaningful way. Above all, trust in the divine unfolding of all things.

August marks a 9 month, signaling the conclusion of a 9-month cycle. It is a time to declutter, finalize loose ends, and relinquish anything that does not contribute positively to your life. Take a moment to reflect on the rewards of your efforts over the past eight months and make space for new beginnings that await you next month. Use your intuition to guide your creative pursuits and focus on serving the greater good as you step into this transformative period.

PERSONAL YEAR 1

KNOW YOUR SUPERPOWERS, KNOW YOUR FUTURE

Personal Day
(August)

1. Take charge of your life; be a leader and make good choices.
2. Collaborate with others toward a mutual goal.
3. Express yourself in any matter of avenues; be open.
4. Schedule your day and follow through to the letter.
5. Be aware of synchronicities happening today.
6. Buy flowers and deliver them to a special someone.
7. Rejuvenate in your happy place.
8. Opportunities abound; take a risk and leap at the chance.
9. Clear out & clean out your physical and metaphysical closets.
10. Decision day: weigh your options and choose.
11. Listen to your intuition and resolve an issue.
12. Throw and impromptu party; be spontaneous.
13. Be practical and use your common sense to be productive.
14. Unpredictability and spontaneity are your foundations today.
15. Straighten up your humble abode; make it beautiful.
16. Don't push the boat upstream, float with the tide.
17. Business and money day; balance accounts.
18. Bring to a close anything not serving you now.
19. Focus forward with a solid base of your aspirations.
20. Apologize; create space for healing.
21. Engage in a fun activity; live joyfully.
22. Clear up any lingering legal or financial issues.
23. Look forward to a great day for sales and promotion.
24. Be available to someone who needs your expertise.
25. Examine your own thoughts; are you where you want to be?
26. Show you have authority; take command.
27. Let go of what you do not want to carry into the next months.
28. Use your intelligent mind and lead the group.
29. Fill in the blanks and complete the outline.
30. Join a group discussion and articulate your opinion.
31. Complete your work for today and make a plan for tomorrow.

September
1 Personal Month

Note: Because September is the ninth month, it is always the same number as your personal year. This means you have double the energy of your personal year for thirty days. If the current year calculates to the same value as your personal year, then you receive triple that number's energy in September.

With more 1 energy this month, you have the opportunity to revisit the manifestation list you crafted back in January. Reflect on whether your dreams and aspirations have evolved over the past eight months. Have you added to this list as the year has unfolded? If not, now is the moment to focus on what your heart truly desires. Return to the three columns you previously established: Must Haves, Would Be Nice Ifs, and Wildest Dreams.

Concentrate on your future and envision how you see yourself over the next nine years. This month emphasizes independence, placing you at the forefront of your journey. Your aspirations take precedence, so summon your courage to embrace this time of new creations that support your ambitions. Although the pace may be bustling with fresh beginnings, rest assured that October will bring a welcome period of recuperation.

Maintain a positive outlook, and if you find yourself in a leadership position, seize the opportunity with confidence. Consider enrolling in a self-improvement course, allowing yourself to grow and gain valuable wisdom.

September is characterized as a 1 month, heralding new beginnings. This is the time to plant the seeds for your goals and intentions for the next nine months. Embrace the busyness of the month, filled with myriad new projects, and have the bravery to step into a leadership role as you navigate this exciting journey ahead.

Personal Day
(September)

1. Strive to maintain a peaceful and harmonious atmosphere.
2. Allow your cheerful and inspirational side shine through.
3. Wear your effective manager hat and get organized.
4. Any changes coming prepare the way for growth opportunities.
5. Find your community and make a contribution to it.
6. Take time to research something which interests you.
7. Action, ambition, and achievement are major vibrations today.
8. Be willing to let go for a higher purpose in the future.
9. Make solid business deals; wear your integrity on the outside.
10. Patience and understanding are required; allow, don't push.
11. Optimism and positive thinking will go a long way.
12. Be sure your moral compass points due north.
13. Curb your impulses and make well-thought-out decisions.
14. Handle any domestic quarrels with love and understanding.
15. Tend to your health. Begin a new exercise regimen.
16. Focus on gratitude and welcome abundance.
17. Success comes to those who serve humanity.
18. Use your independent leadership skills to forge a new path.
19. Good friends day; inspire love and companionship.
20. Silence your inner critic; look on the bright side.
21. Read the fine print on any documents.
22. Be open to new ideas, but don't get overwhelmed.
23. Whatever the responsible thing is, do it.
24. If you are in need of it, this is a favorable day for a rest.
25. Focus on the greater good, not just your own rewards.
26. Clear away useless items; prepare for a shift next month.
27. Make improvements to a project; do not rest on your laurels.
28. Help others first and then yourself.
29. Attend a personal growth seminar or read a related book.
30. Honor your diligent work ethic.

October
2 Personal Month

Note: October is always the same number as your personal year next year. This means October is a brief preview of the coming year.

This year, January and October both resonate with the number energy, offering you a unique opportunity to revisit your earlier aspirations. Reflect on the manifestation list you created at the beginning of the year and consider any necessary upgrades or changes. Does your current list accurately represent what you desire today? Throughout the year, your dreams may have evolved, prompting you to redefine your aspirations and gain clarity on what you truly want.

Now is the time to update your manifestations to align them with your current vision. Pay close attention to details, refining your previous writings to ensure they reflect the future you wish to create over the next nine years.

As you enter this 2 month, turn your focus inward and contemplate what has transpired thus far. Partnerships will flourish if you embrace cooperation and allow the energy to flow naturally. In this phase, it's wise to defer to others, as you may not be in a leadership position. Utilize the slower pace to cultivate a deeper relationship with your intuition.

October is a 2 month in this personal year, which encourages you to concentrate on the finer details. Attend to the little things and nurture the seeds you planted last month. Cooperation in your relationships is paramount after the recent focus on individual pursuits. This month may bring forth emotional dynamics that require the use of your diplomacy skills. Embrace the opportunity to compromise and practice patience as you navigate these circumstances.

Personal Day
(October)

1. Unleash your creativity.
2. Knock out that to-do list.
3. Let the good vibes roll.
4. Celebrate your partner like it's their birthday.
5. Dive into a book that excites you.
6. Make a savvy investment move.
7. Give back and spread the good karma.
8. Kickstart that project you've been dreaming about.
9. Explore some hot real estate deals.
10. Let your imagination run wild.
11. Do your homework before diving in.
12. Get ready for an exciting surprise.
13. Spruce up your home and make it sparkle.
14. Take a leisurely stroll and soak in the sights.
15. Give your finances a little TLC.
16. Step up and help someone in need.
17. Scribble down your action items.
18. Patch things up and kiss and make up.
19. Make today a delightful adventure.
20. Zero in on your work like a pro.
21. Embrace the winds of change.
22. Enjoy a cozy staycation at home.
23. Journey inward and discover your Zen.
24. Take charge and lead the way.
25. Spread a little kindness with a good deed.
26. Dive into fresh beginnings.
27. Be the cheerleader your friend needs.
28. Let your true self shine through.
29. Hustle hard and chase those dreams.
30. Be bold and seek new adventures.
31. Treat yourself and your date to a fun night out.

November
3 Personal Month

As you reach the conclusion of your year dedicated to manifesting your desires for the next nine years, November marks a pivotal moment filled with spiritual energy, aligned with the frequency of the eleventh month. This is a time to deepen your intuitive abilities; listen carefully to the guidance available to you as you engage in fruitful partnerships with others. Collaboration, cooperation, and attentiveness to the advice of those around you are central to this month's vibrations. Embrace the sense of community and camaraderie among friends and associates.

Within your 1 personal year, November embodies the lively energy of a 3 month. This signifies an ideal time for creative self-expression and emotional connection. Allow your artistic passions to flourish; if you are an artist, create; if you are a dancer, let the music move you. Utilize any creative outlet available to you as a means of expressing your innermost thoughts and feelings.

Let your social calendar expand as you revel in the interconnectedness of those around you. Travel opportunities may arise, encouraging you to embrace new experiences. November is a season when your creative juices flow freely, inviting an influx of innovative ideas aimed at fostering abundance. While this period is infused with playfulness, maintain simplicity and focus on your pursuits. Engage in redecorating, redesigning projects, writing stories, or dancing, and fully immerse yourself in this vibrant tapestry of creativity.

Personal Day
(November)

1. Whip up a magical manifestation list.
2. Get set for all the surprises life throws your way.
3. Tune in to your partner's thoughts and ideas.
4. Treat yourself to some glorious 'me' time.
5. Give your finances a fun makeover with an audit.
6. Release what no longer serves you; let it fly.
7. Dive headfirst into a creative project.
8. Channel your inner diplomat and spread the peace.
9. Dance, sing, and express yourself with pure joy.
10. Hone in and sharpen that focus like a laser beam.
11. Embrace distractions; sometimes they can be fun.
12. Transform your space with a fabulous redecorating spree.
13. Dive into an online course and expand your horizons.
14. Balance those accounts like a financial wizard.
15. Show off your compassionate side; let it shine.
16. Splash some color into your life; think vibrant.
17. Trust your gut and listen to that inner voice.
18. Be the mastermind of your own creations.
19. Stand tall on a solid foundation of confidence.
20. Embark on an unforgettable adventure.
21. Gather the family for a delightful dinner together.
22. Delve deep and explore your inner self.
23. Be a whiz at knowing your business inside and out.
24. Champion the greater good in your daily deeds.
25. Craft a sizzling new 'want' list to inspire you.
26. Keep that balance scale perfectly aligned.
27. Spill your thoughts into your journal; let it flow.
28. Check off something from that procrastination list; go you.
29. Soak up the vibes at a fun event and let loose.
30. Great energy for a date night or to have fun with friends.

December
4 Personal Month

As we arrive at the final month of the year, it is essential to roll up your sleeves and diligently tidy up both your physical and metaphorical spaces. Take the time to bring resolution to this bustling chapter of your life. Reflecting on the past eleven months, consider all the seeds you have sown. Have you shared your desires for the next nine years with the Universe? If you have yet to do so, the energy is still present for you to invest in your future.

The number 4 symbolizes a sturdy foundation, making it an ideal energy to conclude this year as you prepare to launch into a new year. Organize your surroundings and eliminate anything unnecessary that no longer serves you. Focus on what you wish to carry forward into the new year rather than what you need to release. What burdens are you ready to let go of? Now is the moment to work with love and discipline to accomplish your tasks.

While staying within your established parameters, strive to complete your to-do list. Embrace the joy of the holiday season and the close of the year, but prioritize your responsibilities first.

December resonates with the energy of a 4 month, which emphasizes organization, discipline, and diligence. Prioritize your health through mindful diet and exercise, and bring the creative endeavors from last month into tangible form. Finish projects that have been on your list and reset your foundation in preparation for the expansive energy of the upcoming year. Enjoy the strong sense of tradition and connection with family during the holidays, even as you acknowledge that financial resources may be limited. Create a schedule and commit to it, ensuring that you balance the completion of your tasks with the warmth of the season.

Personal Day
(December)

1. Get ready for change; adaptability is key.
2. Focus on productive work from home for efficiency.
3. Include regular exercise for overall well-being.
4. Review your finances for stability and informed decisions.
5. Complete your projects; diligence leads to success.
6. Create a monthly to-do list to guide your efforts.
7. Address outstanding tasks by filling in details.
8. Enjoy today; balance is vital for sustained productivity.
9. Remember, diligence pays off in your career.
10. Be prepared to embrace upcoming changes.
11. Prioritize relationships; maintain strong team connections.
12. Reflect on goals and strategies during quiet time.
13. Be open to workplace changes; flexibility leads to innovation.
14. Release anything that doesn't serve your goals.
15. Reflect on new ideas to enhance your approach.
16. Focus on details; they are crucial for effective execution.
17. Engage in activities that bring joy and boost morale.
18. Ensure stability personally and professionally.
19. Embrace new responsibilities to elevate your workload.
20. Improve your home for productivity and comfort.
21. Choose fresh, nourishing foods for optimal health.
22. Leverage your expertise to guide decisions.
23. Complete a to-do list with precision; celebrate achievements.
24. Embrace new opportunities and chapters in your journey.
25. Read between the lines in communications for deeper insights.
26. Keep yourself accountable; integrity builds team trust.
27. Avoid overthinking; trust your instincts and act decisively.
28. Prepare for a busy month; stay organized and proactive.
29. Brighten your space with flowers for beauty and inspiration.

Personal Year 2

In a personal year marked by the number 2, receptivity reigns supreme, inviting balance, harmony, and the resolution of lingering issues. It is a time to embrace cooperation over competition, fostering diplomacy, patience, compassion, and understanding to fuel your progress. Maintain your vision, trust in the process, and allow time to unfold naturally.

Building on the foundations laid in the previous year, pay close attention to details and collaborate with those who share your values. Refine and expand your manifestations with care, as your heightened intuition serves as a trusted guide. Develop a practice of daily intuitive guidance, trusting in the timing and process of integration.

This year calls for honing your diplomatic skills, recognizing that patience is indeed a virtue. It is a time for nurturing compatible friendships and potentially deepening intimacy in romantic relationships. By aiding others, you ultimately help yourself.

As you proceed through this year, take the opportunity to slow down, regroup, and genuinely listen to those around you. Reflect on the achievements of the previous year, nurturing the seeds that were planted. This is not a year for bold outward accomplishments or forcing your way forward; rather, your personal power is subtle and indirect.

Focus on inner growth, welcoming the introspective pace with gratitude. Strengthen your relationship with your intuition, which will enhance your sensitivity to others and may lead you to defer to them more readily. Employ diplomacy and cooperation, making necessary compromises to relate to others effectively.

Allow for slow, steady growth, nurturing the aspirations of the previous year. Protect your ideas and tend to your creations quietly, without broadcasting your plans. This is a favorable year for discovering new love or seeking a new residence. Harmonize with a serene tempo, relish the tranquility, and let the gentle current guide your journey.

PERSONAL YEAR 2

January
3 Personal Month

Last year, you set your intentions for the next nine years, and now, in this year of nurturing your aspirations, you will cultivate those dreams into reality. While this is a slower-paced year, ample work still awaits you, beginning with a joyful month ahead. Embrace your creative side, allowing your imagination to flourish and explore new creative pursuits without reservation.

In this year, relationships and balance take precedence, making effective communication essential. Focus on uncovering and expressing your emotions, stepping into the role of diplomat in your interactions. As your social calendar fills, exercise discernment in how you choose to spend your time. Above all, let your imagination expand and showcase your creative talents, turning this month into a delightful experience.

Make the most of this joyful time, for next month will demand more effort and diligence. The year's energy embodies balance and moderation, so remain mindful of any tendencies toward extravagance. Listen closely to your inner guidance, taking time to meditate for clarity and direction.

Explore various avenues of enjoyment; sing, dance, create, and maintain a positive mindset to foster a fulfilling month. Allow the music to flow through you, keeping your focus while navigating any feelings of being scattered or confused. Engage socially and creatively, embracing the abundant possibilities before you.

January is characterized as a 3 month, where your creative energies will flow freely, bringing forth new ideas and opportunities for abundance. This playful time encourages you to keep things simple while remaining focused. Consider redecorating, redesigning projects, writing stories, or dancing; whatever inspires you to express yourself fully.

PERSONAL YEAR 2

Personal Day
(January)

1. Scribble down your dream wish list.
2. Brace yourself for all the twists and turns today.
3. Tune into your partner's vibes.
4. Indulge in some glorious 'me time.'
5. Spruce up your wallet with a little financial check-up.
6. Wave goodbye to that baggage.
7. Launch into a fun-filled creative adventure.
8. Be the peacemaker in your circle.
9. Let your personality sparkle when you express yourself.
10. Zero in and channel that focus power.
11. Expect a little chaos for some unexpected fun.
12. Give your space a makeover and freshen things up.
13. Enroll in a cool online class and boost your brain.
14. Keep track of those pennies; balance those bucks.
15. Show your soft side, spread some love.
16. Splash vibrant colors onto your canvas of life.
17. Follow that gut feeling; listen to your inner compass.
18. Craft and create like the superstar you are.
19. Build your dreams on a strong foundation.
20. Seek out new adventures; go on a wild ride.
21. Host a cozy family feast and share good times.
22. Dive deep into your personal world; explore within.
23. Get savvy about your biz; know it like the back of your hand.
24. Champion good vibes and commit to the greater good.
25. Add to your creation list.
26. Dance on the balance beam; juggle it all with flair.
27. Pour your heart out onto the pages of your journal.
28. Tackle that project you've been avoiding; it's time to shine.
29. Dive into a lively event and soak up the joy.
30. Take your beloved out to create some quality memories.
31. Time for solitude and regeneration to rebuild your coffers.

February
4 Personal Month

Diligence and discipline emerge as the guiding themes for you this month. While January was characterized by playfulness and unconventional thinking, February introduces the steadfast energy of the number 4, encouraging hard work within established parameters. It is the time to organize and implement the creative endeavors sparked in the previous month.

Prioritize your health through mindful diet and regular exercise, committing to your responsibilities with focus and determination. As you lay the groundwork for the remainder of the year, remember that a stronger and more stable foundation now will keep you grounded throughout the year ahead.

This month is about manifesting those creative ideas from January into tangible form. Take the necessary steps to complete your projects; procrastination is not an option. Keep your focus sharp and your efforts resolute, as next month will bring opportunities for expansion and new experiences. The energy of 4 encourages a concentrated approach; leverage this focused energy to achieve your goals.

While you may encounter certain restrictions and family obligations during this time, it is essential to remain responsible and attentive to detail without becoming overwhelmed.

February, as a 4 month, emphasizes organization, discipline, and diligence. With a commitment to maintaining your health through proper nutrition and exercise, turn your creativity from last month into reality. Conclude any unfinished projects and reset your foundational elements in preparation for the expansive journey awaiting you in the coming 5 month.

PERSONAL YEAR 2

Personal Day
(February)

1. Be ready for change; adaptability is key in a dynamic environment.
2. Focus on productive work from home for efficiency today.
3. Add regular exercise to boost your well-being.
4. Review your finances for stability and informed decisions.
5. Complete your agenda projects; diligence leads to success.
6. Create a monthly to-do list to guide your efforts.
7. Address outstanding tasks by adding necessary details.
8. Enjoy today; balance is key to sustained productivity.
9. Remember, diligence pays off in your career.
10. Accept that change is coming; be ready to embrace it.
11. Prioritize strong connections with your team.
12. Set aside time for reflection on goals and strategies.
13. Be open to workplace shifts; flexibility leads to innovation.
14. Release what no longer serves your objectives or well-being.
15. Reflect on new ideas to enhance your approach.
16. Keep a sharp focus on details for effective execution.
17. Engage in activities that bring joy and fulfillment.
18. Ensure stability both personally and professionally.
19. Challenge yourself with new responsibilities confidently.
20. Improve your home for productivity and comfort.
21. Prioritize fresh, nourishing foods for optimal health.
22. Use your expertise and knowledge to guide decisions.
23. Prioritize your objectives with precision; celebrate successes.
24. Embrace new opportunities as you start a new chapter.
25. Read between the lines in communications for insights.
26. Hold yourself accountable; integrity builds trust.
27. Trust your instincts; avoid overthinking and take action.
28. Prepare for a busy month; stay organized and proactive.
29. Enrich your space with flowers for beauty and inspiration.

March
5 Personal Month

This is your month of freedom and expansion. In February, you diligently established a solid foundation, and now it is time to broaden your horizons. Embrace change, both the anticipated and the unexpected. Let go of the past and remain open to the surprises that lie ahead. Opportunities will emerge across various aspects of your life. Are you seeking a new home, a fresh relationship, or a new career? This is an ideal moment to welcome new possibilities.

Travel and adventure beckon, encouraging you to cultivate curiosity and expand your vision. Now is not the time for hesitation or fear; seize the moment to take risks, as fortune is on your side. Change can be a catalyst for positive transformation, elevating your quality of life. Embrace growth opportunities that arise this month, utilizing the energetic influence of 5 to recalibrate your diet or exercise routine. Allow the energy to flow naturally, avoiding the temptation to row against the current. A positive mindset will help propel you along this dynamic journey.

While navigating the energetic shifts, strive to remain focused, even as distractions may arise. Remember, an influx of information does not always equate to clarity; permit any confusion to dissipate while maintaining a sense of order in the midst of change.

March is characterized as a 5 month, heralding a period of unexpected change that brings travel and adventure. You may find yourself altering your course entirely. Promote your ideas and utilize your communication skills to their fullest potential. Step forward and take risks; the changes that unfold this month are poised to enhance your life. Embrace the flow of energy and let it guide you on this exciting path.

Personal Day
(March)

1. Embrace upcoming opportunities with an open heart.
2. Dive into a self-improvement book that inspires growth.
3. Keep balanced amid life's exciting chaos.
4. Brighten someone's day with a kind gesture.
5. Write down wild dreams; let imagination lead them to reality.
6. Embrace collaboration and cooperation with others.
7. Dance joyfully and freely; celebrate life.
8. Follow paths of adventure confidently.
9. Enjoy a spontaneous day of excitement and exploration.
10. Plan a fun evening with a friend; let laughter abound.
11. Take a day trip to discover new horizons.
12. Focus on business while letting creativity flourish.
13. Trust your inner guidance as your journey's compass.
14. Try something new; embrace the thrill.
15. Trust your intuitive guidance in whatever form it takes.
16. Live and love boldly, beyond comfort zones.
17. Strive for success while enjoying the journey.
18. Let today lead you to new, endless possibilities.
19. Engage deeply with a loved one; connect meaningfully.
20. Meditate in nature; feel grounded and refreshed.
21. Organize but embrace spontaneity.
22. Lift a stranger's spirit with kindness.
23. Explore the unfamiliar; expand your horizons.
24. Silence your inner critic; embrace joy and expression.
25. Let your creativity roam free; explore new artistic paths.
26. Ensure your foundation supports your expansive spirit.
27. Check off a wild desire; let dreams soar.
28. Focus on nurturing and strengthening important connections.
29. Embark on a self-discovery adventure.
30. Express your authority; lead with passion and clarity.
31. Maintain balance and harmony while embracing life's abundance.

April
6 Personal Month

In this 2 year, cooperation and diplomacy reign supreme. The number 6 amplifies relationships, so pay attention to any issues that arise now and process them. April is your month dedicated to home, family, and responsibility. Expect those around you to seek your support and assistance, drawing your attention toward helping others. After the expansive energy of March, you may find yourself yearning for the comforts of home. Ground yourself in familiar surroundings and invest quality time with your loved ones.

Consider undertaking a home improvement project or preparing your garden for planting—these activities will bring satisfaction and a sense of accomplishment. As you transition from a month of exploration and freedom, it is essential to redirect your attention towards nurturing your relationships. This is the perfect time to be of service; schedule one-on-one moments with those close to you and invest energy into building stronger connections. The efforts you make now will yield rewards in the future.

Face your responsibilities head-on, and ensure you complete any obligations you may have set aside. However, be mindful not to deplete your resources—find moments for personal regeneration and renewal. Remember to put on your own oxygen mask first; prioritize self-care to maintain your balance.

Good boundaries are essential during this time to limit the demands placed upon you. Although you may feel pulled in multiple directions, it is crucial to tend to your own needs while being of service to others.

April is a 6 month, centering on home and family dynamics. Embrace your responsibilities by taking care of your relationships and household. Use this time wisely, whether by scheduling a family vacation or focusing on home improvement projects, while simultaneously seeking harmony in your career and personal life. Take the opportunity to realign your priorities and create a sense of balance and fulfillment in your surroundings.

Personal Day
(April)

1. Choose the responsible path that resonates with your heart.
2. Choose the responsible path that aligns with your heart.
3. Enjoy a self-improvement book that inspires your growth.
4. Embrace balance in your life amid delightful chaos.
5. Brighten someone's day with a warm, kind gesture.
6. Write down your wildest dreams to manifest them.
7. Collaborate and build connections with others.
8. Let your spirit soar; dance joyfully and celebrate.
9. Follow clear paths while staying open to spontaneity.
10. Gift yourself a day of adventure and exploration.
11. Enjoy an evening out with a friend, savoring laughter.
12. Treat yourself to a day trip to a new destination.
13. Stay engaged with work while thinking creatively.
14. Trust your inner guidance; it reveals your truths.
15. Dare to try something new; embrace the unknown.
16. Honor your intuition and follow its whispers.
17. Live passionately and love fiercely beyond comfort zones.
18. Focus on success; let your determination shine.
19. Let today guide you to new horizons and possibilities.
20. Have a meaningful talk with a loved one; strengthen your bond.
21. Meditate in nature; appreciate beauty to regenerate yourself.
22. Organize your space and respect the rules for clarity.
23. Uplift a stranger's day with a smile or kind word.
24. Explore new dimensions and seek fresh experiences.
25. Calm your inner critic with compassion and understanding.
26. Ignite your creativity to inspire exploration and expression.
27. Realign your foundation with your heart's true desires.
28. Cross off an item from your wildest desires list; make it happen.
29. Pay full attention to someone close; cherish your time together.
30. Embark on a vision quest for clarity on your journey ahead.
31. Confidently express your inner authority with grace.

May
7 Personal Month

Following a month filled with responsibilities and nurturing relationships, it is essential to carve out time for solitude, and the energy of the number 7 invites you to go inward. This is a period for rest, relaxation, and rejuvenation as you reexamine the trajectory of your life. Utilize this meditative and spiritual time to consider enrolling in a self-improvement class or embarking on a weekend retreat to connect with nature.

As you build up your inner resources, prepare for the busyness that June will bring. In this 2 year, fostering your connection to the Divine is paramount, and now is the perfect moment to engage in meditation. Tune into your intuition, as its strength is heightened this year. Additionally, your diplomacy and mediation skills will be invaluable, so take the time to receive guidance on the best paths forward.

Pay close attention to details, tending to the small matters that require your care. Be aware that you may find yourself feeling more emotional this month. It is crucial to allocate time to process the wisdom you receive from your Divine guidance.

Seek a harmonious balance between moments of solitude and social activities. This month may evoke emotional currents, making it an excellent opportunity to delve into your passions through research and exploration.

May is characterized as a 7 month—a time for rest, relaxation, and rejuvenation. Solitude is necessary for inward focus. Reflect on your past and reconsider the direction in which you wish to go. Engage in the study of metaphysics, immerse yourself in nature, and embrace the tranquility of this transformative month.

PERSONAL YEAR 2

Personal Day
(May)

1. Opportunities are near; carefully consider them before acting.
2. Tie up loose ends and complete tasks.
3. Express your authentic self confidently.
4. Cooperation is key; engage harmoniously with others.
5. Pause to savor the joys of each day.
6. Prioritize health with nutritious food; self-care is essential.
7. Embrace spontaneity and synchronicity for enrichment.
8. Attend to your responsibilities and fulfill your obligations.
9. Find your sacred space to recharge your spirit.
10. Abundance is on the way in various forms.
11. Approach today with patience and understanding for yourself.
12. This is a great time to negotiate; your diplomatic skills will shine.
13. Acknowledge others' contributions and foster reciprocity.
14. Take a break from introspection to socialize.
15. Schedule a wellness check to prioritize your health.
16. Do your inner work; achieve something fantastic. Inspire growth.
17. Beautify your living space with flowers or tidy up.
18. Reflect on your life's path—are you on the right track?
19. Balance your checkbook and manage money mindfully.
20. Release what you can't control; avoid overthinking.
21. Align with your goals and assess your progress.
22. Let others take the lead in collaborative efforts.
23. Reach out to an old friend to nurture connections.
24. Stay practical; find order amidst chaos.
25. Promote yourself and showcase your strengths.
26. Maintain your boundaries while respecting others'.
27. Gather your thoughts during a nature walk for clarity.
28. Use professionalism and confidence to reinforce your authority.
29. Honor our shared humanity; be a volunteer to help others.
30. Channel your ambition; strengthen your foundation for success.
31. Use kindness to resolve conflicts; maintain equilibrium.

June
8 Personal Month

This year, prioritizing harmony and balance across all areas of your life is essential. Relationships, career, home, and family require your energy and attention to achieve equilibrium. In this 2 year, you may also discover a new residence on the horizon. The infusion of 8 energy introduces themes of business, finance, organization, and management into the mix. Expect money to flow in greater quantities this month, making it crucial to monitor your spending carefully.

You may find yourself stepping into a position of authority, so embrace your own power and venture beyond your comfort zone. Remember, wealth is not the sole measure of success; it is vital to allocate time and effort to all facets of your life. Balance is key, particularly as the influences of both number energies guide you in June, so strive to maintain your equanimity.

Both 2 and 8 are intuitive numbers, prompting you to pay heed to your inner guidance. Explore the depths of both your material and spiritual domains to uncover the symmetry within. The energy of 8 also encourages taking calculated risks; however, ensure that you maintain balance throughout the process. This can be a prosperous time, provided you nurture a positive mindset.

Diligently engage in your work, and the rewards will surely follow. Stay vigilant regarding your finances, and remember that it's perfectly acceptable to seek assistance in finding solutions when needed.

In June, you enter an 8 month, a period characterized by a strong emphasis on power and authority. Business becomes the focal point, and your leadership abilities will be called into action. It is time to organize and manage all aspects of your life while striving to harmonize both your material and spiritual worlds. Embrace your role as an authority figure and navigate this month with confidence and clarity.

PERSONAL YEAR 2

Personal Day
(June)

1. Donate to a worthy cause, financially or as a volunteer.
2. Start a new research project or a thought-provoking book.
3. Connect with your core values and trust your intuition.
4. Create a time when you nurture creativity; allow ideas to flow.
5. Prioritize organization to structure your workday efficiently.
6. Embrace variety in your schedule; be open to unexpected change.
7. Be ready to assist those in need with compassion and support.
8. Approach familiar challenges with new perspectives and ideas.
9. Focus on tangible advancements and opportunities for growth.
10. Complete ongoing projects and finalize your ideas.
11. Uphold your independence; express your unique perspective.
12. Focus on details; ensure all is well-considered and complete.
13. Reconnect with an old friend to catch up on each other's lives.
14. Use a solutions-oriented mindset to address challenges.
15. Promote yourself effectively to elevate your initiatives.
16. Strengthen your boundaries and ensure they are respected.
17. Allow time for rest and regeneration to recharge your energy.
18. Keep your financial records balanced and invest wisely.
19. Use your talents to benefit your community.
20. Collaborate with others to maximize the impact.
21. Let your endeavors progress organically; avoid forcing outcomes.
22. Make time for enjoyment & play; find joy in everyday moments.
23. Ensure a solid foundation; stability is crucial for growth.
24. Network with new people; open doors for valuable opportunities.
25. Nurture important relationships as they are key to success.
26. Inspire a space that promotes positive energy.
27. Be mindful of financial matters, consider growth opportunities.
28. Identify solutions to problems; let go of any attachments.
29. Share your knowledge generously; collaboration fosters growth.
30. Use diplomacy to resolve conflicts amicably; promote harmony.

July
9 Personal Month

This year measures a slower pace, encouraging you to focus intently on the finer details of your life. Embrace this introspective time as an opportunity to connect with your higher guidance and cultivate a deeper relationship with your intuition. During this period, nurturing cooperation and compassion is essential, so aim to foster positive interactions with those around you.

Explore creative ways to serve your community, as the rewards of your humanitarian efforts will bear fruit in due time. Prioritize self-care and indulge in travel if circumstances permit, but exercise some caution regarding the pitfalls of gullibility.

As a 9 month, this period signifies the culmination of a 9-month cycle and a time for cleansing, finalizing, and releasing anything that does not contribute positively to your journey. Relish the fruits of your labor from the past eight months and prepare for the new beginnings on the horizon. Trust your intuition as you contemplate what you wish to create next. Embrace your creativity while seeking avenues to serve the greater good.

This year is characterized by heightened intuition, especially in this spiritually resonant 9 month. Take your time and allow yourself to be guided; surrender to the process. Commit to cooperating and being of service within your community. As the final number in the numerological cycle, 9 signifies that certain aspects of your life will come to completion. Welcome the harvest reaped from your efforts over the past nine months and acknowledge the rewards of your accomplishments.

It is time to declutter your life, discarding anything unnecessary as you move forward. Carry forward only what you need into August and the fresh energy of the 1 month.

Personal Day
(July)

1. Lead with compassion and uplift those around you.
2. Collaborate to achieve goals for the greater good.
3. Express yourself openly and be receptive to all views.
4. Plan your day and commit to your priorities.
5. Notice coincidences; they may offer guidance.
6. Brighten someone's day with flowers or kindness.
7. Rejuvenate your spirit in a joyful, peaceful space.
8. Embrace opportunities and take leaps of faith.
9. Clear clutter to make room for personal growth.
10. Align your choices with your core values.
11. Trust your intuition to foster harmony.
12. Celebrate spontaneity with joyful gatherings.
13. Use common sense to boost productivity.
14. Stay open to the unpredictable; let it shape you.
15. Tidy your space to create beauty and warmth.
16. Follow life's natural flow and let things unfold.
17. Focus on financial health by balancing your accounts.
18. Conclude activities that no longer serve you.
19. Look ahead with clarity; build on your dreams.
20. Apologize when needed to allow for healing.
21. Engage in activities that bring you joy.
22. Address outstanding legal or financial issues.
23. Expect success in sales through genuine connections.
24. Share your skills with those who can benefit.
25. Reflect on your thoughts to align with your goals.
26. Show leadership through responsibility and compassion.
27. Release what you don't need to prepare for the future.
28. Lead initiatives promoting understanding and progress.
29. Focus on details to complete tasks and outline steps.
30. Participate in discussions, sharing insights to inspire.
31. End your day fulfilled and prepare thoughtfully for tomorrow.

August
1 Personal Month

In a 2 personal year, August unfolds as a dynamic 1 month, heralding new beginnings. After several months immersed in the introspective energy of the 2, where you have been connecting with your Divine guidance and engaging in collaboration and cooperation, the 1 energy invites you to shift your focus back to yourself and your personal desires.

This month gives you the green light to take the driver's seat— now is not the time to remain passive. Over the next four weeks, concentrate on manifestations and the creation of your aspirations. Use this time to clarify your desires and actively invite them into your future. Channel your courage and determination to establish your goals and intentions for the remainder of the year.

You will likely feel a surge of motivation to embark on new projects, making this a bustling month. Be brave and advocate for your own needs and ambitions, as you may find yourself stepping into a leadership role. It is also an opportune moment to release anything that no longer serves you. Rest assured, you will have the chance to relax come September when the gentle, nurturing energy of double 2 returns.

August is indeed a month of new beginnings, ripe for planting seeds and setting goals and intentions for the next nine months. Embrace the abundance of possibilities before you and have the courage to lead as you navigate this exciting chapter of your life. Stay attuned to the new ideas and resolutions that come forth, and pay careful attention to the individuals who enter your life during this transformative time.

PERSONAL YEAR 2

Personal Day
(August)

1. Create a harmonious space for open communication and collaboration.
2. Let your cheerful spirit uplift those around you.
3. Organize tasks and goals with clarity and purpose.
4. Embrace changes as opportunities for collective growth.
5. Engage with your community in meaningful ways.
6. Dedicate time to research topics that expand your knowledge.
7. Use ambition & action to drive progress and motivate others.
8. Let go of old processes for future success.
9. Today is ideal for making solid business deals; act with integrity.
10. Practice patience and allow situations to unfold naturally.
11. Cultivate optimism and positively impact your environment.
12. Ensure your moral compass guides you in leadership.
13. Take a moment to think before making decisions.
14. Address domestic disputes with love to foster resolution.
15. Prioritize your health by starting a new exercise routine.
16. Focus on gratitude and remain open to abundance.
17. True success comes from serving the greater good.
18. Use independent leadership to find innovative solutions.
19. Make time for friends to strengthen your support network.
20. Silence your inner critic and focus on your positives.
21. Read fine print for clarity and protection.
22. Stay open to fresh ideas while focusing to avoid overwhelm.
23. Commit to actions that prioritize your team and community.
24. Honor your need for a break; rest is essential for productivity.
25. Focus on the greater good and value collective rewards.
26. Clear unnecessary items to make space for positive changes.
27. Strive to improve ongoing projects; don't settle for past success.
28. Prioritize helping others and reinforce a spirit of service.
29. Engage in self-improvement through seminars or books.
30. Uphold your strong work ethic; it sets a standard.
31. Embrace your individuality & courage for rewarding adventures.

September
2 Personal Month

Note: Because September is the ninth month, it is always the same number as your personal year. This means you have double the energy of your personal year for thirty days. If the current year calculates to the same value as your personal year, then you receive triple that number's energy in September.

In a 2 personal year, September brings the energizing influence of a 2 month, enhancing your intuitive abilities and amplifying your diplomatic and negotiation skills. This is not a month for independence; rather, it calls for collaboration and harmony. Embrace your role as a team player, offering support to those who need it.

Take this opportunity to nurture the seeds you've planted last year and the intentions set in August. Flow gracefully with the abundant spiritual energy surrounding you. Dedicate time to quiet meditation, fostering a deeper connection with your Divine intuition. Attend to the details and handle small matters as they arise, as this can be an emotionally charged month. Ensure that you carve out time to process your feelings, as sensitivity may be heightened during this period.

Be attentive and defer to others if questions arise; cooperation is essential. This slower month within a more reflective year invites you to delve deeper into issues, so allow yourself the necessary time for this exploration. Keep your ideas close to your heart; restraint is wise when it comes to sharing your plans.

The number 2 can also signify a change in residence, so remain open to new possibilities—whether it be a shift in your living situation or the potential for a new relationship. As intuition peaks, practice patience and be receptive to the information that may guide you in the future.

Take time for self-care by engaging in activities that nurture you, such as getting a massage.

Personal Day
(September)

1. Create something that showcases your unique creative skills.
2. Organize and prioritize the tasks in your life.
3. Release your worries and let life flow gracefully.
4. Give your partner a delightful meal & engaging conversation.
5. Read a book that broadens your horizons.
6. Make a prudent investment with your resources.
7. Volunteer in a role that resonates with your heart.
8. Assemble the right team and initiate a new project together.
9. Explore real estate for enjoyment or speculation.
10. Harness your imagination to bring something new into existence.
11. Conduct thorough research and ignite a strong work ethic.
12. Stay open to the surprises that come your way.
13. Undertake a home improvement project to enhance its beauty.
14. Spend time in your happy place, immersed in nature.
15. Evaluate your financial portfolio with care.
16. Keep the larger picture in mind as you serve humanity.
17. Create a to-do list and diligently complete them.
18. Foster diplomacy by mediating any disagreements.
19. Enjoy today by engaging in activities that bring you joy.
20. Concentrate on your workload and accomplish your tasks.
21. Embrace the changes that are unfolding with enthusiasm.
22. Find solace at home and enjoy your personal sanctuary.
23. Dedicate time to internal focus and reflection.
24. Be courageous and assert your authority confidently.
25. Perform a good deed to help those in need.
26. Embrace originality as you express your individuality.
27. Offer support and compassion to a friend in need.
28. Find every opportunity to express yourself today.
29. Consider the firm foundation that supports your endeavors.
30. Embrace adventure by trying something completely new.

October
3 Personal Month

Note: October is always the same number as your personal year next year. This means it is a brief preview of the coming year.

As you near the completion of a year devoted to balance, moderation, cooperation, and harmony, you may have experienced a deepening of your intuition, cultivated a relationship with the Divine, or perhaps even changed your residence. This period of introspection is drawing to a close, as next year will propel you into a vibrant social atmosphere.

October, characterized by the energy of 3, is centered on creativity and communication, marking a time that is both highly social and outwardly focused. Utilize this month as a preview of the year ahead—expand your horizons and delve into your emotions, learning to articulate your feelings with clarity. If any unresolved issues linger, now is the opportune moment to address them with your loved ones. Your imagination is particularly heightened during this time; allow it to flourish.

While January was also a 3 month, remember that you have evolved since then. Expect to see a shift in your energy from inward introspection to outward expression this month, providing insight into what the next year holds for you. Embrace the flow of your creative juices, but remain focused and inspired to manifest something meaningful.

This month is ripe with the potential for new relationships and an increase in social engagements. Cultivate a spirit of playfulness while maintaining an optimistic outlook, and do not hesitate to release any lingering issues from the past.

October is indeed a 3 month, where your creativity flows abundantly, leading to fresh ideas for abundance. This playful time invites you to engage in simple, focused projects. Consider redecorating your space, redesigning a project, writing a story, or indulging in dance—each a beautiful expression of your newfound energy.

Personal Day
(October)

1. Use your creative flair to make an agenda and follow it.
2. Be receptive to opportunities that present themselves today.
3. Engage in a heartfelt dialogue with your partner.
4. Enjoy a peaceful environment for reflection and rejuvenation.
5. Conduct a thorough audit of your financial accounts.
6. Embrace forgiveness and unconditional love to foster peace.
7. Launch a creative enterprise in collaboration with others.
8. Allow your intuition to flow freely and trust in its guidance.
9. Express yourself through singing, dancing, painting, or writing.
10. Focus your concentration and teamwork to accomplish tasks.
11. Welcome distractions, as they may lead to new opportunities.
12. Enhance your living space with thoughtful redecorations.
13. Enroll in an online course focused on self-development.
14. Balance your material and spiritual accounts with care.
15. Practice compassion and understanding in all interactions.
16. Embrace both independence and individuality.
17. Sit in stillness and tune into your intuition.
18. Attend a social gathering, relishing the company.
19. Visualize a strong foundation supporting your endeavors.
20. Spark your adventurous spirit by following your heart.
21. Savor a family gathering while respecting personal boundaries.
22. Evaluate whether you remain true to your spiritual path.
23. Accept mutual support when achieving your aspirations.
24. Act in service to humanity and extend kindness to someone.
25. Welcome new experiences and opportunities with openness.
26. Strive for balance, harmony, and peace throughout the day.
27. Document your gratitude in a journal to enhance positivity.
28. Complete and check off an item on your task list.
29. Explore unknown territories with an open mind toward growth.
30. Be bold and embark on new adventures; foster connections.
31. Treat yourself and a companion to an enjoyable night.

November
4 Personal Month

Now is the time to build a solid foundation in preparation for the expansive months that lie ahead. Focus on organizing your workspace, home, and nearly every aspect of your life. This is not the moment for risks or vacations; rather, let structure and discipline guide your daily routines. Leverage the ideas you cultivated last month to invigorate your work ethic, recognizing that this period will heavily emphasize productivity.

While this may prove to be a challenging time marked by a strong focus on work, the rewards will be significant as you assess your progress at month's end. Prioritizing a healthy diet and regular exercise will also serve you well during this time. In a 2 year, harmony and cooperation are essential, so collaborate effectively with others. Remember, you are not alone, and it is perfectly acceptable to seek assistance when needed.

Pay careful attention to the details and address those mundane tasks you may have been postponing. Refrain from taking unnecessary risks; instead, go with the flow and remain adaptable in your approach. Be accommodating and open to the needs of others.

November embodies the energy of a 4 month, emphasizing the values of organization, discipline, and diligence. Focus on your health through mindful eating and exercise, and bring to fruition the creations inspired by last month. Whether you embark on a new project or complete one that has been lingering, take this opportunity to reset your foundation in anticipation of the expansive energy of the upcoming 5 month.

PERSONAL YEAR 2

Personal Day
(November)

1. Stay alert for shifts and greet them with enthusiasm.
2. Focus your energy on productive work from home today.
3. Add exercise to your routine to boost energy levels.
4. Organize your finances; balance is key.
5. Finish your project and take pride in your work.
6. Create a monthly to-do list to stay on track.
7. Address unfinished tasks for clarity and success.
8. Set aside time for enjoyment; celebrate your hard work.
9. Diligence pays off; your efforts will yield results.
10. Embrace upcoming changes for exciting possibilities.
11. Nurture valuable relationships; they need attention.
12. Allow time for quiet reflection to gather insights.
13. Stay open to changes at work and adapt as needed.
14. Let go of what no longer serves you for clarity.
15. Reflect on new thoughts and insights.
16. Focus on details; they are crucial for success.
17. Identify what brings you joy and prioritize those activities.
18. Stay grounded to support your endeavors.
19. Increase your workload with determination and enthusiasm.
20. Enhance your home environment for productivity.
21. Choose fresh, nutritious foods for optimal health.
22. Honor your knowledge; it's a valuable asset.
23. Complete your to-do list and celebrate each task.
24. Embrace the chance to start a new chapter.
25. Seek deeper meanings in your interactions.
26. Hold yourself accountable to foster growth.
27. Avoid overthinking; trust your instincts and act.
28. Prepare for a fast-paced month; stay organized.
29. Brighten your space with flowers for inspiration.
30. Focus on self-improvement to evolve joyfully.

December
5 Personal Month

After a month of diligent work, it is time for a change. December beckons with surprises, extending beyond what might be found beneath the tree. Both anticipated and unforeseen shifts are on the horizon, and it's essential to seize every opportunity that presents itself. Having labored within the confines of your box, you are now poised to leap into the unknown, supported by the strong foundation you have established.

Release the challenges of the past and remain grounded in the present moment. New horizons await you—do not hesitate to forge your own path. Embrace curiosity and explore all of life's offerings. Take risks and allow the expansive energy of the 5 to invigorate you, living with optimism and positivity. As you conclude your 2 year, it is likely that your intuition has sharpened and you have formed new relationships. Everything you have done this year prepares you for the wonderfully creative journey that lies ahead.

Expect that changes may manifest in both short-term opportunities and longer-lasting effects. Embrace travel and relish in your newfound freedom, though you may feel a sense of unease as you navigate through transition.

December is a 5 month—an invitation to welcome unexpected change characterized by travel and adventure. Be prepared for potential shifts in direction. Leverage this time to promote yourself and utilize your communication skills effectively. Step forward and take calculated risks, as the transformations that occur this month are geared toward enhancing your life. Allow the vibrant energy to flow and embrace the possibilities it brings.

Personal Day
(December)

1. Embrace opportunities ahead and choose boldly.
2. Dive into a self-improvement book to fuel your adventure.
3. Cultivate balance amid the exciting chaos around you.
4. Share your adventurous spirit with enthusiastic gestures.
5. Write down your dreams and manifest the extraordinary.
6. Collaborate to build partnerships that enhance your adventures.
7. Dance like nobody's watching and let joy resonate.
8. Follow clear paths to exciting destinations.
9. Enjoy a spontaneous adventure; wander freely.
10. Plan an exhilarating evening out with a friend.
11. Take a day trip to explore something new and exciting.
12. Check in with your business; think outside the box.
13. Follow your inner guidance to discover uncharted territories.
14. Challenge yourself to try something new and adventurous.
15. Trust your intuition to guide you through thrilling experiences.
16. Live and love fully, stepping outside your comfort zone.
17. Use adventure to drive your success.
18. Let each day lead to new horizons and possibilities.
19. Have heartfelt conversations with loved ones to connect.
20. Find serenity in nature; meditate and reconnect.
21. Organize your plans but stay open to unexpected detours.
22. Lift the spirits of others with your adventurous energy.
23. Explore new dimensions in life; let curiosity guide you.
24. Quiet your inner critic and embrace spontaneity.
25. Let your creativity lead you on new explorations.
26. Reassess your foundation; align with your adventurous goals.
27. Check off something from your desires list and act.
28. Give full attention to someone special; nurture the bond.
29. Embark on a vision quest to uncover your adventure within.
30. Confidently express your authority; lead with passion.
31. Commit to balance & harmony as you embrace your journey.

Personal Year 3

In a personal year characterized by the vibrant energy of the number 3, the creative forces cultivated over the past two years come to fruition. This year invites you to express yourself joyfully and embrace the optimism that flows from the seeds sown in your year of beginnings. Let creativity guide you—express yourself, inspire those around you, and harness the power of your imagination.

During this time, friendships and connections with associates reach newfound importance, with travel and an active social life taking center stage. Stay focused on your goals, allowing your imagination and creative energies to flourish. This is a year of growth and expansion through joyful living; however, strive to maintain balance and avoid becoming overwhelmed by the exuberance of creation.

Express yourself through every avenue that arises, embracing the fun, imaginative, and creative journey this year offers. Anticipate the industrious energy of the upcoming year, but for now, indulge in travel and entertainment. Let optimism be your companion and revisit the goals set in your foundational year as you witness the fruits of your efforts.

Resolve lingering emotional issues and delve deeply into your emotions, preferably with the support of a group dedicated to mutual growth. Keep negative thoughts and emotions in check, avoiding the distraction of scattered energies. Focus on what truly matters, using this year as an opportunity for self-improvement.

Allow the dynamic energy of 3 to stimulate your creativity and inspire your artistic talents.

Creativity reigns supreme this year, encouraging pursuits in writing, speaking, drama, and all artistic endeavors. Reach new heights by expanding your imagination and manifesting your dreams. As more social engagements and relationships enrich your life, understand and express your emotions with clarity.

Commit to harnessing your creative power without excess, enjoying the fun while maintaining a disciplined approach. Balance the creative energies with commitment, reaping the great rewards it brings. Indulge in your creative imagination for a joyful year before transitioning into a more industrious phase of hard work and practical focus.

PERSONAL YEAR 3

January
4 Personal Month

A 3 year promises to be filled with joy and excitement, brimming with opportunities for social engagement. You may find yourself communicating more than usual, and emotions are likely to surface during this period. Take the time to connect with your feelings and learn to express them authentically. Unresolved relationship issues may come to the forefront; addressing them now will pave a clear path for the remainder of the year.

With the creative energy of a 3 year, it is essential to have a solid foundation beneath you to ensure success throughout this joyful and vibrant time. As you transition into this new year, the 4 month ahead signifies a period devoted to laying down a new foundation for the year. Structure and discipline will be paramount; consider what aspects of your life require transformation as you set your New Year's resolutions. The energy is now aligned for you to commit to these goals.

Embrace opportunities to organize, remodel, and complete ongoing projects during January. While the creative energies of the year can inspire a multitude of ideas, they may also lead to a scattered focus. Your determination and perseverance will carry you through, allowing you to pay attention to details and establish a stable framework for the year ahead. Prioritize your health through mindful eating and exercise, and let creativity flow freely, utilizing the disciplined energy of 4 to accomplish your tasks.

Be mindful of any tendencies toward extravagance, and strive to stay focused amidst the potential distractions of your vibrant creativity.

January signifies a 4 month, dedicated to organization, discipline, and diligence. Prioritize your health and bring the creations from the previous year into tangible form. Complete your projects and reset your foundation in preparation for the expansive energy of the upcoming 5 month.

PERSONAL YEAR 3

Personal Day
(January)

1. Stay alert for shifts and welcome them enthusiastically.
2. Focus on productive work from home today.
3. Incorporate exercise into your routine to boost energy.
4. Organize your finances; balance is key.
5. Complete your project and take pride in your achievement.
6. Draft a monthly to-do list to keep organized.
7. Address unfinished tasks for clarity and success.
8. Make time for enjoyment; celebrate your hard work.
9. Diligence pays off; expect positive outcomes.
10. Embrace upcoming changes; they bring possibilities.
11. Nurture valuable relationships; they require attention.
12. Set aside time for quiet reflection to gather insights.
13. Be open to workplace shifts and adapt as needed.
14. Let go of what no longer serves you; simplify for clarity.
15. Reflect on new insights and thoughts that arise.
16. Focus on details; they are essential for success.
17. Prioritize activities that bring you joy.
18. Stay grounded and stable for your endeavors.
19. Approach your workload with determination and enthusiasm.
20. Improve your home environment for productivity.
21. Be mindful of your diet; choose fresh, nutritious foods.
22. Honor your knowledge; it's a valuable asset.
23. Complete your to-do list, celebrating each task.
24. Embrace the chance to start a new chapter.
25. Seek deeper meanings in interactions; read between the lines.
26. Hold yourself accountable to foster growth.
27. Avoid overthinking; trust your instincts and act.
28. Prepare for a fast-paced month; stay organized and ready.
29. Brighten your space with flowers for inspiration.
30. Focus on self-improvement to keep evolving.
31. Strive for balance and harmony for a fulfilling experience.

February
5 Personal Month

This year is a canvas of creativity for you, and February invites you to expand your horizons and explore new possibilities. Change is on the horizon, both anticipated and unforeseen, so be prepared to embrace it. Engage in exploration, travel, and adventure, and don't hesitate to take calculated risks.

Harness the imaginative energy of the 3 to think outside the box. Reflect on what you truly desire for this year and utilize your communication skills to promote yourself effectively. The dynamic interplay of the creative 3 and the expansive 5 creates a month brimming with limitless potential. Tap into all your skills and talents as you aim for previously unattainable heights.

Flow with this vibrant energy; resist the urge to paddle against the current. Opportunities are abundant, so remain alert and ready to seize whatever comes your way. Use your communication skills to address unresolved issues, expanding your scope and reaching for new experiences without fear. Luck is on your side; this is not the time for timidity or shyness. Step into the limelight, blaze your own trail, and liberate yourself from conventional boundaries.

Expect a delightful variety of experiences this month, but you may also feel a sense of restlessness as you navigate your newfound freedom. Open yourself to new interests, destinations, and connections as you venture into uncharted territories.

February is characterized as a 5 month; a time of unexpected change that brings opportunities for travel and adventure. Be prepared for potential shifts in direction and take the initiative to promote yourself. Embrace risks, as the transformations this month are poised to enhance your life. Allow the energy to flow and revel in the possibilities.

PERSONAL YEAR 3

Personal Day
(February)

1. Delight in the abundance of opportunities; choose joy and wonder.
2. Open a self-improvement book and let your imagination soar.
3. Navigate chaos with a balanced lifestyle that radiates energy.
4. Spread joy with kind gestures and watch smiles bloom.
5. Write down your dreams and let them come to life.
6. Embrace cooperation to create harmony with others.
7. Celebrate life by dancing and singing; let your spirit shine.
8. Follow clear paths on your whimsical journey.
9. Enjoy a day filled with adventure—exploration awaits!
10. Plan a fun evening out with a friend, filled with laughter.
11. Take a day trip to a new place and follow your curiosity.
12. Check in on your business while letting imagination roam.
13. Trust your inner guidance like a curious child on a quest.
14. Dare to try something new; adventure is calling you.
15. Follow your intuition on delightful escapades.
16. Live boldly; step outside your comfort zone spontaneously.
17. Focus on your success path while adding whimsy.
18. Let the day lead you to joyful new horizons.
19. Engage in meaningful conversations to deepen bonds.
20. Find peace in nature; meditate and hug a tree.
21. Embrace organization with a cheerful approach.
22. Lift others' spirits; your cheerful energy spreads happiness.
23. Explore new dimensions with playful curiosity.
24. Quiet your inner critic and let your heart express freely.
25. Inspire creativity to explore new realms; let imagination lead.
26. Realign your foundation with joyful intentions for adventures.
27. Check off something from your desires list; make dreams real.
28. Devote your attention to someone special and cherish the bond.
29. Embark on a whimsical quest to uncover your inner magic.

March
6 Personal Month

Responsibility takes center stage this month, emphasizing the importance of home and family. Your loved ones will undoubtedly need your support, making this an ideal time to be of service to them. Relationships are in the spotlight, urging you to address any issues as they arise. With the nurturing energy of the number 6 backing you, you have the tools to resolve conflicts and elevate your connections to a higher level. Strive to create harmony in all your relationships, practicing forgiveness and letting go of past grievances.

As you move forward, keep your gaze focused on the future rather than dwelling on previous experiences. Consider taking your beloved on a weekend getaway to strengthen your bond or use this time to organize your space or embark on a home improvement project. Dedicate quality moments to your children, sharing your wisdom and teaching them something new to foster connection and understanding.

This month is your opportunity to manage all of your responsibilities, both at home and work. Following the expansive energy of April, this month invites you to return home and find your center. Embrace your role as caregiver, nurturing those you hold dear. However, remember that to give fully, you must also recharge your own energy; after all, you cannot pour from an empty well.

Feel your creativity coming alive as it directs your focus toward home and family. Make a meaningful contribution and be of service; surround yourself with beauty and positivity to enhance your environment.

March is characterized as a 6 month, a time dedicated to home and family. Embrace your responsibilities and take care of your household and relationships. Prioritize family time by scheduling vacations or initiating home improvement projects, all while seeking harmony in both your career and personal life. Now is the moment to realign your priorities and foster the connections that matter most.

PERSONAL YEAR 3

Personal Day
(March)

1. Set aside sacred time for yourself in an inspiring space.
2. Embrace balance across all aspects of your life.
3. Radiate love and forgiveness to enrich your spirit.
4. Approach responsibilities with grace and compassion.
5. Express gratitude for your family's contributions to you.
6. Emanate joy and positivity, brightening those around you.
7. Strengthen your boundaries and ensure they are respected.
8. Try something new and exciting with a loved one.
9. Share heartfelt conversations with your partner to connect.
10. Transform your inner critic into motivation.
11. Invest energy in expanding your career and ambitions.
12. Perform acts of kindness to spread positivity.
13. Dedicate quality time to nurture your relationships.
14. Use diplomacy to resolve issues and foster harmony.
15. Channel creativity into a home project that brings beauty.
16. Create a clear plan to turn your vision into reality.
17. Reserve a day for soul-nourishing activities.
18. Make lasting memories with loved ones, capturing joy.
19. Meditate and connect with your intuition as your guide.
20. Find your center to maintain harmony amid challenges.
21. Embrace letting go and surrender to higher wisdom.
22. Collaborate with your partner to set shared goals.
23. Be willing to compromise for balance and harmony.
24. Treat yourself to an entertaining evening filled with joy.
25. Keep structure and discipline as foundations for success.
26. Stay open to amazing events and embrace the unexpected.
27. Take charge of your responsibilities with purpose.
28. Retreat to your happy place with a book for escape.
29. Honor your wisdom; embody your authority with confidence.
30. Practice forgiveness and let unconditional love flow.
31. Stay attuned to new ideas; keep your mind open to inspiration.

April
7 Personal Month

This year invites you to embrace your creativity and revel in the joys of social engagement. Allow yourself to fully utilize your creative gifts as you embark on this fun-filled journey. This month, however, encourages you to turn your imagination inward. Dedicate time to meditation and visualization, focusing on what you wish to manifest this year. Next month, the energetic vibrations aligned with you will support the transformation of your visualizations into tangible reality.

Following a month dedicated to serving others, make it a priority to seek solitude and rest. Reflect on the current trajectory of your life and consider whether you are truly fulfilling your highest purpose. The energy of 7 is particularly attuned to spiritual pursuits and personal growth, making this an ideal time to engage in self-improvement activities. Enroll in a class, embark on a retreat, or delve into a self-help book. Now is the perfect moment to explore metaphysical sciences.

Immerse yourself in nature, allowing its tranquility to restore and rejuvenate you. Take this opportunity to listen to your inner voice, exercising trust in your intuition and guidance. Establish a healthy foundation with your inner self and prioritize your well-being this month by developing balanced dietary and exercise routines.

As you review your projects, take the time to analyze everything thoroughly and conduct any necessary research. Remember that it is perfectly acceptable to withdraw from external demands right now; avoid making hasty decisions until you have gained clarity.

April is characterized as a 7 month, a time for rest, relaxation, and rejuvenation. Solitude is essential for personal reflection; take the opportunity to reevaluate your life's journey and assess the direction you wish to pursue. Engage in studies of metaphysics, embark on a retreat, and immerse yourself in the serenity of nature.

PERSONAL YEAR 3

Personal Day
(April)

1. Embrace opportunities as they come; think before acting.
2. Tie up loose ends and complete tasks with pride.
3. Boldly express your individuality and unique essence.
4. Cultivate cooperation; collaborate harmoniously with others.
5. Savor moments to fully enjoy your day.
6. Prioritize health with wholesome eating and exercise.
7. Embrace spontaneity and discover delightful surprises.
8. Tackle responsibilities with commitment and diligence.
9. Seek your sacred space; cherish solitude for reflection.
10. Prepare for abundance; it's not just about money.
11. Cultivate patience and understanding in your interactions.
12. Today is great for negotiations; clarity leads to success.
13. Seek reciprocity by acknowledging others' contributions.
14. Shift from introspection to embrace social connections.
15. Consider a wellness check; prioritize nurturing your health.
16. Embrace variety; challenge yourself to do something extraordinary.
17. Beautify your home with flowers or tidiness for inspiration.
18. Reflect on your path and ensure it aligns with your goals.
19. Manage finances; balance your checkbook and credit cards.
20. Release what you cannot control; free yourself from burdens.
21. Align actions with your highest goals; assess progress.
22. Practice deference; let collaboration flourish today.
23. Reach out to an old friend with a heartfelt message.
24. Create order amidst chaos by grounding yourself in practicality.
25. Promote yourself and your work; share your innovations.
26. Maintain boundaries while respecting others' limits.
27. Gather your thoughts on a nature walk for inspiration.
28. Embrace your authority; present yourself confidently.
29. Show compassion by volunteering your time when possible.
30. Let ambition and success build a foundation for your future.

May
8 Personal Month

The energy of 3 brings forth a year filled with fun, imagination, and social engagement. This is your opportunity to truly enjoy life to the fullest. Recognized as a lucky number, 3 encourages you to embrace calculated risks. Expand your horizons, harness your creative talents, and create something that celebrates this remarkable year.

The 3 also embodies communication, which means unresolved emotions may surface, seeking resolution. Take the time to engage deeply with these feelings and tidy up any emotional clutter to foster a balanced and joyful existence.

As the energy of 8 comes into play, the focus shifts to business, management, financial growth, and stepping into your role as your own authority. If you are an artist, explore ways to expand your brand and reach new audiences. This year holds great potential for financial success, particularly when paired with the creative energy of 3 allowing your business endeavors to flourish. Embrace your personal power and authority throughout May, as this month embodies self-empowerment.

Trust your intuition and summon your courage; maintaining a positive mindset is crucial when navigating the influences of these two powerful numbers. Delight in the joyful aspects of life, recognizing that success encompasses more than just financial wealth.

You are called to fully understand the laws of attraction during this time. Make decisive choices, embrace significant new undertakings, and assess your investments. Remain open to receiving the abundance that comes your way.

May is characterized as an 8 month, focused on work, power, and authority. This is a time when business demands your attention, and stepping into a leadership role is essential. Organize and manage all facets of your life, ensuring you maintain a healthy balance between your material and spiritual pursuits. Embrace your role as an authority, guiding yourself and others toward success.

PERSONAL YEAR 3

Personal Day
(May)

1. Spread love—donate to a worthy cause with time or money.
2. Start an adventure with a research project or a captivating book.
3. Center yourself and trust your gut feeling.
4. Let your creativity flow; unleash your imagination.
5. Organize your fun—structure your workday for creativity.
6. Embrace variety; each day holds delightful surprises.
7. Be a superhero—be ready to help those in need.
8. Put on your explorer hat; twist old ideas into something new.
9. Keep your eyes on the prize; seize upcoming opportunities.
10. Wrap up projects with flair and celebrate completion.
11. Showcase your uniqueness; express individuality boldly.
12. Pay attention to details for a polished finish.
13. Reach out to an old friend; reconnections are rewarding.
14. Activate your practical side; tackle tasks head-on.
15. Promote yourself and share your talents confidently.
16. Establish and protect your boundaries fiercely.
17. Don't forget to recharge; rest to maintain your energy.
18. Balance your accounts; invest wisely for future success.
19. Use your gifts to give back; it feels great!
20. Collaborate with others; teamwork leads to breakthroughs.
21. Go with the flow; let things unfold naturally.
22. Play hard and find joy in the little things.
23. Ensure your foundation is solid; stability boosts confidence.
24. Get out and mingle; new people can lead to opportunities.
25. Nurture key relationships; they are crucial for success.
26. Create a perfect space; invite in positive vibes.
27. Keep an eye on your finances; money matters are important.
28. Identify solutions, then let go for freedom.
29. Share your wisdom; your insights are valuable.
30. Use diplomacy to resolve conflicts smoothly.
31. Communication is your superpower; engage and inspire.

PERSONAL YEAR 3

June
9 Personal Month

This year promises to be a delightful journey filled with joy and creativity. Embrace the opportunity to socialize and fully engage in your artistic pursuits. Connect with your imagination and express yourself freely. Explore your innovative side and create something meaningful that can uplift humanity. As the number 9 is known for its humanitarian spirit, serving others will bring you great fulfillment.

In this 9 month, you stand at the close of a numerology cycle, inviting the energy to cleanse, release, and finish anything that no longer serves your best interests. Prepare for new beginnings that await you in July by letting go of as much as possible, creating space for new possibilities. Both 3 and 9 are powerful creation numbers; allow your imagination to run wild and develop something that contributes to the greater good.

Compassion, forgiveness, and unconditional love resonate with the 9 vibration, as well. It is a time to shed what does not align with your highest purpose and to embrace the rewards that this 9 month presents. Now is your moment to reap the fruits of your labor and to dream about what you wish to manifest in the future.

Expand your generosity and benevolence, seeking out your spiritual truth. Lead with unconditional love and understanding, and remember that forgiveness is essential. Contemplate your future vision and keep your eye on the bigger picture, avoiding the temptation to get lost in fantasy.

June represents a 9 month, signifying the conclusion of a nine-month cycle. Take this time to cleanse, complete your tasks, and release everything that does not serve you. Enjoy the rewards of your hard work from the past eight months, and make room for the exciting new beginnings that lie ahead. Use your intuition as you contemplate what you wish to create next, harnessing your creativity to serve the greater good.

PERSONAL YEAR 3

Personal Day
(June)

1. Take charge of your life; be the visionary artist with intention.
2. Collaborate with creators to bring a shared vision to life.
3. Express yourself through various media; stay open to new forms.
4. Plan your day but allow space for spontaneous inspiration.
5. Stay attuned to synchronicities that add magic to your day.
6. Buy vibrant flowers and share their beauty with someone special.
7. Renew yourself in a sanctuary that fuels creativity and peace.
8. Seize bold opportunities that art presents.
9. Simplify your space to clear the way for new inspirations.
10. Use today to choose your artistic paths thoughtfully.
11. Trust your intuition through creative challenges.
12. Celebrate spontaneity with a lively gathering for creativity.
13. Balance creativity and practicality to boost productivity.
14. Let unpredictability fuel dynamic artistic expression.
15. Order your space to reflect your artistic sensibility.
16. Flow with your creativity; avoid forced direction.
17. Manage finances to ensure balance in your artistry.
18. Release outdated projects to make room for new ones.
19. Align your vision with your dreams to build a foundation.
20. Offer heartfelt apologies to foster creative healing.
21. Engage in joyful activities that uplift your spirit.
22. Address unresolved issues clearly to free your mind.
23. Showcase your work; share your creations with the world.
24. Be ready to offer insights and guidance to others.
25. Reflect on your journey; ensure your path matches your desires.
26. Assert your authority in your artistic domain with confidence.
27. Let go of what no longer serves your creative future.
28. Inspire collective expressions by leading with your intellect.
29. Focus on finishing unfinished projects to bring them to life.
30. Share your unique artistic perspectives in discussions.

PERSONAL YEAR 3

July
1 Personal Month

This is your year of creativity, and this month allows you to envision and articulate what you wish to achieve for the remainder of the year. With the energy of a 1 month promoting new beginnings and the support of 3 energy amplifying your creative endeavors, you are doubly blessed.

Dream without limits; what are your wildest aspirations? Do not hold back; dare to think big, as many individuals do not dream expansively enough. Consider what truly makes your heart sing and what brings you joy. Clarify your desires and invite a spirit of enjoyment into your life. The essence of 3 centers around the pursuit of joy, so allow yourself to discover your bliss throughout this year.

Now is the time to plant the seeds for your future, allowing the Universe the space and time to manifest your intentions. With a plethora of new opportunities ahead, expect this month to be busy. While your social calendar may be filled to the brim, carve out moments to focus on what you want to manifest. Maintain a positive mindset and remember to hold yourself to the discipline and commitment necessary to bring your projects to completion.

Embrace the chance to establish new, healthy habits and take the initiative to try something different. Be original and adventurous as you embark on fresh projects, stretching yourself socially along the way and making new friends.

July emphasizes new beginnings. It is a perfect time to plant seeds, delineate your goals, and set your intentions for the year ahead. With an abundance of exciting projects on the horizon, have the courage to step into a leadership role and make your aspirations a reality.

PERSONAL YEAR 3

121

Personal Day
(July)

1. Create a peaceful environment to boost creativity and collaboration.
2. Let your cheerful spirit inspire others to embrace innovation.
3. Be an effective manager by organizing your thoughts and resources.
4. View changes as opportunities for growth and innovation.
5. Engage with your community and make meaningful contributions.
6. Research topics that excite you to fuel your innovative mindset.
7. Focus on action, ambition, and achievement to drive initiatives.
8. Be open to letting go of outdated practices for a greater purpose.
9. Today is ideal for forging solid business deals with integrity.
10. Exercise patience to foster a free-flowing atmosphere for ideas.
11. Maintain optimism to inspire your team and enhance creativity.
12. Align your values with ethical leadership and innovation.
13. Make thoughtful decisions; curb impulsiveness and focus long-term.
14. Approach conflicts with kindness to nurture collaboration.
15. Prioritize health by starting a new exercise routine.
16. Cultivate gratitude and welcome abundance into your initiatives.
17. True success comes from serving humanity; lead with this mindset.
18. Use your leadership skills to chart new paths for others.
19. Value friendships; nurture love and companionship in your network.
20. Quiet your inner critic and focus on the positives.
21. Read fine print in documents for clarity and to avoid pitfalls.

22. Stay open to fresh ideas without getting overwhelmed.
23. Commit to responsible actions for your mission's advancement.
24. Embrace rest; it's vital for renewal.
25. Focus on the greater good; prioritize collective benefits.
26. Clear clutter to prepare for transformative opportunities.
27. Strive to improve projects; aim for progress, not complacency.
28. Support others to reinforce a culture of service.
29. Attend self-improvement seminars or read inspiring books.
30. Honor your work ethic; it sets a powerful example for others.
31. Ignite your individuality by pursuing adventurous ideas.

PERSONAL YEAR 3

August
2 Personal Month

The energy of 3 significantly enhances every creative endeavor, regardless of the medium you choose to express yourself. Whether through writing, acting, singing, dancing, or speaking, all pursuits are particularly fruitful now. This month is likely to be vibrant and social, with a full calendar of engaging activities.

Expressing your emotions is vital, especially in August, as you may find yourself more sensitive under the influence of the 2 vibration. Cooperation, diplomacy, and negotiation will be prominently featured, making this an ideal time to resolve any relationship issues.

As the month unfolds at a slower pace, you will have ample opportunity to turn inward and connect with your inner guidance. Pay keen attention to the details and strive for balance and harmony in all your endeavors. Nurture the aspirations you planted last month, and take care of the small things that matter.

Allow yourself to go with the flow; this is not the time to struggle against the current. Above all, remember to enjoy life and make space for playfulness, as 2025 will be defined by hard work.

Embrace simplicity and slow your pace. Remain cautious, receptive, and accommodating as you gather information for future considerations. Your ultimate goal during this time is to cultivate peace and harmony.

August represents a 2 month; a period focused on the finer details. Attend to the small matters and nurture the seeds you planted last month. Cooperation in relationships is essential, particularly after last month's emphasis on individuality. Prepare for an emotional journey this month that may call for the application of your diplomatic skills.

PERSONAL YEAR 3

Personal Day
(August)

1. Unleash your artistic talent; create a masterpiece of your soul.
2. Organize chaos; prioritize tasks like a maestro.
3. Release worries and let life flow gracefully.
4. Treat your partner to a delicious meal and great conversation.
5. Dive into a book that leads to new adventures.
6. Develop a smart investment strategy for prosperity.
7. Volunteer where your spirit thrives and make a positive impact.
8. Assemble a dream team and start an ambitious project.
9. Explore real estate opportunities and imaginative ideas.
10. Use imagination to innovate something wonderful.
11. Fuel ambition with hard work and strong ethics.
12. Embrace the unexpected; let surprises brighten your day.
13. Start a home project to enhance your sanctuary.
14. Recharge in nature and enjoy the earth's tranquility.
15. Take charge of your finance by assessing your portfolio.
16. Seek ways to uplift humanity as you reflect on life.
17. Create order from chaos with an epic to-do list.
18. Promote peace as a diplomatic figure in conflicts.
19. Seize the day with joy as your guide; enjoy your pursuits.
20. Focus on tasks and eliminate distractions.
21. Embrace change; dance with life's transformations.
22. Enjoy the comforting embrace of your home.
23. Reflect inwardly, exploring the depths of your mind.
24. Lead with courage, embracing your authority and vision.
25. Perform acts of kindness to spread goodwill.
26. Express your individuality boldly and creatively.
27. Support a friend with compassion and a listening ear.
28. Make today a canvas showcasing your essence.
29. Reflect on the foundations supporting your growth.
30. Step into the unknown with courage and pioneer horizons.
31. Respect boundaries and avoid giving unsolicited advice.

PERSONAL YEAR 3

September
3 Personal Month

Note: Because September is the ninth month, it is always the same number as your personal year. This means you have double the energy of your personal year for thirty days. If the current year calculates to the same value as your personal year, then you receive triple that number's energy in September.

Create. Create. Create. The energy surrounding you now is amplified, granting you double the imagination to bring forth whatever your heart desires. With a bustling social calendar this month, relish the time spent in the company of others. Understanding your emotions and learning to articulate them is essential this year, particularly during this month of creativity.

Three is a lucky number, and it's exhilarating to witness the wonderful manifestations that result from your belief. Embrace your creative power to infuse joy into your life. As you anticipate the upcoming year, a year defined by diligence and discipline, make the most of the enjoyable energy that flows around you now.

Maintain a positive mindset while being mindful of a potential tendency toward unnecessary drama. Choose your words carefully; gossip and negativity serve no one. Keep life simple and remain focused. If you're not feeling particularly inspired creatively, consider redesigning something or making improvements to an existing project.

Allow for personal growth as you broaden your horizons. Let your imagination run free and seek out activities that bring you joy. Utilize your creative skills, for entertainment and enjoyment are paramount at this juncture. Embrace romance and forge new relationships, expressing yourself fully while reveling in the joyful vibrations that surround you. Be wary, however, of a tendency toward extravagance.

September unfolds as a 3 month, where your creative juices flow abundantly, unveiling fresh ideas that can lead to prosperity. Embrace this playful time, yet remember to keep things simple and maintain your focus.

126

Personal Day
(September)

1. Create a playful agenda and enjoy checking off tasks.
2. Watch for delightful surprises today.
3. Share a laughter-filled chat with your partner.
4. Treat yourself to a blissful retreat for "me" time.
5. Audit your finances and check your bank account thoroughly.
6. Let forgiveness and love fill your life with joy.
7. Gather your creative crew for a fun project.
8. Allow your intuition to guide you freely.
9. Express yourself through fun activities like singing or dancing.
10. Bring playful focus to your day and create magic.
11. Embrace delightful distractions for new adventures.
12. Add flair to your home with spontaneous redecorating.
13. Sign up for a lively online course to boost your spirits.
14. Balance earthly and spiritual matters with grace.
15. Let compassion and understanding light your path.
16. Celebrate your wild side by embracing independence.
17. Find a cozy spot for reflection and listen to your intuition.
18. Dive into a social gathering and enjoy the fun.
19. Envision a whimsical foundation supporting your dreams.
20. Ignite your adventurous spirit and follow your heart.
21. Enjoy family gatherings while maintaining joyful boundaries.
22. Take a lighthearted view of your spiritual journey.
23. Shine your aspirations brightly and level up with a smile.
24. Spread good vibes like confetti to bless those around you.
25. Open the doors to welcome new delights into your life.
26. Juggle life's demands with a twinkle in your eye.
27. Write down what you're grateful for; let joy overflow.
28. Celebrate the thrill of crossing tasks off your list.
29. Embark on a joyful adventure into the unknown.
30. Channel your inner explorer and seek new escapades.

PERSONAL YEAR 3

October
4 Personal Month

Note: October is always the same number as your personal year next year, so it is a brief preview of the coming year.

This year is intended for enjoyment, yet October introduces a shift toward structure and discipline. This transition from creative expression to diligent focus can feel quite radical; it is wise to start by completing any unfinished projects you initiated earlier. Now is the time to transform your creative ideas into tangible realities.

Embrace the energy of the number 4, which emphasizes the importance of building a solid foundation beneath you, preparing you for the months to come. As you anticipate the opportunities of the next year, pay close attention to the details and address any issues as they arise. Procrastination is not conducive to the energy of 4, nor is this a month for taking risks. Instead, keep your head down, concentrate on your tasks, and embrace the diligence required at this time.

The rewards for your efforts will manifest as you reflect on the work you accomplished this month, rather than postponing your energy. Understand that this is not a time for vacations or leisurely pursuits; instead, prioritize getting your life in order. Approach the month with a practical and pragmatic mindset, resisting any temptations toward laziness or procrastination.

October is characterized as a 4 month, emphasizing the need for organization, discipline, and diligence. Prioritize your health through mindful diet and exercise, and ensure that you bring your creations from last month into physical form. Conclude any outstanding projects and reset your foundation in preparation for the expansive journey that lies ahead in the coming 5 month.

PERSONAL YEAR 3

128

Personal Day
(October)

1. Embrace the excitement of a shift; get ready for the thrill.
2. Dive into remote work today; blend comfort with productivity.
3. Fit in some exercise to boost energy and mood.
4. Manage your finances while dreaming of rewards.
5. Finish your project and treat yourself afterward.
6. Create an inspiring to-do list for the month.
7. Update your tasks to keep the momentum going.
8. Schedule time for fun; life is too short to miss out.
9. Remember, hard work pays off, especially with enjoyment.
10. Prepare for upcoming changes with enthusiasm.
11. Strengthen relationships this month; they enrich your life.
12. Take quiet moments for reflection to gain clarity.
13. Stay open to work changes; they can lead to new opportunities.
14. Release what hinders you and make space for fun.
15. Reflect on new ideas and let creativity flow.
16. Pay attention to details while seeing the bigger picture.
17. Discover what brings you joy and engage fully.
18. Balance ambition with enjoyment for a solid foundation.
19. Increase your workload while keeping the mood light.
20. Enhance your home environment to inspire passion.
21. Focus on your diet; fresh food energizes your spirit.
22. Value your knowledge while being open to new insights.
23. Complete monthly tasks, celebrating each achievement.
24. Welcome the chance to start a new chapter of possibilities.
25. Seek deeper meanings in conversations for delightful surprises.
26. Hold yourself accountable for your goals; it's your journey.
27. Avoid overthinking; trust your instincts and act boldly.
28. Prepare for a fast-paced month; let excitement motivate you.
29. Bring home flowers to brighten your space and mood.
30. Focus on personal growth; it leads to greater joy.
31. Seek balance and harmony while enjoying life's pleasures.

PERSONAL YEAR 3

November
5 Personal Month

As this year of fun draws to a close, November ushers in a period of exhilarating freedom and expansion. Throughout the year, you have likely embraced numerous opportunities to explore your creative outlets. The vibrational energy of 5 this month heralds a wealth of possibilities for liberating experiences and personal growth.

If you find yourself hesitating, now is the time to take a bold step. With 3 representing luck and 5 providing the motivation to transcend your comfort zone, your guiding mantra this month is: "Go for it." Shun timidity, put yourself out there, and be open to the wonders that await you.

While neither number is particularly associated with balance, strive to maintain some sense of order amidst the vibrant energy of this month. Avoid getting swept away in chaos or drama, and remember to cultivate a positive mindset throughout your endeavors.

Expect a return to the energy reminiscent of February, but now infused with a heightened vibration. This month promises a rich variety of experiences and creativity, though you may also feel a sense of restlessness. Embrace this newfound freedom, allowing yourself to explore new interests, travel to exciting destinations, and connect with new people.

November is indeed a 5 month, a time marked by unexpected changes that invite travel and adventure. You may find yourself altering your path entirely. Take advantage of this momentum to promote yourself and leverage your communication skills effectively. Step forward and embrace the risks that come your way, as the transformations of this month will contribute positively to your life. Allow the energy to flow freely and enjoy the journey ahead.

Personal Day
(November)

1. Embrace opportunities around you; choose joyfully.
2. Dive into a self-improvement book that inspires happiness.
3. Strive for balance amid life's delightful chaos.
4. Spread joy with kind gestures that warm hearts.
5. Write down your biggest dreams and let them shine.
6. Collaborate joyfully with others to uplift everyone.
7. Dance freely, allowing joy to guide your spirit.
8. Embrace the guiding principles in your life now.
9. Enjoy a day of adventure and celebrate your freedom.
10. Plan a fun evening with a friend for joyful memories.
11. Take a day trip to discover something new and exciting.
12. Check in on your business while exploring creatively.
13. Trust your inner guidance and follow your instincts toward happiness.
14. Dare to try something new; venture into the unknown.
15. Follow intuitive nudges and let your heart guide you.
16. Live and love boldly; step out of your comfort zone.
17. Focus on success; celebrate each achievement along the way.
18. Let today lead you to new, joyful horizons.
19. Engage in meaningful conversations to deepen connections.
20. Meditate in nature; embrace tranquility and hug a tree.
21. Organize your space to promote positivity.
22. Brighten a stranger's day; your kindness creates joy.
23. Explore new aspects of life to ignite curiosity.
24. Calm your inner critic and foster self-compassion.
25. Inspire creativity through new explorations and adventures.
26. Realign your foundation to support your happiness.
27. Check off a wishlist dream; celebrate your courage.
28. Offer full attention to someone; gift them presence.
29. Go on a vision quest that brings dreams to life.
30. Express your inner authority confidently; be heard.

PERSONAL YEAR 3

December
6 Personal Month

As the holiday season approaches, the nurturing energy of the number 6 graces your chart, inviting you to create a truly special atmosphere. Embrace this time by utilizing your creative talents to enhance the festive spirit. Decorate with flair and immerse yourself in the joy of the season, reveling in the energy of shopping, giving, and receiving, while also reconnecting with old friends. Delight in the vibrant tapestry of lights, sights, and sounds that define this joyous time of year.

Family plays an important role during this period, and their needs may be more pronounced than usual. Ensure you carve out time for your loved ones as you conclude your year of creative expression. With the appearance of 6, all relationships come into focus, so be proactive in addressing any issues that may arise.

December marks your last month of vibrant energy before you transition into a dedicated year of hard work in January. This month offers a chance to revisit the excitement of March, albeit with a festive twist. Allow your creativity to flow toward nurturing your home and family. Make meaningful contributions and be of service to those around you; surround yourself with beauty and warmth as you celebrate the holidays.

December is defined as a 6 month, emphasizing home and family. Take responsibility for your surroundings and attend to your relationships. Dedicate quality time to family, whether by scheduling a vacation or taking on home improvement projects. Balance your priorities between career and home life, ensuring harmony in all areas. Now is the time to realign your intentions and focus as you embrace this heartfelt season.

PERSONAL YEAR 3

Personal Day
(December)

1. Immerse yourself in a peaceful space to nurture your spirit.
2. Reflect on achieving balance in body, mind, and soul.
3. Emit love and forgiveness to create a soothing presence.
4. Approach tasks gracefully, adding a loving touch.
5. Express gratitude for your family's contributions; it strengthens bonds.
6. Radiate joy and positivity to brighten others' lives.
7. Set and maintain boundaries for your well-being.
8. Enjoy a playful adventure with a loved one to create memories.
9. Have a heartfelt conversation with your partner to deepen connection.
10. Build a constructive relationship with your inner critic for growth.
11. Dedicate time to advance your career and align your passions.
12. Spread kindness through uplifting deeds for positivity.
13. Nurture relationships by spending quality time with loved ones.
14. Use diplomacy to resolve issues and foster understanding.
15. Channel creativity into your home, reflecting inner beauty.
16. Create a clear plan to bring your project ideas to life.
17. Take a personal day for activities that rejuvenate your spirit.
18. Make lasting memories with loved ones by celebrating moments.
19. Meditate to explore your inner self and connect with intuition.
20. Find your center during challenges; maintain balance.
21. Embrace letting go; trust in higher wisdom to guide you.
22. Collaborate with your partner to align future goals.
23. Be flexible to maintain harmony in relationships.
24. Enjoy an entertaining evening to infuse joy and strengthen bonds.
25. Recognize the importance of structure in nurturing your environment.
26. Acknowledge today's opportunities; seize them.
27. Take responsibility for your role with purpose and integrity.

PERSONAL YEAR 3

28. Retreat to your happy place with a good book for inspiration.
29. Honor your wisdom and step confidently into your authority.
30. Practice forgiveness, let love open doors to new experiences.
31. Stay open to new ideas as gifts for inspiration and growth.

PERSONAL YEAR 3

Personal Year 4

A personal year signified by the number 4 calls for practicality and pragmatism, where organization and patience are your guiding principles. This period prioritizes self-management, leaving no room for procrastination or indolence. Exercise sound judgment and maintain order in every facet of your life, with particular attention to business, legal matters, and general paperwork. Monitor your finances closely and practice thriftiness, remaining cautious in all business or legal dealings. Ensure a thorough understanding of the facts and details before proceeding. Seek opportunities through professional connections, embodying dependability, organization, and loyalty.

This is a year dedicated to building a strong foundation for both career and personal growth, paving the way for lasting happiness and harmony. Embrace the routine and commit to your work, yet remain open to self-improvement, avoiding stagnation.

This is your year to construct a solid groundwork for the upcoming nine years. Structure and discipline are essential, allowing you to reset your life and prepare for future endeavors. Establish a foundation robust enough to support your plans as you clear away clutter and refocus your efforts. While last year was about ideation and brainstorming, this year demands focus to bring those creative ideas to fruition. With the prospect of greater freedom and expansion next year, a solid foundation is critical.

Harness this year's energy to cultivate discipline, a lesson that will serve you throughout your life. Pay attention to details and address issues promptly. Organization at home and work is vital to securing a stable future. Consider revamping your home and completing unfinished projects, supported by the steadfast energy of 4. Unresolved family matters may surface, presenting an opportunity for resolution. Legal matters may also arise, calling for patience but not procrastination. Avoid taking significant risks this year; instead, focus on health and well-being, as health concerns may emerge.

Determination and commitment are your allies through this industrious year. Maintain a positive outlook and adhere to rules for a rewarding experience. Although a 4 year can be challenging, your diligent focus will leave you reflecting on it with satisfaction and gratitude.

PERSONAL YEAR 4

January
5 Personal Month

This marks the beginning of your hardworking year, as you lay the groundwork for the entire nine-year cycle ahead. Diligence and determination will be your guiding principles over the next twelve months, but fortunately, you are greeted with a spirited January. Your year kicks off with an expansive and transitional month, where change becomes the central theme as you hit the ground running.

Seize every opportunity for freedom and growth, as the remainder of your 4 year journey will be centered around hard work and commitment. Embrace new experiences that broaden your horizons and be prepared for surprises along the way. Travel and adventure await, potentially leading you down a completely new path in life.

Allow the vibrant energy of 5 to flow through you as you prepare for next month's focus on home and family. The stabilizing force of the 4 energy will help ground you amid the exciting chaos that the 5 can inspire, enabling you to fully appreciate the benefits this month has to offer. This is your chance to reorganize, rebuild, and eliminate what no longer serves you.

January embodies the essence of a 5 month, characterized by unexpected changes that invite travel and adventure. You may find yourself shifting directions entirely, so take the initiative to promote yourself and leverage your communication skills effectively. Embrace the risks before you, for the changes unfolding this month are designed to enhance your life. Allow the energy to flow seamlessly, welcoming the opportunities that arise.

PERSONAL YEAR 4

137

Personal Day
(January)

1. Seize the opportunities ahead of you; make bold choices.
2. Dive into a self-improvement book to enhance your skills.
3. Maintain balance in your life amidst the chaos of adventure.
4. Show your power through uplifting acts of kindness.
5. Write down your dreams and pursue them with determination.
6. Collaborate with others to create impactful alliances.
7. Dance and sing; let your energy fill the room.
8. Now is the time to follow the clear paths to your goals.
9. Embrace spontaneous adventure and savor your freedom.
10. Plan a fun evening out with a friend for genuine connection.
11. Take a day trip to a new destination and explore.
12. Check in on your business, thinking creatively to innovate.
13. Trust your intuition as it guides you toward greatness.
14. Try something new to push your boundaries.
15. Follow your instincts and embrace spontaneity.
16. Live and love boldly, stepping out of your comfort zone.
17. Focus on achieving success with unwavering ambition.
18. Let each day lead you to new opportunities and excitement.
19. Engage in deep conversations to strengthen bonds.
20. Meditate in nature and reconnect with the Earth's energy.
21. Organize your goals; adhere to the rules that support them.
22. Lift a stranger's spirits with your positive energy.
23. Explore new possibilities; curiosity is your greatest ally.
24. Silence your inner critic and unleash your adventurous spirit.
25. Nurture your creativity and inspire yourself to explore.
26. Adjust your foundation to support your ambitious future plans.
27. Cross something off your desires list; make it a reality.
28. Give full attention to someone close to deepen ties.
29. Embark on a vision quest to gain insights for your journey.
30. Express your authority and take control of your destiny.
31. Commit to balancing activities and interactions while thriving.

February
6 Personal Month

As the year has unfolded, you may have already embraced a new work ethic, and this month is no exception. In this 4 year, you are diligently laying the groundwork for the forthcoming nine-year cycle. February brings your home and family into sharper focus, as the energy of 6 emphasizes relationships and responsibilities. Expect your family to require your support more than usual during this time, with added significance in November.

Pay particular attention to your primary relationship; it may reach a new plateau that calls for nurturing and understanding. Be proactive in addressing any issues that arise, as relationships are likely to come under scrutiny this month. Attend to your home as well; consider brightening up your winter space with fresh decor or embarking on a painting project.

With the combination of the 4's strong work ethic and the emphasis on home and family, you have the potential to accomplish significant home improvement projects. Remember that relationships offer valuable lessons about ourselves, so seize this opportunity to deepen your self-awareness. Plan a brief holiday with loved ones to give yourself a well-deserved break from work and strive to find harmony and balance in all your endeavors.

February embodies the energy of a 6 month, dedicated to home and family. It is vital to face your responsibilities head-on and care for both your household and your relationships. Utilize this time to strengthen family bonds by scheduling a vacation or focusing on home improvement projects. Seek harmony in both your career and home life, aligning your priorities to create a more fulfilling experience.

PERSONAL YEAR 4

Personal Day
(February)

1. Spend time in a sacred space for your well-being.
2. Prioritize balance in all aspects of life for success.
3. Embrace love and forgiveness to foster peace.
4. Handle responsibilities with grace and kindness as a leader.
5. Show gratitude for your family's contributions; recognition matters.
6. Radiate joy and positivity; it boosts productivity.
7. Set clear boundaries to ensure mutual respect.
8. Go on a fun adventure with a loved one; try something new.
9. Have open conversations with your partner; foster understanding.
10. Build a constructive relationship with your inner critic.
11. Dedicate time to advancing your career and prioritizing growth.
12. Act kindly through service; every good deed counts.
13. Nurture relationships by spending quality time together.
14. Use diplomacy to resolve issues and create harmony.
15. Channel creativity into improving your home environment.
16. Follow a detailed plan to complete your project successfully.
17. Take a day for engaging in self-care activities; it's essential.
18. Create cherished memories with loved ones; value those moments.
19. Meditate and trust your intuition to guide you.
20. Find your center and maintain balance during challenges.
21. Let go of what no longer serves you and trust your intuition.
22. Work with your partner to set new shared goals.
23. Be flexible to maintain balance in relationships.
24. Enjoy a fun evening out; embrace joy in life.
25. Embrace structure & discipline; they are essential for success.
26. Recognize the amazing opportunities unfolding today.
27. Be responsible; leadership requires accountability.
28. Retreat to your happy place to nourish your mind and spirit.
29. Honor your wisdom and be confident in your authority.

March
7 Personal Month

This month invites you to turn your attention inward, as the spiritual essence of the number 7 encourages deep reflection on your beliefs. You may find yourself reconsidering some of these beliefs during this time. Embrace a spiritual path; consider enrolling in a personal growth seminar or engaging in activities that nurture your soul.

After a month dedicated to serving your family, it is essential to carve out time for solitude and introspection. Utilize this opportunity to develop your intuition and strive for inner peace. Prioritize your health this month, as both the energies of 4 and 7 emphasize well-being. Now is an ideal time to establish new dietary and exercise regimens that support your physical vitality.

Be aware that legal matters may arise during both 4 and 7 months, so address any outstanding legal issues promptly. Reevaluate your current direction in life and make the necessary adjustments that align with your intuitive insights. Self-awareness is paramount at this time, and your commitment to personal growth will yield rewarding benefits in the future.

Take the opportunity to rest and rejuvenate in nature, allowing its serenity to replenish your spirit. You deserve this month of soulful focus dedicated to your own self-improvement.

March is characterized as a 7 month, a time for rest, relaxation, and rejuvenation. Solitude is essential for inward focus, providing you the space to reflect on where your life has been and the direction you wish to pursue. Engage in the study of metaphysics, take a retreat, and immerse yourself in the tranquility of nature.

PERSONAL YEAR 4

Personal Day
(March)

1. Prepare for new opportunities; think things through first.
2. Tie up loose ends by completing tasks for closure.
3. Embrace your individuality and express your true self.
4. Foster cooperation and harmony in your interactions.
5. Savor joyful moments; enjoy each day fully.
6. Prioritize health with a balanced diet and exercise.
7. Embrace spontaneity; welcome unforeseen opportunities.
8. Approach responsibilities diligently with focus.
9. Seek your sacred space; value solitude for reflection.
10. Recognize abundance is coming in forms beyond money.
11. Cultivate patience and understanding for growth.
12. Today is ideal for business negotiations; be intentional.
13. Aim for reciprocity; acknowledge others' contributions.
14. Step away from introspection and engage socially.
15. Consider a wellness check; self-care is essential.
16. Add variety to life and seek extraordinary experiences.
17. Enhance your home environment with flowers or tidiness.
18. Review your path to see if you're where you want to be.
19. Balance your checkbook for precise financial management.
20. Let go of what you cannot control; focus on the present.
21. Align with your highest goals and evaluate your progress.
22. Collaborate with others when needed for best results.
23. Reconnect with an old friend to strengthen the bond.
24. Stay practical; create order within chaos.
25. Promote yourself and your work; share your contributions.
26. Maintain boundaries while respecting others' limits.
27. Clear your mind on a nature walk; let tranquility inspire.
28. Be your own authority; exude confidence and professionalism.
29. Honor your commitment to help others through volunteering.
30. Your ambition and success lay the foundation for your endeavors.
31. Use diplomacy to navigate challenges while staying balanced.

PERSONAL YEAR 4

April
8 Personal Month

This year presents a unique opportunity to establish a solid foundation for your future. Since January, you have been diligently working, and your efforts will be rewarded if you choose to stay the course. Focus intently on your tasks, resist the temptation to take unnecessary risks, and remain committed to completing your work.

The energy of 8 draws attention to themes of money, management, and assuming your rightful authority. Business and career take center stage this month, and you may find your authority challenged or feel compelled to step into a leadership role. While this year may not be as expansive as the forthcoming year will be, governed by the vibrant 5 energy, the 8 vibration encourages you to stretch your capabilities.

April is a month dedicated to self-empowerment, providing you with the chance to learn what it means to be your own authority. Prioritize the organization and management of both your career and home life, striving to maintain a balance between your material pursuits and spiritual well-being. Uphold a strong moral code, as doing so will yield rewards in return.

Stay positive and take the time to envision what you wish to manifest in your future.

As April unfolds as an 8 month, the emphasis lies on work, power, and authority. Business becomes the focus, and you are called to embrace a leadership role. Organize and manage all aspects of your life, ensuring harmony between your material and spiritual worlds as you navigate this pivotal period.

PERSONAL YEAR 4

Personal Day
(April)

1. Donate time or money to a worthwhile cause.
2. Start a research project or read to expand your knowledge.
3. Center yourself; connect with thoughts and trust instincts.
4. Let your creativity thrive for innovative workplace solutions.
5. Prioritize order and organization for an efficient workday.
6. Embrace variety; adapt to surprises that enhance productivity.
7. Be ready to help those in need; it's responsible leadership.
8. Use imagination to find new approaches to familiar tasks.
9. Focus on advancing your goals; consistently seek growth.
10. Complete projects with precision; finalize details before moving on.
11. Embrace independence and express your individuality.
12. Pay attention to details to ensure accuracy and completion.
13. Reach out to an old friend; maintaining connections is key.
14. Activate practical skills; efficiency is vital in all endeavors.
15. Promote your accomplishments confidently; self-promotion matters.
16. Set clear boundaries; discipline requires maintaining limits.
17. Allocate time for rest and rejuvenation; it's essential.
18. Review finances regularly; invest wisely for good outcomes.
19. Use your gifts for the greater good; contributing is key.
20. Collaborate effectively; teamwork leads to greater achievements.
21. Allow progress to unfold naturally; avoid forcing outcomes.
22. Set aside time for enjoyable activities to boost productivity.
23. Ensure your foundation is solid; a strong base is crucial.
24. Network regularly; meeting new people opens opportunities.
25. Nurture key relationships; they are vital for support.
26. Create a productive space that inspires your work.
27. Stay vigilant with finances; monitor your investments.
28. Identify solutions to problems and move on; don't dwell.
29. Share your knowledge; teaching enhances your learning.
30. Use diplomacy to resolve conflicts; harmony boosts productivity.

PERSONAL YEAR 4

May
9 Personal Month

The energy of 4 represents discipline and structure, lessons you likely explored in the first quarter of the year. This year, your focus is on establishing a solid foundation for the next five years, so prioritize organization and maintain your sense of stability. This is not a time for risk-taking; instead, concentrate on building a secure base beneath you. Strive to complete any projects you initiated this year, if possible.

As the 9 vibration takes center stage in May, this month emphasizes completion and the art of letting go. It's essential to declutter your life, finalize tasks, and release anything that no longer serves your journey. Be discerning about what you wish to carry forward into the future. With changes on the horizon in June, now is the moment to make space for new beginnings.

The number 9 is also associated with rewards, so if you have diligently applied yourself, be prepared to accept the accolades that come your way. Themes of compassion, forgiveness, unconditional love, and understanding resonate powerfully this month. Make it a point to invest time in serving your community and supporting humanitarian causes; strive to see the Divine in all things.

May represents a 9 month, the conclusion to a nine-month cycle. Take this opportunity to clean out, finalize, and release anything that does not enrich your life. Reap the rewards of your hard work from the past eight months and prepare for new beginnings next month. Use your intuition to guide your next steps, allow your creativity to flourish, and dedicate yourself to serving the greater good.

PERSONAL YEAR 4

Personal Day
(May)

1. Take responsibility by leading with purpose and informed decisions.
2. Collaborate to achieve community goals that uplift everyone.
3. Share your ideas openly through various expressions.
4. Plan your day efficiently and follow through on commitments.
5. Stay mindful of meaningful connections & patterns each day.
6. Brighten someone's day with flowers or kind acts.
7. Recharge in your favorite peaceful spot to refresh.
8. Embrace opportunities and take calculated risks for growth.
9. Clear your space and thoughts for clarity and focus.
10. Make informed choices by weighing your options carefully.
11. Trust your intuition to guide you through challenges.
12. Organize spontaneous gatherings to enjoy others' company.
13. Approach tasks practically to enhance productivity.
14. Use unpredictability to adapt and thrive in life.
15. Beautify and organize your home for a welcoming space.
16. Go with life's natural flow; let things unfold organically.
17. Focus on finances by balancing accounts & staying organized.
18. Let go of tasks that no longer serve you for growth.
19. Keep an eye on the future, supported by strong foundations.
20. Offer apologies when needed to foster healing in relationships.
21. Engage in joyful activities to enrich your life.
22. Address any outstanding legal matters for smoother progress.
23. Prepare for productivity by showcasing achievements today.
24. Be available to share skills and expertise with others.
25. Reflect on your thoughts to ensure alignment with aspirations.
26. Lead with authority and confidence to guide others effectively.
27. Release what no longer benefits you for upcoming months.
28. Use intelligence to lead groups and foster cooperation.
29. Complete unfinished tasks by filling in details and steps.
30. Participate in discussions; share insights for meaningful chats.
31. Finish today's responsibilities and plan thoughtfully for tomorrow.

June
1 Personal Month

You are currently immersed in a year of hard work, where diligent efforts serve as your driving force. Focus on staying grounded and committed to your tasks, keeping your attention fixed on fulfilling your obligations while solidifying a strong foundation for the year ahead.

This month, however, encourages new beginnings. Reflect on what you truly wish to create for the remainder of the year. Compile a list of your must-haves and greatest desires, and do not hold back; dream expansively. Employ your imagination to visualize these aspirations and then harness the disciplined energy of 4 to reset your foundation and turn those dreams into reality.

It is essential to muster the courage to take on a leadership role during this transformative time. Both number vibrations emphasize the importance of cleaning out and letting go of what no longer serves you, making room for that which truly enhances your life. Organize all aspects of your existence and prioritize your health through mindful diet and exercise.

Utilize structure and discipline to achieve your objectives. Set your intentions for the next nine months and draw on the supportive energy of 4 to bring those aspirations into the material realm.

As June unfolds as a 1 month, it heralds new beginnings. Now is the ideal time to plant seeds for your future; set your goals and intentions for the months to come. Embrace the busyness of this month, filled with fresh projects and opportunities. Have the confidence to take on a leadership role and guide your endeavors toward success.

PERSONAL YEAR 4

147

Personal Day
(June)

1. Create a peaceful atmosphere to maintain control and order.
2. Use your charisma to inspire loyalty and motivation.
3. Be an effective manager; organization is key to your vision.
4. Prepare for changes as opportunities for growth.
5. Identify your community and strengthen your leadership.
6. Dedicate time to research topics that align with your goals.
7. Foster a culture of action and ambition in your leadership.
8. Let go of practices that no longer serve a greater purpose.
9. Today is ideal for securing solid business deals; show integrity.
10. Exercise patience, allowing situations to develop naturally.
11. Promote optimism and positive thinking in your leadership.
12. Align your moral compass with your principles; be steadfast.
13. Practice discipline; control impulses and make wise choices.
14. Address conflicts with compassion to maintain harmony.
15. Prioritize health by starting a new exercise routine.
16. Focus on gratitude and embrace abundance as your power.
17. Recognize that true success comes from serving humanity.
18. Use independent leadership to forge new paths for your goals.
19. Value close allies; inspire loyalty and strengthen bonds.
20. Suppress self-doubt and focus on positive leadership aspects.
21. Scrutinize documents carefully; vigilance protects you.
22. Stay open to new ideas while maintaining your focus.
23. Take decisive actions to demonstrate responsible authority.
24. Rest when needed; rejuvenation sustains your power.
25. Concentrate on the greater good to enhance your leadership.
26. Remove unnecessary items to prepare for upcoming changes.
27. Always seek improvements in your projects; avoid complacency.
28. Support others to foster loyalty and strengthen position.
29. Engage in self-improvement through seminars or reading.
30. Maintain a strong work ethic; it earns respect and authority.

PERSONAL YEAR 4

July
2 Personal Month

Throughout this year, you have worked diligently, establishing a strong foundation driven by the energy of structure, boundaries, and discipline. These elements will continue to support you as you prepare for the freedom and opportunities that next year will bring.

However, July's energy may bring a slightly slower pace, encouraging a more inward focus. This is an ideal time to attune yourself to your intuition, which is heightened in a 2 month. Make space for introspection and heed the guidance that emerges during this reflective period. Employ your diplomatic skills and strive for cooperation with those around you.

Seek balance and harmony in all your endeavors while maintaining the structure you have meticulously crafted this year. Don't hesitate to lean on others for advice; collaboration will serve you well during this time. You may notice heightened sensitivity in your emotions over the next few weeks, and that's perfectly acceptable. Just be mindful not to let your inner critic overshadow your experiences.

Take this opportunity to consider the potential for new relationships or to reflect on what such connections might look like in your life. Cherish the peaceful energy of this month and allow yourself to go with the flow.

July is a 2 month, where attention to detail is paramount. Focus on the small tasks at hand, nurturing the seeds of intention you planted last month. Cooperation within your relationships is essential after the self-focused energy of the previous month. Prepare for an emotional journey that may call upon your diplomacy skills as you navigate this gentle, yet profound, time.

PERSONAL YEAR 4

149

Personal Day
(July)

1. Use creativity to create something meaningful.
2. Organize and prioritize your tasks systematically.
3. Let go of concerns; let events unfold naturally.
4. Engage your team to complete work effectively.
5. Read a book that expands your intellectual horizons.
6. Make informed investment decisions with your resources.
7. Volunteer for causes that align with your values.
8. Build a capable team and start a structured project.
9. Review real estate options for enjoyment or investment.
10. Use your imagination to generate innovative ideas.
11. Conduct research and develop a strong work ethic.
12. Stay open to unexpected opportunities as they arise.
13. Focus on a home project to enhance aesthetics.
14. Allocate time to relax in your favorite natural setting.
15. Evaluate your financial portfolio carefully.
16. Consider how your actions can benefit humanity.
17. Create a detailed to-do list and complete tasks.
18. Facilitate communication to resolve disagreements.
19. Plan a delightful day centered on activities you love.
20. Stay focused on responsibilities and complete efficiently.
21. Prepare for change and adapt as necessary.
22. Find comfort in your home environment.
23. Set aside time for introspection and self-reflection.
24. Show courage and take on a leadership role when needed.
25. Help those in need through charitable actions.
26. Embrace your uniqueness and express individuality.
27. Offer support and empathy to a friend in need.
28. Communicate openly and explore self-expression.
29. Reflect on the stability of your foundational principles.
30. Try a new activity that challenges your routine.
31. Respect boundaries and avoid giving unsolicited advice.

PERSONAL YEAR 4

August
3 Personal Month

August presents the vibrant energy of a 3, offering you a much-needed reprieve from your diligent efforts this year. In stark contrast to the disciplined nature of 4, the energy of 3 invites you to embrace joy and creativity. For the next few weeks, allow yourself to take a break; consider going on a vacation to rejuvenate your spirit.

Tap into your creative potential and express the imagination that has been waiting to unfold. This month encourages you to connect with your emotions and learn to communicate your feelings more effectively. While this is a time for relaxation, keep it simple and maintain your focus.

Engage in activities such as redecorating your office or redesigning a project that sparks your interest. Dedicate extra time to journaling, as this can be both productive and creatively fulfilling. By harmonizing the grounded, focused energy of the number 4 with the imaginative spirit of 3, you can achieve remarkable results.

Savor August, as it provides a playful interlude before the intensity returns in September, when both the month and the year resonate with the energy of 4.

August is indeed a 3 month, providing an opportunity for your creative juices to flow freely and leading to fresh ideas that can cultivate abundance. Embrace this playful time but remember to keep things simple and focused. Whether you choose to redecorate, redesign an ongoing project, write a story, or dance, allow the joy of creativity to guide you this month.

PERSONAL YEAR 4

Personal Day
(August)

1. Set your agenda and follow through; no excuses.
2. Be ready to seize any opportunity with confidence.
3. Have a heartfelt conversation with your partner; listen attentively.
4. Dedicate "me" time in a peaceful environment; you deserve it.
5. Audit your bank account and credit cards to stay in control.
6. Embrace forgiveness and love; they maintain your peace.
7. Launch a creative project with others; collaboration succeeds.
8. Trust your intuition; let it guide you freely.
9. Express joy through singing, dancing, painting, or writing.
10. Focus your attention to complete tasks efficiently.
11. Welcome distractions; they may lead to new opportunities.
12. Enhance your living space through redecorating.
13. Invest in yourself with an online self-development course.
14. Balance your material and spiritual accounts for harmony.
15. Show compassion and understanding to foster goodwill.
16. Celebrate your independence and individuality; shine!
17. Listen to your intuition for valuable insights.
18. Prioritize social gatherings to enjoy camaraderie.
19. Visualize a strong foundation to support your ambitions.
20. Ignite your adventurous spirit and pursue opportunities.
21. Enjoy family gatherings while maintaining your boundaries.
22. Ensure your spiritual path aligns with your true self.
23. Focus on aspirations and elevate yourself without limits.
24. Honor the greater good and bless others with kindness.
25. Open yourself to new experiences; invite change.
26. Strive for balance, harmony, and peace in your actions.
27. Keep a gratitude journal to document your blessings.
28. Complete tasks and check them off; stay organized.
29. Explore the unknown earnestly, embrace new opportunities.
30. Be bold and seek new adventures; this is your moment.
31. Treat yourself and a companion to a delightful night out.

PERSONAL YEAR 4

September
4 Personal Month

Note: Because September is the ninth month, it is always the same number as your personal year. This means you have double the energy of your personal year for thirty days. If the current year calculates to the same value as your personal year, then you receive triple that number's energy in September.

If you are in a 4 personal year, September embodies the energy of a 4 month. This is the time for work, structure, discipline, and organization; key components that are magnified this month. As you focus on building a solid foundation for the expansive opportunities awaiting you in the coming year, remember that the more stable your platform, the higher you can soar, ultimately gaining greater freedom.

Now is the moment to transform your creative ideas from last year and last month into tangible reality. Embrace your responsibilities and remain committed to your tasks. With the upcoming year on the horizon, a year marked by change, it is crucial to prepare yourself now. This period may present challenges, but by staying focused on your work, you will find that rewards will indeed follow.

Consider reorganizing your workspace or completing any outstanding projects. Clear away unfinished tasks to ensure you are ready for the next chapter. Prioritize your health by maintaining a balanced diet and regular exercise; establishing a routine during this 4 energy period greatly enhances the likelihood of success.

September is a 4 month, emphasizing the importance of organization, discipline, and diligence. Take care of your health through mindful dietary choices and physical activity. Focus on bringing your creations from last month into material form, and take this opportunity to finalize projects. Reset your foundation in preparation for the expansive energy that lies ahead in the 5 month.

PERSONAL YEAR 4

Personal Day
(September)

1. Prepare for change; adaptability is key in a dynamic environment.
2. Use your home office today to boost productivity and focus.
3. Schedule regular exercise to maintain health and energy.
4. Review finances thoroughly to ensure stability and growth.
5. Complete outstanding projects for overall progress.
6. Create a comprehensive to-do list for the month; be organized.
7. Address unfinished tasks for clarity and completeness.
8. Allow moments of enjoyment; balance work and leisure.
9. Diligence pays off; consistent effort brings results.
10. Be ready for imminent change; navigate new opportunities.
11. Focus on relationships; they are vital for success.
12. Dedicate time for contemplation to gain strategic insights.
13. Stay flexible and open to changes at work.
14. Release obligations or resources that hinder your goals.
15. Reflect on new ideas to enhance your strategies.
16. Pay attention to details; precision is vital in leadership.
17. Incorporate joyful activities into your routine; happiness fuels productivity.
18. Operate from a solid foundation personally and professionally.
19. Embrace additional responsibilities for growth & development.
20. Improve your home office to enhance your workspace.
21. Make mindful dietary choices; prioritize fresh foods.
22. Trust your knowledge and instincts in decision-making.
23. Complete your monthly to-do list efficiently and intentionally.
24. Get ready for a fresh start; embark on a new chapter.
25. Read between the lines for deeper understanding & strategies.
26. Hold yourself accountable; integrity is crucial in leadership.
27. Avoid overthinking; make informed decisions and act.
28. Prepare for a fast-paced month; stay agile and adaptable.
29. Bring home flowers to brighten your space & inspire creativity.
30. Prioritize self-improvement and continual learning; grow as a leader.

October
5 Personal Month

Note: October is always the same number as your personal year next year. This means it is a brief preview of the coming year.

If in a 4 personal year, October ushers in the dynamic energy of a 5 month. Throughout this year, you have diligently maintained your focus and discipline, but fortunately, this month brings a refreshing reprieve. Not only do you get a glimpse of the exciting year ahead, but you also enjoy a break from the structured demands of the current year. The number 5 embodies freedom, expansion, and the pursuit of a life fully lived; qualities that may have eluded you thus far amid your hard work.

In October, the pace of life quickens as surprises and changes unfold before you. Embrace the opportunities that come your way. Adventure and travel await you, but remember to maintain your balance as the year draws to a close. Be mindful of falling into the overwhelm of drama or chaos; instead, focus on thoughtful improvements for your life that can be implemented next year.

Consider adopting a new diet or exercise program, or perhaps enrolling in a self-improvement course. The energy of 5 signifies change, and positive transformations will elevate your life in remarkable ways.

October is a 5 month, marked by unexpected changes that invite travel and adventure. You may find that you alter your direction entirely. Seize the moment to promote yourself and utilize your communication skills with confidence. Step into opportunities and take calculated risks, for the changes that occur this month are designed for your greater benefit. Allow the energy to flow freely and savor this exhilarating transition.

PERSONAL YEAR 4

Personal Day
(October)

1. Seize opportunities; approach each choice boldly.
2. Read a self-improvement book to fuel your ambition.
3. Maintain a balanced lifestyle amid leadership chaos.
4. Highlight your authentic self through uplifting gestures.
5. Write down your dreams and aspirations for manifestation.
6. Collaborate with others to build strong partnerships for success.
7. Celebrate life with singing and dancing; savor the joy.
8. Follow established paths that lead to success with discipline.
9. Enjoy a day of freedom and adventure; let curiosity guide you.
10. Plan an enjoyable evening with a friend to strengthen bonds.
11. Take a spontaneous day trip to explore new perspectives.
12. Stay engaged in your business while thinking innovatively.
13. Trust your inner guidance when making decisions.
14. Challenge yourself to try something new for growth.
15. Follow intuitive prompts, even if unpredictable.
16. Live and love fully; discover new dimensions of experience.
17. Focus on success; let determination pave your way.
18. Allow today to lead you to new opportunities.
19. Engage in deep conversations with loved ones.
20. Meditate in nature to recharge and connect with the earth.
21. Organize your goals to enhance productivity.
22. Lift the spirits of those around you with positivity.
23. Explore new dimensions in work & life; embrace the unfamiliar.
24. Calm your inner critic and let creativity flourish.
25. Inspire creativity to explore new frontiers confidently.
26. Realign your foundation to support your vision.
27. Cross something off your desires list; pursue your passion.
28. Offer full attention to someone special to strengthen connections.
29. Go on a vision quest for insights that guide your future.
30. Confidently express your authority; embrace leadership.
31. Commit to balance and harmony in all ventures for fulfillment.

PERSONAL YEAR 4

November
6 Personal Month

As the energy of 6 takes center stage, relationships come into focus, particularly as family members may seek your support during this holiday season. Throughout this year of hard work in a 4 personal year, you have diligently established structure and discipline in your life. Now, as you reflect on the progress and accomplishments of the past year, take a moment to celebrate the projects you've completed and the personal growth you've achieved.

This is an opportune time to address any unresolved issues in your relationships. Reach out to others and endeavor to finish the year with a clean slate. Adhere to established boundaries and remain committed to following the rules. Be of service to your loved ones, as they will undoubtedly need your attention during this period.

Strive to foster harmony and balance in every aspect of your life, while also ensuring that you take care of yourself as you fulfill your obligations.

November resonates with the energy of a 6 month, a designated time for home and family. Embrace your responsibilities, tending to both your household and your relationships. Dedicate quality time to your family; consider scheduling a vacation or engaging in home improvement projects. Seek to find harmony in your career as well as your home life, and take the opportunity to realign your priorities for a fulfilling end to the year.

PERSONAL YEAR 4

157

Personal Day
(November)

1. Carve out personal time for reflection and rejuvenation.
2. Consider balance; equilibrium nourishes the spirit.
3. Radiate love and forgiveness for inner and outer peace.
4. Approach responsibilities with grace and kindness.
5. Express gratitude for your family's contributions.
6. Emanate joy; your positivity uplifts those around you.
7. Establish and maintain boundaries for your well-being.
8. Embrace adventure with loved ones; try something fun.
9. Engage in heartfelt talks with your partner to bond.
10. Build a compassionate relationship with your inner critic.
11. Dedicate time to career growth and align with aspirations.
12. Perform kind acts that positively impact the world.
13. Nurture relationships by spending quality time together.
14. Use diplomacy to resolve lingering conflicts gracefully.
15. Start a home improvement project that reflects your values.
16. Create a detailed plan to complete your projects.
17. Take a day for activities that nourish your soul.
18. Create cherished memories; celebrate joyful moments.
19. Meditate to connect with your intuition for guidance.
20. Find your center amid challenges; balance is key.
21. Release what no longer serves you and surrender wisely.
22. Set new goals with your partner to align visions.
23. Be willing to compromise for harmony in relationships.
24. Enjoy a fun evening out; embrace laughter and connection.
25. Emphasize structure and discipline for success.
26. Stay open to amazing events today; embrace opportunities.
27. Take initiative in your responsibilities; lead as needed.
28. Retreat to your favorite spot with a good book.
29. Honor yourself and the wisdom gained on your journey.
30. Practice forgiveness to let go and allow love to flow.

PERSONAL YEAR 4

December
7 Personal Month

After a month devoted to serving your loved ones, you now have the opportunity to rest and rejuvenate. The energy of 7 invites solitude, which is essential for inward reflection. This serene period marks a fitting conclusion to your year of hard work, allowing you to contemplate and reevaluate the direction of your life.

Take a moment to ask yourself: Are you where you envision yourself? Have you put forth the necessary effort this year? Have you achieved the goals you set for yourself? Now is the time for introspection and thoughtful decision-making. Prioritize your health during this time, listening closely to your intuition and heeding its guidance. Seek inner peace, as prayer and meditation will be particularly beneficial now.

Reflect on your spiritual, mental, and physical ideals. Consider any shifts you wish to implement as you move forward into a new year. What changes do you want to embrace in the coming months?

December embodies the essence of a 7 month, emphasizing rest, relaxation, rejuvenation, and the necessity of solitude for focused introspection. Use this time to reassess where your life has journeyed and the path you wish to pursue. Engage in the study of metaphysics, consider attending a retreat, and immerse yourself in the tranquility of nature.

PERSONAL YEAR 4

Personal Day
(December)

1. Embrace opportunities, but take time to contemplate before acting.
2. Tidy up loose ends; complete tasks for closure.
3. Let your individuality shine and express your true self.
4. Recognize cooperation's importance; cultivate harmony with others.
5. Pause to savor beauty; take moments for quiet enjoyment.
6. Nourish your body with healthy food and regular exercise.
7. Embrace spontaneity and synchronicity to enrich your day.
8. Handle responsibilities with intention and focus.
9. Seek your sacred space; enjoy solitude for inner exploration.
10. Recognize that abundance is coming in various forms.
11. Cultivate patience and understanding in your interactions.
12. Today is good for business negotiations; approach openly.
13. Honor reciprocity by matching others' contributions; succeed together.
14. Step out of introspection and socialize genuinely.
15. Schedule a wellness check; prioritize your well-being.
16. Add variety to your inner work; engage in inspiring experiences.
17. Beautify your space; buy flowers or organize for tranquility.
18. Reflect on your life's journey; assess if you're where you want to be.
19. Manage finances carefully; balance checkbooks and credit cards.
20. Release what you can't control; free your mind from worries.
21. Align with your highest goals; evaluate your current path.
22. Allow others to lead today; support their efforts.
23. Reach out to an old friend with a heartfelt note or call.
24. Be pragmatic; create order in chaos for a peaceful environment.
25. Promote your work confidently; share your vision boldly.
26. Maintain and respect your boundaries and those of others.

27. Spend time in nature to gather thoughts and find serenity.
28. Embody authority and present yourself with conviction.
29. Honor humanity by volunteering and helping those in need.
30. Acknowledge that ambition and success are your foundation.
31. Use diplomacy to navigate challenges while maintaining balance.

PERSONAL YEAR 4

Personal Year 5

The personal year 5 stands as a pinnacle within the nine-year cycle, a period ripe for transformation, surprises, and new opportunities. It invites you to view the world through fresh eyes and make necessary changes in alignment with this new perspective.

Dedicate time to exploring and investigating emerging opportunities, releasing anything that hinders your progress. Strive for balance, avoiding excess while enhancing and adding value to your life. The energy of the 5 year revolves around change, offering new perspectives across various facets of life.

While growth opportunities abound, be mindful not to pursue change merely for its own sake. Avoid dispersing your energies yet give each opportunity at least a thoughtful glance. This is an ideal time for travel and discovering new vistas, allowing your curiosity to guide you toward novel experiences. Be flexible while avoiding impulsivity, and manage restlessness with openness to the new.

This year is excellent for promoting yourself and your creative pursuits, meeting people who can elevate your career and enrich your life. Balance remains key; explore possibilities without overindulgence. Situated as the pivotal midpoint in the nine-year cycle, the 5 year is a harbinger of transition and dynamic change, both anticipated and unexpected.

In this year of renaissance, release the burdens of the past and chart a new course. Unlike the restrictive nature of the previous year, liberty now takes center stage, making it a suitable time to expand horizons and embrace risks. Opportunities abound for finding a new home, career, or relationship, with travel and adventure leading the way.

With freedom and expansion at the forefront, this is not a time for timidity or excessive caution. Embrace opportunities for increased freedom, maintaining balance to avoid attracting undue chaos or drama. Implement changes that enhance your quality of life, whether through new diets, exercise regimes, or self-improvement initiatives. Adapt to the fast pace, maintain a positive outlook, and welcome the good fortune that accompanies this transformative year. The changes embraced this year will elevate your life and set the stage for the years to come.

PERSONAL YEAR 5

January
6 Personal Month

A year of freedom, expansion, and transformation lies ahead of you. Prepare for surprises, as they are certain to arrive whether you feel ready or not. Abundant opportunities for growth await, presenting new horizons in every direction, should you choose to embrace them. Almost every aspect of your life is ripe for expansion, including your awareness and perspective.

This year begins with a focus on the vibration of 6, which emphasizes home and family. During this month, your loved ones will likely need your support more than usual, and relationships may undergo significant shifts. Make time to both give and receive love; the energy surrounding you is conducive to healing past issues.

Embrace this month as an opportunity to take responsibility for nurturing a balanced and harmonious life. Prioritize your loved ones by resolving any lingering issues in your relationships. Consider scheduling a family vacation to strengthen those bonds or refurbishing an area of your home to enhance your living space.

Realign your priorities and ensure that you foster harmony in all your endeavors. As this month unfolds, face your responsibilities with grace, attending to your home and relationships with care. Use this time to find equilibrium between your career and family life, ensuring that you create a space of beauty and tranquility.

PERSONAL YEAR 5

Personal Day
(January)

1. Carve out time for yourself in a nurturing sacred space.
2. Embrace balance in all areas of your life for harmony.
3. Radiate love and forgiveness to create a warm atmosphere.
4. Handle responsibilities with grace to make caregiving joyful.
5. Express gratitude for your family's efforts to strengthen bonds.
6. Emanate joy and happiness to uplift those around you.
7. Set and maintain healthy boundaries for your well-being.
8. Go on a fun adventure with a loved one; try something new.
9. Engage in heartfelt conversations with your partner for intimacy.
10. Build a friendly rapport with your inner critic for growth.
11. Invest time in your career while embracing your free spirit.
12. Show kindness by performing a good deed; let it shine.
13. Dedicate quality time to nurture your relationships.
14. Use diplomacy to resolve lingering issues with compassion.
15. Unleash creativity with a home project that reflects you.
16. Craft a clear plan to execute your project effectively.
17. Dedicate a day to yourself; nourish your soul with joy.
18. Create lasting memories; celebrate the moments that matter.
19. Meditate and reconnect deeply with your intuition today.
20. Find your center and maintain grace through challenges.
21. Let go and surrender to higher wisdom guiding your path.
22. Set new goals with your partner to align your aspirations.
23. Be willing to compromise to maintain balance in relationships.
24. Enjoy an entertaining evening out; relish time with others.
25. Approach days with structure and discipline, keeping focus.
26. Embrace amazing events unfolding today; welcome opportunities.
27. Step up & fulfill responsibilities; your dedication uplifts others.
28. Retreat to your happy place with an inspiring book.
29. Honor yourself and embrace your wisdom; be your authority.
30. Practice forgiveness and let love illuminate your path.
31. Stay open to new ideas; each insight offers growth.

PERSONAL YEAR 5

February
7 Personal Month

This year heralds a time of change, brimming with surprises both anticipated and unforeseen. It is a year dedicated to growth and expansion. With the arrival of the 7 energy this month, you are encouraged to turn inward. Take a moment to reflect on life's profound questions: What do I truly want for my life? What is my purpose? Allow yourself the grace to pause, relax, rejuvenate, and rest before the more dynamic energy of 8 enters your experience come March.

Seek solace in nature, reconnecting with your inner self as you reassess your direction in life. This month focuses on your needs after a period where all attention was directed toward family. Consider enrolling in a class centered on metaphysics or embarking on a vision quest; this is your time to invest in inner growth. Engage in reading, research, and introspection, the key components for your personal development right now. Any effort spent on self-improvement will yield significant rewards.

You will have another opportunity later this year in November to delve deeper into your innermost desires, so approach this reflective time with intention. Prioritize your health with a balanced diet and exercise, recognizing that solitude and rest are essential for deep introspection.

You deserve this dedicated time to focus on yourself; remember that timing is everything.

February is characterized as a 7 month, a time for rest, relaxation, and rejuvenation. Embrace solitude as a necessary component for inward focus, reevaluating the path your life has taken and determining the direction you wish to pursue. Engage in the study of metaphysics, consider taking a retreat, and immerse yourself in the tranquility of nature.

PERSONAL YEAR 5

166

Personal Day
(February)

1. Opportunities are coming; consider them thoughtfully before acting.
2. Tie up loose ends; complete tasks to create mental space.
3. Express your individuality; let your true self shine.
4. Recognize the importance of cooperation; engage harmoniously.
5. Take moments to enjoy life and soak in the present.
6. Nourish your body with wholesome foods & regular exercise.
7. Allow spontaneity to guide your experiences; embrace surprises.
8. Meet responsibilities with focus; work diligently on tasks.
9. Seek a sacred space for solitude and reflection.
10. Abundance is on its way in forms beyond currency.
11. Cultivate patience and understanding in your interactions.
12. Today is great for negotiating; approach with clarity.
13. Acknowledge contributions of others to foster reciprocity.
14. Embrace social opportunities; connection is vital.
15. Consider a wellness check; prioritize your overall well-being.
16. Infuse variety into your work; challenge yourself with the new.
17. Enhance your home environment with flowers or tidiness.
18. Reflect on your path; check if you align with your desires.
19. Maintain financial awareness by balancing your accounts.
20. Let go of what you can't control; avoid excessive rumination.
21. Align your actions with your aspirations; assess your journey.
22. Defer to others' guidance; allow partnerships to flourish.
23. Reconnect with an old friend with a heartfelt note or call.
24. Embrace practicality; find order in chaos for stability.
25. Promote your work confidently; share your unique contributions.
26. Honor your boundaries while respecting others' limits.
27. Gather thoughts while walking in nature; find peace & clarity.
28. Be your own authority; present yourself confidently.
29. Honor our shared humanity; consider volunteering your time.

PERSONAL YEAR 5

March
8 Personal Month

You find yourself in an expansive year filled with change, where the vibration of 8 highlights themes of money management, business acumen, and personal empowerment. Your career is under the spotlight, and with the energetic influence of 5, significant shifts in your livelihood are likely on the horizon. Prepare for the possibility of a promotion or increased freedom in your responsibilities, as well as the potential for a career change or a completely new position, which may materialize as early as March.

Both the energies of 8 and 5 encourage you to think outside the box and embrace risks. The positive energy surrounding you will bolster your endeavors, allowing money to flow abundantly in both directions this month. However, it is crucial to maintain balance within your finances. You may also encounter someone from your past who once disempowered you; now is the time to summon your courage, assert yourself, and embrace your role as your own authority.

The number 8 embodies balance, and maintaining equilibrium is paramount, especially in this 5 year. Strive to harmonize your financial aspirations with your humanitarian spirit.

March represents an 8 month, a period that emphasizes hard work, power, and authority. Business takes precedence, and you will be called upon to assume a leadership role. Organize and manage every aspect of your life while ensuring that you maintain a healthy balance between your material pursuits and spiritual well-being. Step confidently into your authority and guide your journey with intention.

PERSONAL YEAR 5

Personal Day
(March)

1. Embrace giving; donate time or money to a meaningful cause.
2. Start a new research project or dive into an inspiring book.
3. Center yourself and trust your intuition for decisions.
4. Let creativity soar; encourage imagination to flow freely.
5. Establish flexible order in your workday; structure matters.
6. Embrace variety; be open to surprises and new opportunities.
7. Stand ready to support those in need; helping others is powerful.
8. Use imagination to reimagine familiar paths and innovate.
9. Keep pushing towards your material goals; freedom follows.
10. Complete projects with creativity; celebrate your accomplishments.
11. Be your authentic self; express individuality without fear.
12. Focus on details; small pieces matter in the bigger picture.
13. Reach out to an old friend; reconnecting brings joy.
14. Activate practical skills to tackle challenges efficiently.
15. Make self-promotion a priority; showcase your successes.
16. Strengthen your boundaries to protect your values and freedom.
17. Allow time to rest and rejuvenate; downtime is essential.
18. Review finances regularly; balance accounts and invest wisely.
19. Use talents to give back; share what you can with others.
20. Collaborate with others; joining forces enhances impact.
21. Let currents take you; avoid forcing progress; go with the flow.
22. Dedicate time to play; find joy in your pursuits.
23. Ensure stability beneath you; a solid foundation supports freedom.
24. Expand your circles; meet new people for potential ventures.
25. Prioritize important relationships; nurture connections for fulfillment.
26. Find your personal space; create an inspiring environment.
27. Keep finances at the forefront; recognize potential for growth.
28. Identify solutions to problems and let them go; don't dwell.

PERSONAL YEAR 5

29. Share knowledge generously; teaching enriches understanding.
30. Use diplomacy to resolve disputes; harmony fosters collective freedom.
31. Communicate effectively; connecting with others is vital for growth.

PERSONAL YEAR 5

April
9 Personal Month

As you enter the fourth month of this year of expansive change, April presents itself as a 9 month, focused on the themes of letting go, decluttering, and completing matters that no longer serve you. The essence of 9 is completion; the more you release, the more space you create for new beginnings.

Take the time to lighten your load; clean out your closet and eliminate anything unnecessary from your life at this moment. With May approaching, which heralds the energy of a 1 month and the opportunity to create your desired future, it's vital to embrace this process of closure. Allow yourself to be of service to others, as compassion and forgiveness are integral aspects of the 9 vibration.

Use this month to resolve any lingering differences, demonstrating courage and trust in the Divine order of all things as you let go. The personal growth challenges you've navigated over the past year will bear fruit during this 9 month, presenting you with rewards.

Channel your creativity into manifesting your aspirations for the future, aiming to serve the greater good with your endeavors.

April signifies a 9 month, marking the conclusion of a nine-month cycle. Now is the time to clean, finish, and release anything that does not enhance your life. Reap the benefits of your hard work from the past eight months and prepare to welcome new beginnings in the upcoming month. Trust your intuition as you contemplate what you want to create next, embrace your creativity, and continue to serve the greater good.

PERSONAL YEAR 5

171

Personal Day
(April)

1. Embrace your autonomy; lead with choices reflecting your values.
2. Collaborate to achieve shared goals, fostering unity and freedom.
3. Express yourself through diverse channels; stay open to sharing.
4. Plan your day flexibly; allow room for unexpected adventures.
5. Stay attuned to meaningful coincidences guiding your journey.
6. Spread joy by gifting flowers, creating moments of connection.
7. Rejuvenate in your sanctuary; recharge your spirit in peace.
8. Embrace abundance; take bold risks to pursue your passions.
9. Clear clutter to create space for new experiences and growth.
10. Make thoughtful decisions by evaluating options for freedom.
11. Trust your intuition to navigate challenges & find resolutions.
12. Celebrate spontaneity with an impromptu gathering of joy.
13. Stay grounded; use common sense to boost your productivity.
14. Embrace unpredictability and spontaneity for fluidity.
15. Enhance your space by creating beauty and order.
16. Flow with life's currents, embracing ease as you move.
17. Attend to finances, ensuring resources support your freedom.
18. Release commitments that no longer align with your purpose.
19. Focus on the future with a strong foundation of dreams.
20. Offer apologies to create space for healing and understanding.
21. Engage in joyful activities that foster happiness and freedom.
22. Address legal or financial matters to clear your path.
23. Anticipate a productive day filled with opportunities.
24. Be present to support those in need with your skills.
25. Reflect on your direction to ensure alignment with desires.
26. Demonstrate leadership confidently, guiding others as needed.
27. Let go of burdens that no longer serve your journey.
28. Leverage your intellect to inspire collaborative discussions.
29. Complete projects by addressing unfinished details.
30. Join conversations with an open mind, sharing perspectives.

May
1 Personal Month

Dynamic change and transformation await you this year, which is characterized by expansion and the exhilarating sense of freedom that comes with the 5 vibration. After four months of boundless energy, you are now poised to embrace new beginnings with the influence of the number one, empowering you to create the reality you desire for the remainder of the year.

Take this opportunity to articulate your greatest desires and most ambitious dreams for the year. Allow your imagination to flow freely; do not censor yourself or shy away from reaching for new heights. Embrace courage as you confront your fears, recognizing that true growth often lies just outside your comfort zone.

As you list your aspirations, ensure that you encompass every aspect of your life to maintain balance. Embrace the fast pace of this month, knowing that luck is on your side. Expect a multitude of new projects and avenues to explore, and strive to cultivate harmony throughout your endeavors.

You are leveling up this year, so harness the power of the number 1 vibration to plant the seeds for your future and aim high.

May is a 1 month, a time for fresh starts. This is the moment to set your goals and intentions for the next nine months. Embrace the busyness of this time, filled with new projects, and have the courage to step into a leadership role as you navigate this exciting chapter of your journey.

PERSONAL YEAR 5

Personal Day
(May)

1. Cultivate a peaceful environment that fosters collaboration.
2. Let your cheerful nature shine, uplifting those around you.
3. Be an effective organizer, empowering those around you.
4. View changes as exciting opportunities for growth.
5. Connect with your community and aid its well-being.
6. Explore subjects that spark your curiosity and passion.
7. Harness ambition and action to propel initiatives forward.
8. Let go of outdated practices for greater success.
9. Seize the day for impactful business negotiations.
10. Foster patience; allow ideas to flourish naturally.
11. Embrace optimism; it's a strong tool for resilience.
12. Align your moral compass with your leadership vision.
13. Curb impulsive decisions; choose well-considered actions.
14. Approach home matters with compassion and understanding.
15. Prioritize health by starting an invigorating exercise routine.
16. Cultivate gratitude and welcome abundance into your life.
17. True success comes from serving humanity; let it guide you.
18. Use leadership to create inspiring paths for others.
19. Celebrate friendships that strengthen supportive bonds.
20. Quiet your inner critic; focus on positive possibilities.
21. Read fine print in agreements; attention to detail matters.
22. Stay open to fresh ideas while avoiding distractions.
23. Commit to actions that align with your values.
24. Take breaks; rest is vital for creativity.
25. Focus on the greater good; ensure actions benefit all.
26. Eliminate clutter to welcome new opportunities.
27. Seek to enhance projects; aim for progress today.
28. Promote others' well-being to reinforce support and success.
29. Engage in self-improvement with seminars or books.
30. Honor your work ethic; it underpins your leadership.
31. Embrace individuality and courage in pursuing goals.

June
2 Personal Month

Dynamic change awaits you this year, and it's likely you've already encountered it on multiple occasions so far. This renaissance year invites you to broaden your horizons and embrace freedom in all aspects of your life. Seize every opportunity that comes your way and do not shy away from taking calculated risks.

The energy of 2 encourages introspection and balance, highlighting the importance of listening to your intuition. Trust in your Divine guidance and follow its lead. Seek to cultivate peace in your relationships as you work to establish equilibrium amidst the changes. This year may stretch your limits, but the 2 energy serves as a reminder to stay level-headed.

Allow yourself to slow down, step back, and explore your inner landscape. Dedicate time to your personal growth, nurturing the aspirations you cultivated last month. June holds the potential for new beginnings, whether it be a new residence or a blossoming romantic relationship.

Cooperation and diplomacy are crucial during this period; pay attention to the finer details, as subtle and indirect energy is present to guide you. Be open to compromise and work harmoniously with others.

June is characterized as a 2 month, an invitation to focus on the details and attend to the small things that matter. Nurture the seeds you've planted and foster cooperation in your relationships, particularly after the previous month's emphasis on individual pursuits. This month may be emotionally charged, requiring the application of your diplomacy skills.

PERSONAL YEAR 5

Personal Day
(June)

1. Unleash your creativity; craft something reflecting your vision.
2. Embrace a broader perspective while prioritizing your endeavors.
3. Release inhibitions; let life flow with ease and spontaneity.
4. Celebrate your partnership with a lavish meal and deep dialogue.
5. Dive into literature that broadens your horizons and perspectives.
6. Make wise investments for personal growth and better understanding.
7. Engage in volunteer work that aligns with your passions.
8. Rally diverse minds and embark on a groundbreaking project.
9. Explore real estate for joy or opportunity, locally and globally.
10. Let your imagination soar and cultivate innovation in all forms.
11. Conduct research to ignite a strong work ethic with global impact.
12. Open to unexpected wonders and lessons that life presents.
13. Enhance your space with projects that inspire beauty and serenity.
14. Immerse yourself in nature, finding solace within.
15. Evaluate your financial strategies from a broader perspective.
16. Envision your role in humanity's tapestry; seek to contribute.
17. Craft a purposeful to-do list; enjoy the satisfaction of completion.
18. Exercise diplomacy to foster harmony in resolving conflicts.
19. Create a joyful day, embracing activities that bring delight.
20. Dive into responsibilities and achieve your goals with vigor.
21. Embrace change as constant and thrive in its embrace.
22. Find peace in the sanctuary of your home.
23. Dedicate time to introspection, exploring your inner world.
24. Embrace courage and take charge as a leader in your domain.
25. Extend kindness through good deeds that ripple through the world.

PERSONAL YEAR 5

176

26. Express your individuality with bold originality and flair.
27. Offer unwavering support and compassion to those in need.
28. Communicate freely and express yourself in every medium available.
29. Reflect on the strength and stability of your foundational beliefs.
30. Embark on adventures that open new vistas of experience.

PERSONAL YEAR 5

July
3 Personal Month

With the myriad of changes this year has brought, July proves to be no exception. Expect more surprises this month, and many of them may even bring a sense of joy. The energy of 3 infuses this time with a delightful emphasis on FUN. Take a well-deserved break, gather with friends for a social outing, or indulge in activities that bring you joy.

Creativity will flourish during this period, so seize the opportunity to leverage the inspirational energy that the number 3 offers. Maintain a positive outlook despite the expansiveness of the year thus far, and strive to keep your focus as best as you can, aiming to see your projects through to completion.

Be mindful that both the 3 and 5 vibrations can lead to a sense of scattered energy, so it's important to find moments to center and ground yourself. A walk in nature, meditation, or simple introspection can serve as powerful tools to help maintain your equilibrium. Fully embrace your creative talents this month and allow them to shine brightly.

Cultivate a positive mindset and consciously seek the silver linings in every encounter. Savor this period of leisure, for you will have work to tackle in August.

July is a 3 month, when your creative juices overflow with new ideas that have the potential to generate abundance. This is a playful time, so remember to keep things simple while remaining focused. Whether you choose to redecorate, redesign a project, write a story, or dance, allow the vibrant energy of creativity to guide your actions.

PERSONAL YEAR 5

178

Personal Day
(July)

1. Set a flexible agenda and allow room for spontaneity.
2. Embrace each opportunity ready to soar to new heights.
3. Engage in heartfelt conversations, exploring horizons together.
4. Carve out "me" time in a serene space to rejuvenate.
5. Review finances for opportunities that inspire growth.
6. Let forgiveness and love pave the way to inner peace.
7. Launch a creative venture with like-minded collaborators.
8. Trust your intuition to guide you toward expansive paths.
9. Indulge in self-expression through song, dance, or art.
10. Harness focus to achieve your ambitions with clarity.
11. Embrace distractions as gateways to exciting directions.
12. Revitalize your space with creative enhancements and energy.
13. Dive into an online course to expand your horizons.
14. Harmonize your financial and spiritual worlds for balance.
15. Radiate compassion to cultivate enriching connections.
16. Celebrate your independence as you explore new possibilities.
17. Tune into your intuition to guide your journey.
18. Immerse yourself in social gatherings to welcome joy.
19. Visualize a solid foundation ready to support your explorations.
20. Ignite your adventurous spirit; trust your heart's compass.
21. Enjoy family gatherings while respecting your own boundaries.
22. Reflect on your path to ensure it aligns with your freedom.
23. Focus on your aspirations, breaking barriers to new heights.
24. Serve the greater good with acts of kindness and abundance.
25. Open your heart to new, exciting experiences.
26. Cultivate balance, harmony, and peace during adventures.
27. Document gratitude in a journal to enhance appreciation.
28. Tackle tasks with enthusiasm, checking them off as you go.
29. Venture into the unknown with open arms, ready to grow.
30. Seek out thrilling new adventures with confidence.
31. Share a joyous night out with your date, savoring freedom.

PERSONAL YEAR 5

August
4 Personal Month

Surprises in your year are governed by the energy of 5, and you have likely encountered more expansive changes this year than in any other. Alongside these transitions, you have also experienced a wealth of opportunities for growth and development. If you find yourself teetering on the edge and in need of stability, you are in luck; the energies of 5 and 4 complement each other beautifully.

August brings a much-needed chance to pause, focus, and concentrate on your work. If your imagination ran wild in July, resulting in the initiation of new projects, now is the time to keep your nose to the grindstone and see them through to completion. The principles of organization, discipline, and diligence are now firmly rooted in your life, providing the support necessary to create a month that is both productive and rewarding.

Regaining your balance during this time will serve you well as you transition into September, which carries a double 5 vibration that emphasizes further expansion and freedom. By channeling your energies towards finishing your projects, you will look back on this time with gratitude and a profound sense of accomplishment.

As August unfolds as a 4 month, focus on organization, discipline, and diligence. Take care of your health by implementing a balanced diet and exercise regimen. Ensure that the creations inspired last month are brought into tangible form, and commit to completing projects that have been in progress. Use this time to reset your foundation in preparation for the expansive energy that awaits you in the upcoming 5 month.

PERSONAL YEAR 5

180

Personal Day
(August)

1. Embrace the excitement of a shift on the horizon.
2. Enjoy the freedom of working from home today.
3. Get up and move; exercise celebrates your vibrant spirit.
4. Balance your finances and make them dance in alignment.
5. Wrap up that project you've been toying with; finish strong.
6. Create a fun to-do list for the month; adventure awaits.
7. Fill in the blanks to bring clarity to your plans.
8. Make time to enjoy today; savor every moment.
9. Remember, diligence pays off; your efforts set you free.
10. Get ready; change is just around the corner.
11. Give extra love to your relationships; they bring vibrancy.
12. Find quiet time to reflect; explore your inner landscape.
13. Stay open to shifts at work; they may lead to new paths.
14. Shed what no longer serves you; feel the lightness.
15. Reflect on new ideas to ignite your curiosity.
16. Focus on details while keeping the big picture in mind.
17. Identify what brings you joy and dive into it.
18. Stay grounded and embrace new experiences with confidence.
19. Rise to the occasion; level up your workload today.
20. Breathe life into your home with inspiring improvements.
21. Nourish your body with fresh, vibrant foods.
22. Honor your knowledge; trust what you've learned.
23. Complete your to-do list with flair; celebrate accomplishments.
24. Welcome a new chapter; adventure awaits you.
25. Read between the lines to find hidden meanings.
26. Hold yourself accountable; own your journey with pride.
27. Avoid overthinking; embrace spontaneity and flow.
28. Prepare for a fast-paced month; let excitement propel you.
29. Brighten your space with flowers; let nature uplift you.
30. Focus on self-improvement; explore new facets of life.
31. Strive for balance and harmony while exploring life's offerings.

PERSONAL YEAR 5

September
5 Personal Month

Note: Because September is the ninth month, it is always the same number as your personal year. This means you have double the energy of your personal year for thirty days. If the current year calculates to the same value as your personal year, then you receive triple that number's energy in September.

September arrives with the invigorating energy of a 5, amplifying the dynamic change and transitions that define your year. Prepare yourself, for heightened surprises and growth experiences are on the horizon. Abundant opportunities await, each promising freedom and expansion.

Seize every chance that comes your way. This is not the month for timidity or fear; instead, embrace your courage and take calculated risks. The essence of 5 encourages you to fully engage in opportunities that promote personal growth and broaden your horizons. Expect changes across all facets of your life, whether it involves a new home, career advancement, or the blossoming of a new relationship.

Pack your bags, as travel and adventure are likely to knock at your door, as well. Stay open and ready for the unexpected. Amidst this whirlwind of transition, strive to maintain your balance; grounding yourself will help mitigate any potential drama that may arise.

This is a time of rapid movement, so do your best to keep pace. Cultivating a positive attitude will attract positive experiences in return. The number 3 is often seen as lucky, and the 5 energy carries its own share of fortuitous opportunities.

September is a 5 month, characterized by unexpected changes that invite travel and adventure. You may find yourself altering your path significantly. Take this time to promote yourself and effectively utilize your communication skills. Embrace risks, as the transformations this month are designed to enhance your life. Allow the vibrant energy to flow freely, and prepare to explore the exciting possibilities that await you.

PERSONAL YEAR 5

Personal Day
(September)

1. Embrace the opportunities before you; choose boldly and adventurously.
2. Dive into a self-improvement book that sparks your growth.
3. Strive for balance as you navigate life's exhilarating chaos.
4. Express your spirit through kind gestures that spread joy.
5. Capture wild dreams in writing; let your imagination roam.
6. Collaborate with adventurers; together, create magic.
7. Dance freely, letting your spirit soar in joy.
8. Follow paths guiding you to your goals while staying open.
9. Savor a day of adventure; embrace spontaneity.
10. Plan an exciting evening out with a friend; relish the thrill.
11. Take a day trip to explore uncharted territory.
12. Check your commitments but think outside the box.
13. Trust your guidance as you navigate life's journey.
14. Try something new; embrace the thrill of new experiences.
15. Honor your intuition and let it guide your spirit.
16. Live and love beyond the ordinary; seek thrilling experiences.
17. Stay focused on success while infusing fun into pursuits.
18. Let today lead you to new horizons of excitement.
19. Engage in heartfelt talks with loved ones to deepen bonds.
20. Find peace in nature; hug a tree and connect with the world.
21. Stay organized while following safety guidelines in adventures.
22. Lift a stranger's spirits with your vibrant energy.
23. Explore new dimensions; let curiosity lead your discoveries.
24. Quiet your inner critic to make space for joy.
25. Inspire your creativity to explore untraveled paths.
26. Adjust your foundation to align with your adventurous spirit.
27. Check off something from your desire list; make it real.
28. Give full attention to someone close and nurture the bond.
29. Embark on a vision quest for self-discovery and treasures.
30. Boldly express your inner authority while pursuing passions.

PERSONAL YEAR 5

October
6 Personal Month

Note: October is always the same number as your personal year next year, meaning it is a brief preview of the coming year.

If you are in a 5 personal year, October brings the energy of a 6, and just like January, it shines a spotlight on your relationships. This year has undoubtedly been marked by change, and October continues that trend. Both October and January resonate with the same vibrational energy, albeit with eight months in between for expansion and growth during this dynamic 5 year.

You are not the same person you were in January, and your perspectives on relationships may have evolved significantly. This month presents an opportunity to be of service to your loved ones once more, allowing you to reassess how to move forward with a fresh perspective. You may also encounter new career opportunities that complement this interpersonal focus.

October is your month to embrace responsibility and set an example for those around you. Strive to cultivate harmony and balance in what can be an otherwise tumultuous year. Prepare yourself for November, when you will turn inward to reflect on your current path.

Take some time to be at home with family, dedicating yourself to meaningful projects or planning a vacation with loved ones. By the time November arrives, you will likely find that your priorities have realigned.

October is indeed a 6 month; emphasizing your home and family. It's crucial to face your responsibilities and nurture both your living space and your relationships. Dedicate quality time to your family by scheduling a vacation or engaging in home improvement projects. Seek to create harmony in both your career and your domestic life, taking this time to realign your priorities for the months to come

Personal Day
(October)

1. Carve out sacred time for yourself in a tranquil space.
2. Cultivate balance in every area, weaving harmony daily.
3. Embrace unconditional love and forgiveness from your heart.
4. Approach responsibilities with grace and kindness.
5. Express gratitude for your family's contributions; deepen connections.
6. Emanate joy and happiness; uplift yourself and others.
7. Establish boundaries essential for maintaining your well-being.
8. Embark on a delightful adventure with a loved one.
9. Engage in meaningful conversations to deepen connections.
10. Cultivate a compassionate friendship with your inner critic.
11. Dedicate time to align your career with your values.
12. Share kindness through acts of service; small gestures matter.
13. Nurture relationships by spending quality time with loved ones.
14. Use diplomacy to resolve ongoing issues; seek harmony.
15. Unleash creativity with a home improvement project.
16. Develop a clear plan to guide your projects to fruition.
17. Set aside a day for activities that nourish your soul.
18. Create cherished memories with those closest to you.
19. Meditate to connect with your intuition; trust its guidance.
20. Find your center amidst challenges; maintain balance.
21. Let go and surrender to wisdom for clarity on your journey.
22. Collaborate with your partner to align future goals.
23. Be open to compromise to uphold balance in relationships.
24. Enjoy an entertaining evening out; savor shared joy.
25. Embrace structure and discipline to support your growth.
26. Acknowledge amazing events today; welcome life's offerings.
27. Step up and manage your responsibilities diligently.
28. Retreat to your happy place with a good book for inspiration.
29. Honor yourself & your wisdom; be confident in your authority.
30. Practice forgiveness; let go and fill your heart with love.
31. Stay receptive to new ideas; embrace them as growth opportunities.

PERSONAL YEAR 5

November
7 Personal Month

This has been marked by transitional growth experiences, and this month offers you the opportunity to turn inward and evaluate your response to these changes. Take the time to sit with everything that has unfolded throughout the year; embrace the freedom, expansion, and opportunities that have come your way.

With the influx of 7 energy, now is the moment to pause and reflect on your journey thus far. Are you where you wish to be in life? This is the time to contemplate the deeper questions of your identity and aspirations. Engage in meditation to connect with your inner guidance and wisdom.

Designated as a month for rest and regeneration, consider spending time on nature walks, if the weather permits. Conduct a mini vision quest wherever you find yourself; seek insights that will illuminate your path forward. You may also explore self-improvement courses as a means of further enhancing your personal growth.

November is characterized as a 7 month; an invitation to rest, relax, and rejuvenate. Solitude is essential for inward focus during this time. Use this period to reevaluate where your life has been and the direction you wish to pursue. Dive into the study of metaphysics, go on a retreat, and immerse yourself in the tranquility of nature as you embark on this transformative journey.

PERSONAL YEAR 5

Personal Day
(November)

1. Embrace opportunities; ponder them deeply before acting.
2. Tie up loose ends; complete tasks to create mental space.
3. Express your individuality boldly; let your true self shine.
4. Enjoy solitude, but remember cooperation nurtures connections.
5. Savor moments to relish the beauty of your day.
6. Honor your body with nourishing food and regular exercise.
7. Immerse in spontaneity today; the Universe holds surprises.
8. Attend to responsibilities intentionally; diligence brings freedom.
9. Find your sacred space for peace and solitude.
10. Open your heart to abundance; prosperity takes many forms.
11. Cultivate patience and understanding in your encounters today.
12. Excellent day for negotiating; use intuitive insights wisely.
13. Acknowledge contributions; mutual support strengthens bonds.
14. Step out and embrace the joy of social interaction.
15. Consider a wellness check; self-care promotes vitality.
16. Welcome variety in your work; engage in something extraordinary.
17. Enhance your space with flowers or tidiness for warmth.
18. Reflect on your life path; ensure alignment with your desires.
19. Balance your checkbook; financial mindfulness is key.
20. Release what you can't control; avoid overthinking.
21. Align with your highest goals and assess your journey.
22. Let others lead today; offer support and insights instead.
23. Reach out to an old friend; reconnect with a heartfelt message.
24. Find order amid chaos; clarity breeds peace.
25. Promote yourself confidently; let your voice be heard.
26. Maintain boundaries while respecting others'; balance is vital.
27. Collect your thoughts on a calming nature walk; let serenity guide you.
28. Present your authority with poise and assurance.
29. Honor humanity by volunteering to uplift others.
30. Recognize that ambition & achievement build your foundation.

PERSONAL YEAR 5

December
8 Personal Month

December is a powerful few weeks where the vibrations of abundance and business come to the forefront. You can anticipate a significant flow of money this month, potentially more than in previous months. It is essential to remain mindful, ensuring that this energy flows both ways; keep a close watch on your spending.

The number 8 also embodies themes of authority, presenting an opportunity for you to step up and take charge. You may encounter challenges or confrontations, but these will serve as catalysts for your personal development. Stand your ground confidently, as this month is one of empowerment. Coupled with the energy of a 5 year, you are invited to embrace profound changes in your self-perception.

Face your fears and summon your courage to step outside of your comfort zone. Let your dreams and aspirations propel you forward. Throughout this month, aim to maintain balance and harmony in all aspects of your life. Cultivating a positive mindset will enhance your capacity to serve the greater good.

December is indeed an 8 month, emphasizing hard work, power, and authority. Business becomes the focus, and you are called to embrace a leadership role. Strive to organize and manage every facet of your life, ensuring that you achieve equilibrium between your material ambitions and spiritual well-being. Step into your role as an authority and navigate these transformative energies with purpose and clarity.

PERSONAL YEAR 5

Personal Day
(December)

1. Seize the chance to make an impact; donate your time or money.
2. Dive into a research project or a captivating book for insights.
3. Center yourself; connect with values and trust your instincts.
4. Let your creativity run wild; unleash innovative financial ideas.
5. Establish a structured workday; organization enhances your spirit.
6. Embrace variety and be open to unexpected opportunities.
7. Stand ready to assist those in need; your skills can change lives.
8. Use imagination to explore familiar paths with fresh perspectives.
9. Keep pushing forward in your material pursuits; aim high.
10. Add final touches to your projects and celebrate your success.
11. Be independent; express your individuality in finance.
12. Pay attention to details; they are key to solid planning.
13. Reconnect with an old friend; it may spark new ideas.
14. Activate your practical skills; action leads to adventure.
15. Make self-promotion a priority; attract attention with expertise.
16. Strengthen boundaries; assert your needs to protect your pursuits.
17. Remember to rest and recharge for upcoming challenges.
18. Analyze your accounts regularly; invest wisely for returns.
19. Use your gifts to contribute to the greater good; every bit helps.
20. Collaborate with others; teamwork amplifies your impact.
21. Let your journey unfold naturally; go with the currents.
22. Carve out time for joy and play; it fuels your adventures.
23. Ensure your foundation is solid; strong ground supports exploration.
24. Meet new people to expand your network and open doors.
25. Nurture important relationships; they are invaluable assets.

PERSONAL YEAR 5

26. Create a space for positive energy; a vibrant environment inspires.
27. Stay attuned to financial matters; think strategically about opportunities.
28. Identify solutions, then let them go; free yourself from burdens.
29. Share knowledge generously; teaching leads to rewarding collaborations.
30. Use diplomacy to resolve conflicts; harmony promotes success.
31. Communicate effectively; open pathways for growth and exploration.

Personal Year 6

A personal year marked by the number 6 emphasizes the importance of responsibility and service to others. It is a time to cultivate harmony across all spheres of your life: career, home, and relationships. Approach endeavors with fairness and selflessness, seeking truth and justice while upholding high ideals. Honor your obligations to others with an unselfish spirit, serving humanity for the greater good, and you shall be rewarded.

This year highlights the balance between personal growth and caregiving opportunities. Engage with your community and loved ones, working towards truth and justice while embracing balance and harmony. The focus is on prioritizing the needs of others over your own, emphasizing giving back rather than engaging in self-centered activities. Practice generosity and forgiveness, greeting each day with unconditional love. Selfless sacrifice yields rich rewards, and this year is ripe for forming long-lasting relationships. Be mindful of codependency tendencies, fostering new connections, and maintaining healthy relationships.

As home, family, and relationships take center stage, responsibility becomes paramount. This year may pose challenges as familial needs increase, but it is a period for expressing and receiving the expanding love characteristic of a 6 year. Strive for harmony in relationships, health, and career, finding that forgiveness and letting go are inevitably rewarded. Gain fulfillment through caregiving and service, imparting your values to children and nurturing those you love, including yourself.

Romance and relationships flourish, presenting opportunities to renew commitments and deepen bonds. Whether you choose to strengthen marital vows or reassess commitments, this is a pivotal year for relationship evolution. Positive developments in career and finances may arise, alongside community obligations, requiring delicate balance with family and home priorities. Now is the time to harmonize all facets of your existence, moving forward in personal growth while honoring responsibilities. Remember to take care of yourself, ensuring that you are well-equipped to support those around you.

January
7 Personal Month

In a 6 personal year, January unfolds with 7 energy, a time for inward reflection and introspection. This year invites you to prioritize home and family, placing your relationships at the forefront of your experiences. In its most pronounced form, a 6 year may either signify a period of divorce or serve as an opportunity to renew your vows. The importance of your primary relationships cannot be overstated, making this an ideal time to address and heal any unresolved issues.

As the focus shifts to home and family, you will likely find yourself spending quality time with loved ones. Consider embarking on a renovation project or enhancing your property's landscape. Seek opportunities to upgrade your living space in ways that resonate with your personal aesthetic.

January provides an opportunity to dive deep within and pose profound questions to yourself: What do I truly want? Explore this inquiry across all facets of your life, including career, relationships, and lifestyle. Use this month to uncover your genuine desires and cultivate a healthy relationship with yourself. Foster communication with the Divine and heed the guidance you receive.

This month is about focusing on yourself and clarifying your aspirations, as the remainder of the year will center on serving others.

January is characterized as a 7 month, one that champions rest, relaxation, and rejuvenation. Solitude becomes essential for introspection. Take the time to reevaluate the path your life has taken and the direction you wish to pursue. Engage in the study of metaphysics, consider taking a retreat, and immerse yourself in nature as you navigate this transformative and contemplative period.

PERSONAL YEAR 6

Personal Day
(January)

1. Embrace opportunities; think them through before acting.
2. Tie up loose ends; complete tasks for a sense of closure.
3. Let your individuality shine; express your authentic self.
4. Remember, cooperation is vital; interact with kindness.
5. Savor moments each day; take time to enjoy life.
6. Nourish your body with healthy foods and regular exercise.
7. Embrace spontaneity and be open to life's surprises.
8. Approach responsibilities with intention and commitment.
9. Find your sacred space; cherish solitude for reflection.
10. Recognize abundance is on its way in various forms.
11. Cultivate patience and understanding to nurture relationships.
12. Today is great for negotiating; approach with clarity.
13. Honor others' contributions; reciprocity strengthens bonds.
14. Nurture social connections; engage with others today.
15. Schedule a wellness check to prioritize your health.
16. Add variety to your routine; engage in inspiring activities.
17. Beautify your home with flowers or tidy up for comfort.
18. Reflect on your path; ask if you're where you want to be.
19. Balance your checkbook; financial awareness is key.
20. Let go of what you can't control; release distractions.
21. Align with your highest goals and assess your journey.
22. Practice deference; let others take the lead today.
23. Reconnect with an old friend through a heartfelt note.
24. Stay practical; find order in chaos for calm.
25. Promote your work confidently; share your talents.
26. Uphold your boundaries while respecting others' limits.
27. Collect thoughts on a walk; let nature inspire clarity.
28. Embrace your authority; present yourself with professionalism.
29. Honor humanity by dedicating time to volunteer.
30. Recognize ambition and achievement as your foundation.
31. Use diplomacy to resolve tensions and maintain balance.

PERSONAL YEAR 6

February
8 Personal Month

This year places responsibilities front and center, with the energy of 8 focusing on career, finances, and business growth. It's an ideal time to understand how you earn a living and advance professionally. Partnerships, especially with business associates, will be highlighted, urging you to strengthen connections.

Encourage the free flow of financial resources and energetic exchanges, while ensuring balance in all interactions. Reflect on enhancing your workspace; with the number 8 emphasizing authority, you may be called to step into a leadership role. Although challenges may arise, recognize them as opportunities for personal growth and expansion.

Adopt a broader perspective; practice detachment and let things unfold naturally. Be disciplined with finances and address any fears that might surface.

This month is characterized by hard work, power, and authority. Business is at the forefront, inviting you to embrace a leadership role. Use this time to organize and manage every facet of your life, while balancing material pursuits with spiritual well-being. Step confidently into your authoritative role and navigate this transformative period with clarity and purpose.

February manifests as an 8 vibration, the number associated with organization and business. Invest wisely in your living situation. At the very least, seize this opportunity to declutter and organize your space. Clean out the garage, tidy your home office, or refresh the decor of your living room. Expect a more pronounced flow of money this month compared to others.

The number 8 signifies self-empowerment and claiming authority. Even as you navigate this relationship-focused time, remember to dedicate attention to your own needs and well-being. Your authority may be tested—embrace the challenge with confidence.

PERSONAL YEAR 6

Personal Day
(February)

1. Contribute to a cause that touches your heart; donate or volunteer.
2. Engage in learning with a new project or soul-nurturing book.
3. Center yourself; listen to your heart and trust your intuition.
4. Let creativity flow; bring joy with imaginative ideas.
5. Organize your day with love and intention for harmony.
6. Embrace variety; welcome unexpected joys and experiences.
7. Support those in need with compassion & a willingness to help.
8. Use imagination to revive old paths with fresh perspectives.
9. Enrich your material world with love and meaningful growth.
10. Complete projects with care; add loving final touches.
11. Be true to yourself; express individuality and spread positivity.
12. Pay attention to details; they show you care.
13. Reconnect with an old friend; share love & strengthen bonds.
14. Ignite practical skills with a loving, pragmatic approach.
15. Embrace your strengths; let your light shine brightly.
16. Establish boundaries with love, protecting your energy.
17. Take time to rest and renew your spirit for others.
18. Manage resources wisely to ensure a secure future.
19. Share your unique gifts generously for the greater good.
20. Collaborate with others to create a nurturing environment.
21. Let go and let life unfold, trusting love will guide you.
22. Dedicate time to play; find joy and nurture your soul.
23. Ensure your foundation is strong; love flourishes on solid ground.
24. Connect with new people; nurture friendships to blossom love.
25. Cherish important relationships; give them time and attention.
26. Create a space of love and peace; inspire positive energy.
27. Be mindful of finances; think how they serve your intentions.
28. Resolve problems gently; find solutions and release worries.
29. Share your knowledge openly; teach with love in every interaction.

March
9 Personal Month

March unfolds with 9 energy, heralding a time of reflection and completion. This year emphasizes service to your home and family; take your responsibilities to heart and cherish the moments spent with loved ones. As the final month of the numerology cycle, 9 brings an opportunity to bring closure to various aspects of your life.

Now is the time to wrap up any home improvement projects you have initiated. Tackle those cluttered spaces by cleaning out your closets and garage, discarding anything unnecessary. Lighten your load as you prepare to embark on a new cycle in April, ensuring clarity about what you wish to carry forward.

Reflect on the past months, and make space to let go, forgive, and release any burdens. While you transition into new beginnings next month, take this opportunity to enjoy the rewards of your hard work from previous months.

The energy of 9 is inherently spiritual, so remain attuned to your intuition. Dedicate time to meditation and rejuvenate yourself, preferably in nature. Use this month to serve the greater good, enhancing your compassion and understanding as you accept the rewards that come your way.

March symbolizes a 9 month, the culmination of a nine-month cycle. Embrace the process of cleaning out, finishing tasks, and letting go of anything that does not serve you. Reap the benefits of your diligence from the past eight months and create space for the exciting new beginnings that await you next month. Trust your intuition as you contemplate what you wish to manifest moving forward, and continue to focus on serving the greater good.

PERSONAL YEAR 6

Personal Day
(March)

1. Embrace your role as your journey's guide; lead with compassion.
2. Work harmoniously with others toward shared goals.
3. Express yourself through varied channels; stay open to connection.
4. Plan your day thoughtfully while welcoming growth and change.
5. Stay attentive to meaningful synchronicities on your path.
6. Share kindness by delivering flowers to spread love.
7. Rejuvenate your spirit in a cherished place of peace.
8. Embrace opportunities with bold steps and grace.
9. Clear physical and emotional clutter for renewal.
10. Make careful choices guided by empathy and wisdom.
11. Trust your intuition for resolutions promoting peace.
12. Celebrate spontaneity with joyful gatherings and fun.
13. Approach tasks with practicality and kindness for productivity.
14. Embrace unpredictability as a chance for growth and connection.
15. Bring beauty and order to your home, creating harmony.
16. Move with life's flow, allowing events to unfold naturally.
17. Manage finances carefully to support humanitarian efforts.
18. Conclude activities that don't serve your well-being.
19. Focus on future aspirations with love and forgiveness.
20. Offer apologies to create space for healing.
21. Engage in joyful activities that bring laughter and contentment.
22. Address unresolved issues with clarity and compassion.
23. Embrace opportunities to showcase your talents today.
24. Be present to offer wisdom to those seeking guidance.
25. Reflect on your journey to ensure alignment with your true self.
26. Lead with gentle authority, guiding with kindness.
27. Release burdens weighing on your spirit for growth.
28. Use your intellect to inspire positive change collaboratively.
29. Attend to unfinished business; complete projects with care.
30. Participate in discussions, sharing insights with respect.
31. Finish today's tasks; create a compassionate plan for tomorrow.

April
1 Personal Month

April brings the dynamic energy of the 1. This 6 year invites you to prioritize home, family, and relationships, areas that likely demand your attention more than usual. Now is the time to invest your energy in nurturing these connections. With the supportive vibration of 1, this month offers you the opportunity to define what you wish to cultivate within your relationships.

While the energy of 6 emphasizes connections, the number 1 is inherently solitary, placing a spotlight on your individual needs amid these associations. Harness the 1 vibration to visualize new projects and endeavors. Reflect on what you truly desire to bring into your life for the remainder of the year. Be determined, decisive, and clear about your intentions, setting goals across all facets of your existence.

You carry leadership energy this month, empowering you to summon the courage to become the person you aspire to be. Focus on the positive aspects of your desires, as maintaining an optimistic outlook will yield favorable results. The clearer you are in articulating your aspirations, the easier it will be to manifest your visions.

April is indeed a 1 month, an invitation for new beginnings. Plant seeds, set your goals, and establish your intentions for the next nine months. This is a bustling month filled with opportunities for new projects, so embrace the courage to step into a leadership role and shape your journey ahead.

Personal Day
(April)

1. Foster a peaceful, harmonious environment for everyone's well-being.
2. Let your cheerful nature shine to uplift those around you.
3. Be an effective manager; organization is key to purposeful leading.
4. View upcoming changes as opportunities for growth and improvement.
5. Engage with your community; seek ways to contribute positively.
6. Explore and research topics that enrich your knowledge and leadership.
7. Focus on action, ambition, and achievement to drive initiatives.
8. Let go of outdated practices for a higher purpose moving forward.
9. Today is great for sound business decisions; maintain integrity.
10. Practice patience; allow situations to unfold naturally.
11. Cultivate positivity; an optimistic mindset can be empowering.
12. Ensure your moral compass aligns with your leadership values.
13. Exercise self-control; prioritize thoughtful, wise choices.
14. Approach disagreements with love and understanding for harmony.
15. Prioritize health by starting a new exercise regimen.
16. Focus on gratitude; invite abundance & appreciation into life.
17. True success comes from serving humanity; let this guide you.
18. Use your leadership skills to carve new paths for others.
19. Recognize friendships; inspire love & camaraderie among peers.
20. Quiet your inner critic; focus on the positives of your journey.
21. Read fine print in documents; diligence is key to good leadership.
22. Stay open to ideas while avoiding distractions that scatter focus.

23. Commit to responsible actions to support your team & goals.
24. If needed, take time to recharge; your well-being matters.
25. Focus on the greater good; ensure actions benefit the community.
26. Clear clutter to make room for positive changes ahead.
27. Continuously seek to improve your projects; avoid complacency.
28. Prioritize helping others; extend support before your own needs.
29. Attend a self-improvement seminar or read for personal growth.
30. Honor your strong work ethic; it sets a standard for your team.

PERSONAL YEAR 6

May
2 Personal Month

May unfolds as a 2 energy, offering a heightened focus on relationships infused with the energies of both 6 and 2. The 6 energy emphasizes responsibility and caring for home duties, reminding you that your family will need your support during this time. This may also be a period for addressing home repairs and maintenance.

The dual influence of 2 encourages cooperation and balance, urging you to embrace a collaborative spirit. You are not in charge at the moment; instead, practice deference to others. Listen attentively to your loved ones as well as to your intuition, which is especially refined during this period. The energies present now are conducive to developing a deeper relationship with your inner guidance, so trust and follow it.

With May offering a slower, more relaxed pace than April, use this time for introspection and inner work. Nurture the new ideas that you have already begun to cultivate. Embrace the role of diplomat and be ready to negotiate when challenges arise within your relationships.

Pay close attention to the details, making sure that nothing falls through the cracks, both at work and at home. In this month dedicated to partnerships and relationships, remember that compromise is essential. Avoid rowing against the current; instead, flow with the energy around you. Strive to find harmony in all your endeavors and relish the peaceful moments of the coming weeks.

May is indeed a 2 month, a time to focus on the finer details and take care of the little things that matter. Nurture the seeds you planted last month, as cooperation in relationships becomes paramount after the preceding month's emphasis on individual pursuits. This month may evoke strong emotions, requiring you to utilize your diplomatic skills effectively.

Personal Day
(May)

1. Gather loved ones to create something meaningful together.
2. Organize tasks to enhance harmony and efficiency in life.
3. Foster peace by letting go of control; allow natural flow.
4. Cherish your partner with a thoughtful meal and conversation.
5. Read a book together that inspires personal growth.
6. Make financial decisions to support shared goals and duties.
7. Volunteer as a family in areas that align with your hearts.
8. Unite with loved ones to start a fulfilling group project.
9. Explore real estate opportunities for fun or potential investment.
10. Encourage loved ones' creativity to foster new ideas.
11. Practice diligence in responsibilities to strengthen work ethic.
12. Stay open to unexpected joys and challenges in relationships.
13. Undertake a home project that reflects shared values.
14. Enjoy nature together, finding joy in shared spaces.
15. Review your financial portfolio to meet mutual goals.
16. Envision how to serve humanity together, making an impact.
17. Compile a to-do list for both individual and shared tasks.
18. Mediate disagreements, fostering diplomacy & understanding.
19. Create a joyful day filled with activities to strengthen bonds.
20. Support each other in responsibilities and shared objectives.
21. Embrace changes together, adapting with mutual support.
22. Find comfort and unity at home, enjoying your sanctuary.
23. Spend time reflecting on personal and shared growth.
24. Lead with confidence, stepping up in your responsibilities.
25. Perform kind acts for those in need, strengthening community ties.
26. Encourage originality and express your individuality together.
27. Offer compassion to friends and deepen your connections.
28. Allow open expression, ensuring every voice is heard.
29. Reflect on your relationships, reinforcing their stability.
30. Embark on new adventures together, exploring as a team.
31. Respect boundaries, offering advice only when solicited.

June
3 Personal Month

You have likely devoted considerable time to home and family this year, and that emphasis will continue. Your responsibility to those you love remains paramount, but it is equally important to carve out moments for yourself in order to replenish your reserves. Remember, an empty cup serves no one.

The energy of 3 brings a spirit of enjoyment and creativity this month. Consider planning a project to undertake together or embarking on a joyful outing. Seek ways to celebrate life and embrace playfulness in June. Think about redecorating or redesigning some aspect of your home, dancing to your favorite music, and exploring any creative outlet that resonates with you. Allow your imagination to expand, committing to finding joy in the present.

Be mindful that unresolved issues may surface, and it's essential to address them promptly before they develop into larger concerns. Take the time to delve deeper into your emotions and learn effective ways to express yourself. Maintain a positive mindset to attract abundance into your life.

Avoid scattering your energy across too many projects; instead, focus on one endeavor at a time. The number 3 is often associated with luck, so be sure to seize any opportunities that come your way.

June is a 3 month, where your creative juices will flow abundantly, revealing new ideas to cultivate abundance. This is a playful time, but remember to keep things simple and focused. Engage in activities such as redecorating, redesigning a project, writing a story, or dancing, allowing your creativity to shine.

Personal Day
(June)

1. Create a family agenda and complete it for harmony at home.
2. Prepare for any opportunity that benefits your family today.
3. Have heartfelt conversations with friends; listen genuinely.
4. Dedicate time for personal reflection in a quiet space.
5. Review your family's finances, including bank accounts.
6. Embrace forgiveness and love to foster family peace.
7. Collaborate to start a creative project with loved ones.
8. Trust your intuition when making household decisions.
9. Encourage self-expression through art and creativity.
10. Focus to effectively manage your family responsibilities.
11. Allow distractions that enrich interactions or bring change.
12. Enhance your home with thoughtful redecorations.
13. Enroll in an online course for personal and family growth.
14. Balance material and spiritual matters at home.
15. Practice compassion to strengthen family bonds.
16. Honor your individuality while considering family dynamics.
17. Find quiet moments to listen to your intuition.
18. Attend social gatherings as a family for shared joy.
19. Visualize a strong foundation for your family's future.
20. Stir your relationship's spirit and pursue shared goals.
21. Savor family gatherings while maintaining healthy boundaries.
22. Reflect on your spiritual journey and family values.
23. Focus on family aspirations to uplift and support each other.
24. Serve the greater good, blessing your family and community.
25. Welcome new experiences that enhance family life.
26. Foster balance and peace within the home environment.
27. Document gratitude with your family to cultivate appreciation.
28. Complete tasks for smooth family operations; check them off.
29. Explore new opportunities as a family for growth.
30. Encourage bold family adventures that bring joy and learning.

July
4 Personal Month

For the past six months, your life has primarily centered around home and family, emphasizing your responsibilities to your loved ones. Those closest to you will likely continue to require your support in July. The energy of 4 brings forth diligence, perseverance, and discipline, encouraging you to focus on remodeling or upgrading your living environment in some capacity. At a minimum, consider tidying the garage or decluttering your space.

Your attention, regardless of your career, should be directed toward your home. This time may also prompt you to establish new boundaries with family members. Reflect on whether co-dependence has become an issue for you; are you taking on so much that life feels like a burden? If so, use these upcoming weeks to redefine those boundaries.

Prioritize your health through mindful choices in diet and exercise. Be clear about how you wish to proceed in the future. If you invest the necessary effort to establish a solid foundation for your life now, you will be well-prepared for what lies ahead. August promises expansion and new opportunities, setting the stage for your growth.

As July is a 4 month, emphasize organization, discipline, and diligence during this time. Attend to your health and ensure that you care for your body through proper nutrition and exercise. Focus on bringing to fruition the plans and projects you initiated last month, and take the opportunity to reset your foundation in anticipation of the expansive energy that will emerge in the upcoming 5 month.

Personal Day
(July)

1. Be open and ready for a shift; change is life's journey.
2. Dedicate efforts to working comfortably at home today.
3. Engage in exercise to nurture your body and spirit.
4. Balance your finances; stability brings peace of mind.
5. Wrap up projects; completion brings a sense of fulfillment.
6. Create a thoughtful to-do list for the month ahead.
7. Fill in the blanks on tasks needing your attention.
8. Enjoy today; take a break to savor beauty around you.
9. Diligence pays off; your efforts will be rewarded.
10. Embrace change; welcome it with an open heart.
11. Pay attention to relationships; they are essential.
12. Find moments for quiet contemplation and reflection.
13. Stay open to work shifts; adaptability brings opportunities.
14. Release what you don't need, physically or emotionally.
15. Reflect on new thoughts and insights during introspection.
16. Focus on details; they matter greatly in daily life.
17. Make time for activities that bring you joy.
18. Ensure you're on solid ground, emotionally & physically.
19. Challenge yourself to level up your workload with enthusiasm.
20. Improve your home; a nurtured space fosters peace.
21. Be mindful of your diet; choose fresh, nourishing foods.
22. Honor your knowledge; let it guide your decisions.
23. Complete your monthly to-do list; take pride in achievements.
24. Be ready for a new chapter; embrace upcoming opportunities.
25. Read between the lines for deeper understanding in interactions.
26. Hold yourself accountable for actions to foster growth.
27. Avoid overthinking; trust the process and listen to your heart.
28. Prepare for a fast-paced month; flow with life's momentum.
29. Brighten your space with flowers to invite joy and beauty.
30. Prioritize self-improvement for your growth and well-being.
31. Strive for balance and harmony; nurture yourself and others.

August
5 Personal Month

Throughout this year, your focus has been on responsibilities toward family and nurturing your relationships. Home projects, caregiving, and interpersonal dynamics have defined your journey thus far. However, with the advent of August and the energy of 5, expect significant expansion and forward momentum.

The number 5 embodies change, both anticipated and unexpected, so be prepared for shifts in your relationships, career, and home life. This is an opportune month for travel or a family vacation, encouraging you to explore new horizons. Embrace self-promotion and find the courage to put yourself out there; if an opportunity presents itself, don't hesitate to take the leap.

August promises to be a busy month, infused with unpredictable events. Your best strategy for navigating this lively time is to adopt a flexible mindset and allow the dynamic energy to flow around you. Embrace the possibility of completely altering your course as necessary. Looking ahead, September introduces a double 6 energy into your life, intensifying your relationships further. Any changes made now will contribute positively to your growth.

While it is important to honor your responsibilities during this time, do not forget to prioritize your well-being.

In summary, August is characterized as a 5 month, marked by unexpected change that brings opportunities for travel and adventure. You may find yourself charting a new course entirely, therefore, promote yourself and leverage your communication skills boldly. Take risks, as the transformations this month are ultimately aimed at enhancing your life. Allow the energy to flow freely and immerse yourself in the potential that awaits you.

Personal Day
(August)

1. Embrace opportunities around you; choose thoughtfully for well-being.
2. Discover growth through a self-improvement book for your spirit.
3. Maintain balance in life despite the chaos that may arise.
4. Express kindness through thoughtful gestures that uplift others.
5. Jot down your wildest dreams; manifesting begins with clarity.
6. Practice cooperation to foster mutual support and harmony.
7. Dance joyfully; celebrate and share your happiness.
8. Follow the straight paths that lead you to your goals.
9. Savor a day filled with adventure; explore with an open heart.
10. Enjoy an evening out with a friend; create lasting memories.
11. Plan a day trip to discover new places and enrich connections.
12. Check in on business; think creatively and embrace innovation.
13. Trust your inner guidance; it nurtures your journey.
14. Dare to try something new; embrace joy in new experiences.
15. Heed your intuitive nudges; they are your compass.
16. Live and love authentically; step outside conventional expectations.
17. Focus on success while being mindful of your well-being.
18. Let today guide you towards new horizons of hope and opportunity.
19. Engage in meaningful conversations with loved ones; connection matters.
20. Meditate in nature; find peace and connect with the earth.
21. Organize tasks and adhere to rules for structure in caring.
22. Lift spirits with kindness; your positivity can heal.
23. Investigate new experiences; curiosity enriches understanding.
24. Quiet your critic; allow self-compassion to flourish.
25. Encourage creativity and explore new self-expression avenues.
26. Realign beliefs to support your growth and nurturing spirit.

PERSONAL YEAR 6

27. Act on your wildest desires; make them a joyful reality.
28. Give full attention to someone close; cherish that bond.
29. Embark on a vision quest for self-discovery and growth.
30. Confidently express your authority while attending to others.
31. Maintain balance in your actions; your care enriches the world.

September
6 Personal Month

Note: Because September is the ninth month, it is always the same number as your personal year. This means you have double the energy of your personal year for thirty days. If the current year calculates to the same value as your personal year, then you receive triple that number's energy in September.

The energy of 6 amplifies your focus on loved ones. Throughout the year, you have likely prioritized these connections, but this month brings a heightened emphasis on home and family. Enjoy this time together, as you will have the opportunity to rejuvenate next month, and the entirety of the next year will be dedicated to your inner work.

All of your relationships will be under scrutiny during this period, making it essential to address any issues that arise promptly. Now is the perfect opportunity to renew your commitments; consider taking a weekend getaway with your beloved. If your perceptions have shifted, take the time to ponder your true feelings and emotions.

Honor your responsibilities to both yourself and others by fulfilling your obligations. Strive to create harmony and balance in all areas of your life, reflecting the essence of the 6 energy. Additionally, you may find that your career and finances progress this month, so take care to nurture your own well-being; remember, you cannot pour from an empty cup.

September is defined as a 6 month; a time centered on home and family. Embrace your responsibilities, attending to both your household and relationships with care. Dedicate quality time to family, perhaps by scheduling a vacation or engaging in home improvement projects. Seek harmony in both your career and home life, and take this opportunity to realign your priorities effectively.

Personal Day
(September)

1. Prioritize self-care by creating time for yourself to recharge.
2. Cultivate balance in all areas of life for daily harmony.
3. Embrace unconditional love and forgiveness for everyone.
4. Approach responsibilities with grace and kindness for others.
5. Express gratitude for your family's support; appreciation fosters closeness.
6. Radiate joy and happiness; your positivity uplifts others.
7. Maintain healthy boundaries to protect your well-being.
8. Embark on an adventure with a loved one to strengthen bonds.
9. Engage in heartfelt conversations with your partner for openness.
10. Build a compassionate relationship with your inner critic.
11. Spend time expanding your career; align growth with your values.
12. Perform acts of kindness; good deeds create ripples of positivity.
13. Nurture relationships by spending quality time with loved ones.
14. Use diplomacy to resolve lingering issues calmly and effectively.
15. Unleash creativity with a home improvement project.
16. Formulate a clear plan to ensure your projects come to fruition.
17. Dedicate a day to nourish your soul and bring joy.
18. Create meaningful memories to cherish with loved ones.
19. Meditate to connect with your intuition and guide your actions.
20. Find your center, maintaining balance amid life's challenges.
21. Let go of what no longer serves you; surrender to wisdom.
22. Set new goals with your partner, aligning future visions.
23. Be willing to compromise for harmony in your relationships.
24. Enjoy an entertaining evening out; savor connection and relaxation.

PERSONAL YEAR 6

25. Embrace structure and discipline in caregiving and growth.
26. Stay receptive to amazing events; celebrate each moment.
27. Step up to fulfill responsibilities as a supportive caregiver.
28. Retreat to your happy place with a book to restore energy.
29. Honor yourself and the wisdom gained on your journey.
30. Practice forgiveness and release burdens to let love flow.

PERSONAL YEAR 6

October
7 Personal Month

Note: October is always the same number as your personal year next year, making it a brief preview of the coming year.

This month offers you a well-deserved reprieve from the caregiving and nurturing that have marked your year. It is a time to turn inward and reflect on your beliefs, as well as to consider how you wish to move forward. Prioritize rest and seek solitude, for this is your opportunity to recharge before the demands of next year.

Embrace your spiritual path and take this moment to redefine the direction of your life. October is an introspective month, granting you the space to connect with the Divine and cultivate your intuition. Use this time for self-improvement, enabling you to realign your priorities in preparation for November.

Make it a point to care for yourself and seek inner peace, a much-needed respite after a year dedicated to family and relationships. You might even find the chance for a spiritual retreat where you can gather insights and reflect on whether you are on the right spiritual path. The energy at this time supports deep questioning and self-discovery, offering you clarity and answers to your inquiries.

October embodies the essence of a 7 month, one dedicated to rest, relaxation, and rejuvenation. Solitude is essential for inward focus as you reevaluate the trajectory of your life. Engage in the study of metaphysics, consider taking a retreat, and spend time in nature to replenish your spirit.

Personal Day
(October)

1. Embrace opportunities but reflect deeply before deciding.
2. Focus on completing unfinished tasks; closure brings peace.
3. Celebrate your uniqueness; let it shine through your actions.
4. Foster cooperation; nurture harmonious relationships.
5. Gift yourself moments to simply savor your day.
6. Nourish your body with healthy food and regular exercise.
7. Welcome spontaneity and notice beautiful coincidences.
8. Tend to your responsibilities; fulfilling commitments matters.
9. Create a sacred space for solitude and recharge.
10. Remember that abundance comes in many forms; it's coming.
11. Cultivate patience and understanding in your interactions.
12. It's a good time for negotiating business dealings.
13. Acknowledge & reciprocate others' contributions; seek balance.
14. Step out of introspection; enjoy the company of others.
15. Schedule a wellness check; your health is worth it.
16. Introduce variety into your work; try something extraordinary.
17. Bring beauty into your home; get flowers or tidy up.
18. Reflect on your journey; are you aligned with your aspirations?
19. Review finances; clarity in budgeting promotes peace of mind.
20. Release what you cannot control; let go of unneeded worries.
21. Align actions with your highest aspirations; evaluate progress.
22. Allow others to lead today; support their initiatives.
23. Reach out to an old friend; send a heartfelt letter or call.
24. Stay grounded; seek order amid chaos around you.
25. Share your talents and ideas; promote your work confidently.
26. Maintain boundaries while respecting others; mutual respect is key.
27. Clear your mind while enjoying nature; take a walk.
28. Take charge of your path; present yourself with confidence.
29. Honor humanity by volunteering your time or skills.
30. Let ambition & achievement lay a strong foundation for your future.
31. Approach conflicts with diplomacy; maintain balance and composure.

November
8 Personal Month

This year, responsibilities take center stage as the energy of 8 brings your career, financial matters, and business into sharp focus. It is the ideal time to dedicate your efforts toward understanding how you earn a living and to concentrate on your professional growth. Partnerships and relationships, including those with business associates, will also be under scrutiny, urging you to strengthen these connections.

Allow both financial resources and energetic exchanges to flow freely while ensuring you maintain a state of balance in your interactions. Reflect on what aspects of your workspace require improvement; the number 8 emphasizes authority, suggesting that you may be called upon to step into a leadership role. While you might encounter challenges, recognize that they serve a greater purpose in your personal growth and expansion.

Adopt a higher perspective as you assess the situations before you; practice detachment and allow the natural process to unfold. Be vigilant with your finances and confront any fears that may arise.

November is an 8 month; a time characterized by hard work, power, and authority. Business becomes the focal point, and you are expected to embrace a leadership role. Take this opportunity to organize and manage every aspect of your life while striving to balance your material pursuits with your spiritual well-being. Step confidently into your role as an authority and navigate this transformative period with intention and clarity.

Personal Day
(November)

1. Support a worthy cause with a meaningful contribution.
2. Engage in learning by starting a new research project or book.
3. Ground yourself and connect with instincts for business decisions.
4. Foster an environment encouraging creativity and innovation.
5. Maintain order and organization in your workday; structure benefits all.
6. Embrace variety; be open to unexpected opportunities.
7. Be ready to assist colleagues in need with compassion.
8. Innovate by revisiting methods with fresh perspectives.
9. Focus on advancing business goals and seizing growth opportunities.
10. Complete projects with attention to detail and professionalism.
11. Express individuality and leverage your unique strengths.
12. Remember details count; addressing them enhances quality.
13. Reconnect with past contacts to renew valuable relationships.
14. Apply practical skills effectively to achieve business goals.
15. Promote yourself and achievements to maintain industry visibility.
16. Establish boundaries to protect your work-life balance.
17. Allow time for rest to maintain energy and effectiveness.
18. Review and balance financial accounts; invest strategically.
19. Share talents and resources for the greater good.
20. Collaborate with others to optimize results and partnerships.
21. Let processes unfold naturally; adapt as needed.
22. Allocate time for leisure; balance is key to well-being.
23. Ensure business foundations are secure for long-term success.
24. Network actively; meet new people and form strong alliances.
25. Invest time in nurturing important personal and professional relationships.
26. Create a workspace that supports productivity and positive energy.

27. Stay attentive to financial opportunities; manage resources wisely.
28. Address problems with a solution-oriented mindset.
29. Share knowledge generously; collaboration strengthens community.
30. Use diplomacy in conflicts, aiming for respectful resolutions.

December
9 Personal Month

This month marks the culmination of both the year and a nine-month cycle in your life. This is a time for cleansing, decluttering, and releasing all unnecessary energy that no longer serves you. Reflect on what you wish to carry forward into the next year, shifting your focus to the positive rather than dwelling on what you must let go. Consider the burdens you are no longer willing to bear; how have you changed, and can you identify the excess baggage that you no longer need?

As you navigate this period of completions, resolutions, and the rewarding fruits of your diligence throughout this year, the energy of 9 highlights themes of unconditional love, forgiveness, and compassion. Take a moment to reflect on the past year: did you accomplish your goals? What lessons would you carry forward? Use this newfound wisdom to inform your intentions for the future and the aspirations you set for yourself in the year ahead.

In this 9 month, embrace the opportunity to clean out, finalize, and release anything that does not contribute positively to your life. Reap the rewards of your hard work from the preceding eight months, making room for the fresh beginnings that lie ahead. Trust your intuition as you contemplate what you want to create next, and seek ways to express your creativity while serving the greater good.

PERSONAL YEAR 6

Personal Day
(December)

1. Take charge of your life; lead with integrity and responsibility.
2. Collaborate with others to achieve common goals and teamwork.
3. Communicate openly and express ideas through various channels.
4. Organize your day with care; ensure tasks are completed.
5. Stay mindful of connections and events that guide your actions.
6. Brighten someone's day with flowers; spread kindness.
7. Find renewal in places that bring you peace and rejuvenation.
8. Recognize and seize opportunities; take calculated risks.
9. Declutter your physical and mental spaces for clarity.
10. Evaluate options thoroughly; make informed decisions.
11. Trust your intuition to address and solve issues responsibly.
12. Embrace spontaneity and joy while balancing responsibilities.
13. Apply common sense to enhance productivity and effectiveness.
14. Allow flexibility to guide your day; it fosters growth.
15. Beautify your home, creating a respectful environment.
16. Go with the flow; adapt naturally to changes in life.
17. Manage finances diligently; keep accounts balanced and healthy.
18. Conclude activities that no longer serve your purpose.
19. Focus on future goals, building on a strong aspiration foundation.
20. Apologize when needed to foster healing in relationships.
21. Engage in joyful activities that uplift your spirit.
22. Address legal or financial matters with clarity and responsibility.
23. Anticipate a productive day to showcase your accomplishments.
24. Offer expertise to those in need; be a reliable resource.
25. Reflect on your path to ensure alignment with your values.

26. Lead with authority, guiding others toward positive outcomes.
27. Let go of burdens, preparing for the months ahead.
28. Use your intelligence to support collaborative efforts.
29. Complete tasks, filling in details and closing gaps.
30. Participate in discussions, sharing insights respectfully.
31. Complete today's tasks diligently; plan responsibly for tomorrow.

PERSONAL YEAR 6

Personal Year 7

A personal year marked by the number 7 invites you into a realm of silence and regeneration, where the primary focus is on inner growth. It is a time for deep reflection, contemplation, and the exploration of your inner world through prayer and meditation.

By looking inward at your past, you gain a healthier perspective on your future personal growth. Allow yourself the space to withdraw and engage in internal study, for this journey will lead to a profound understanding of who you truly are and your core values.

Employ your analytical abilities to revisit the goals you set in your foundational year, assessing your progress and being open to changing direction as a result of this self-reflection. Start a new journal to commit your thoughts and ideas to paper, recognizing that this year is meant for internal development rather than outward action.

The inner work you undertake now will manifest as decisive action in the following year.

Connect with your higher intuition and embrace its guidance. Spend time immersed in nature to rejuvenate your spirit. The vibrational energy of this year calls for seeking knowledge and wisdom, prioritizing time alone for study and intellectual enrichment over social engagement. This is an ideal period for refining your skills and expanding your knowledge base, focusing not on business expansion but on research and personal development.

Gather your inner strength and relish in solitude. Pause to reevaluate your life, shedding what no longer serves you. Engage in self-examination and philosophical inquiry, delving deeply into self-discovery and exploring life's mysteries. This internal work can lead to an elevated state of consciousness.

Following a year of service and family engagements, now is the moment to turn inward, seeking solitude, rest, and a reevaluation of your life's path. The energy of the 7 year encourages spiritual pursuits and the study of life's mysteries. Consider embarking on a vision quest or enrolling in self-improvement courses. Prioritize self-care and explore new health regimes, with introspection and intuition taking center stage to achieve inner peace.

Recognize that this focus on your internal self may pose challenges in relationships; however, time dedicated to self-improvement will ultimately enrich your daily life. Pursue the study of science, technology, or metaphysics, developing a well-rounded regime that attends to your physical, mental, and spiritual well-being. Trust in your intuition and have the courage to follow it, for this year is about heeding your inner guidance.

Strengthen the foundation of your inner self through self-awareness and personal growth, with the rewards to follow in subsequent years. Take care to rest and prioritize health more so than in other years. Be aware of legal matters, as the number 7 can also draw attention to such issues.

January
8 Personal Month

January unfolds with 8 energy, presenting a unique opportunity to delve inward after a year dedicated to serving and supporting others. This is a time to confront significant life questions and reflect on what you truly desire. Focus on enhancing your personal growth, honing your intuition, and cultivating inner peace and wisdom.

Use this month for rest and relaxation, taking the time to reevaluate your aspirations. While the energy of 8 typically encourages outward expansion, take advantage of this period to turn your focus inward. The 8 vibration emphasizes self-empowerment and the exploration of authority issues, making it an excellent moment for reorganization, both in your personal life and business endeavors.

January is a month where financial matters may ebb and flow more significantly, marking it as a period of material focus. However, remember that achieving balance between your spiritual and material goals is essential, as true fulfillment encompasses more than just your bank account. Your career will also be in focus this month, and changes may be on the horizon.

This is your year to channel your energies toward self-improvement. Consider undertaking a body cleanse, embarking on a retreat, or dedicating time to your personal development.

As you navigate this 8 month, embrace the calling to take the lead and exercise authority over your life. Organize and manage all aspects of your circumstances while seeking harmony between your material ambitions and spiritual well-being. Step confidently into your role as an authority figure and pursue this transformative journey with intention.

KNOW YOUR FUTURE

Personal Day
(January)

1. Contribute to a cause with a strategic donation or skills.
2. Embark on a research endeavor or read to expand your acumen.
3. Center yourself and follow intuition for financial insights.
4. Let creativity guide you in developing financial strategies.
5. Structure your workday to ensure order in evaluations.
6. Create variety in research; stay open to unexpected data.
7. Offer your expertise to those who could benefit from insights.
8. Reimagine financial paths using your imagination for new strategies.
9. Focus on expanding your horizons in investments and gains.
10. Refine your work with attention to finalize reports and projects.
11. Maintain independence and express your analytical style.
12. Pay attention to details; each data point is critical.
13. Reconnect with colleagues to share insights and perspectives.
14. Use practical skills to solve complex financial challenges.
15. Promote your skills subtly; let your work speak volumes.
16. Fortify boundaries to maintain a focused analytical environment.
17. Allocate time for rest to replenish analytical reserves.
18. Balance accounts and invest with precision for returns.
19. Use your gifts to support societal prosperity thoughtfully.
20. Collaborate with like-minded individuals for better outcomes.
21. Allow markets to guide your analysis, avoiding assumptions.
22. Schedule moments of enjoyment for fresh analytical insights.
23. Ensure a solid foundation for stability in your work.
24. Network to strengthen alliances and share insights.
25. Nurture professional relationships for better collaboration.
26. Create a workspace that fosters focus and positive energy.
27. Stay attuned to developments; assess opportunities for growth.
28. Identify solutions to challenges, then release them.
29. Share knowledge sparingly; ensure value in your contributions.
30. Use diplomacy to navigate professional disagreements gracefully.
31. Communicate findings clearly; use concise mediums for insights.

PERSONAL YEAR 7

February
9 Personal Month

Now is a time for introspection and self-discovery. This year invites you to turn your focus inward and deepen your spiritual connection. Reflect on the profound questions regarding your life's purpose and what brings true meaning to your existence. 9 energy symbolizes completion, preparing you for the onset of a new nine-month cycle beginning in March.

This is the time to declutter your life, letting go of anything you do not wish to carry forward throughout the year. While you will have another opportunity to release in November, do not procrastinate; take the initiative to eliminate what is unnecessary for a more productive year ahead. The 9 energy enhances your divine spiritual connections, aligning beautifully with the reflective qualities of the 7.

Embrace daily meditation, consider embarking on a vision quest, or enroll in a self-improvement class during this time. Rely on your heightened intuition to delve deeper within yourself. Additionally, the number 9 embodies service to humanity, so carve out time to contribute to the greater good and graciously accept the rewards for your efforts from previous months.

February is indeed a 9 month, marking the conclusion of a nine-month cycle. Clean out, finish up, and let go of anything that does not serve you. Reap the benefits of your hard work from the past eight months, making room for new beginnings in the upcoming month. Trust your intuition as you contemplate what you wish to create next, and allow your creativity to flourish as you dedicate yourself to serving the greater good.

Personal Day
(February)

1. Take charge of your journey; lead with informed choices.
2. Collaborate with researchers and partners to achieve goals.
3. Share your findings through diverse channels and insights.
4. Plan your day with precision, allowing focused research time.
5. Stay attuned to patterns that emerge in your studies today.
6. Show kindness with a thoughtful gesture, even from afar.
7. Rejuvenate your mind in spaces that inspire contemplation.
8. Seize exploration opportunities; take calculated risks in research.
9. Organize your workspace and ideas to clear space for insights.
10. Evaluate options carefully; align decisions with your mission.
11. Trust your intuition to resolve academic issues effectively.
12. Let spontaneity inspire creativity and discovery in your work.
13. Use practical reasoning to ensure productive outcomes.
14. Harness unpredictability for innovative ideas & breakthroughs.
15. Keep your environment orderly for intellectual reflection.
16. Let your research flow naturally; adjust as data emerges.
17. Manage financial matters wisely to support your research.
18. Conclude projects that no longer serve your investigative goals.
19. Focus on the future with a solid research foundation.
20. Apologize when needed to maintain harmonious collaboration.
21. Engage in joyful activities that fuel your passion for discovery.
22. Resolve any outstanding logistical issues in your work.
23. Prepare for fruitful collaboration and sharing of findings.
24. Offer expertise to colleagues or humanitarian causes.
25. Reflect on thoughts and findings; ensure alignment with goals.
26. Demonstrate leadership in guiding research with compassion.
27. Release ideas that don't align with your current focus.
28. Use your intelligence to lead discussions and contribute meaningfully.
29. Complete necessary details in your research for clarity.

PERSONAL YEAR 7

March
1 Personal Month

March ushers in the promise of new beginnings. This month invites you to prioritize yourself and channel your energy toward your aspirations. Take this opportunity to plant the seeds of your desires for the remainder of the year, as everything you undertake this month will profoundly impact your future.

Embrace courage in your manifestations, and cultivate the determination needed to see them through to fruition. This is a month marked by independence, and you may find yourself stepping into a leadership role. With numerous new opportunities on the horizon, approach them with fearlessness and take full advantage of what comes your way.

Reflect on your true desires and articulate what you wholeheartedly want in your life. Create lists that include your must-haves, wishes, and even your wildest dreams. Let your imagination flourish without self-censorship. Given that this month is outwardly focused and bustling with activity, time will pass quickly; thus, clarity and decisiveness are essential.

While the energy of 7 encourages introspection, make sure to carve out time for meditation and listen to your intuition. This number also relates to health, and paired with the fresh start energy of one, it may be a perfect moment to initiate a new diet or exercise regimen that aligns with your goals.

March is indeed a 1 month focused on new beginnings. Use this time to plant seeds, set your goals, and establish your intentions for the next nine months. This bustling month is filled with exciting new projects, so gather your courage and step confidently into your leadership role.

Personal Day
(March)

1. Cultivate a peaceful environment; tranquility nurtures growth.
2. Let your cheerful essence radiate & illuminate paths for others.
3. Be an effective manager by organizing thoughts and actions.
4. Recognize change as growth; transitions deepen understanding.
5. Seek your community; our contributions weave collective existence.
6. Dedicate time to explore ideas that spark your curiosity.
7. Today is full of action, ambition, and achievement; harness it.
8. Release what no longer serves you for higher purposes ahead.
9. Today holds potential for business dealings; act with integrity.
10. Cultivate patience; allow life's currents to guide you.
11. Nurture optimism, the seed from which possibility blossoms.
12. Ensure your moral compass points to truth; guide your actions.
13. Practice self-restraint; thoughtful choices open insights.
14. Address conflicts with love; resolution comes from empathy.
15. Attend to your health; a sound body nurtures a clear mind.
16. Choose gratitude; welcome abundance in all forms.
17. True success comes from serving humanity; let this guide you.
18. Use independent leadership to chart a new course; innovate.
19. Celebrate friendship; inspire love as a key human experience.
20. Quiet self-doubt; focus on possibilities and life's beauty.
21. Approach written matters diligently; details hold keys.
22. Greet new ideas with an open mind; stay centered & focused.
23. Commit to actions that align with your values and vision.
24. If rest is what you seek, grant yourself that favor.
25. Focus on the greater good; collective well-being enriches all.
26. Clear out the unnecessary to make way for transformations.
27. Seek to improve projects; complacency hinders growth.
28. Prioritize others' needs; offer support before your own.
29. Engage in self-improvement through seminars or literature.
30. Honor your work ethic; it shows commitment to your pursuits.
31. Embrace individuality & courage for adventurous exploration.

April
2 Personal Month

During this time, you may have sought ample alone time to rejuvenate, rest, and deepen your connection with the Divine. As you continue your journey of introspection, take a moment to reflect on the intentions you set in the Universe last month.

In April, the focus shifts from solitude to connection, as you are called to actively listen to others. While last month encouraged you to establish your goals for the year, now it's time to relax a bit and nurture the manifestations you wish to cultivate. The energy of 2 brings a slower, more measured pace, which you may find refreshing.

It's perfectly acceptable to emerge from your meditative sanctuary and engage in communication with those around you. In fact, the 2 vibration encourages collaboration and the building of partnerships. Diplomacy and cooperation become essential for creating harmony in your relationships.

Pay close attention to the details and address the smaller tasks you may have overlooked previously. This month may also evoke emotions, so leverage your best negotiation skills to resolve any issues that arise. Embrace the opportunity to connect with others while fostering an atmosphere of understanding and support.

Personal Day
(April)

1. Tap into creativity to craft something uniquely meaningful.
2. Reflect on priorities; organize tasks to align with purpose.
3. Release and trust the natural flow of life.
4. Share a nourishing meal and engage in soulful conversations.
5. Explore literature that broadens your mental and spiritual horizons.
6. Invest resources thoughtfully, guided by inner wisdom.
7. Volunteer in spaces that resonate with your calling.
8. Connect with like-minded individuals for meaningful projects.
9. Consider real estate opportunities with curiosity.
10. Let your imagination soar; create something inspired.
11. Approach responsibilities with diligence and higher principles.
12. Stay responsive to the unexpected gifts life offers.
13. Beautify your space with projects reflecting inner harmony.
14. Spend time in nature to reconnect with your tranquil center.
15. Review your finances with clarity and foresight.
16. Envision your contributions to the greater good.
17. Organize your thoughts on a list; check them off mindfully.
18. Apply diplomacy as you navigate conflicts toward resolution.
19. Craft a joyful day filled with inspiring activities.
20. Focus on work and complete tasks with intention and grace.
21. Welcome change as an opportunity for growth.
22. Find comfort and contemplation in your home sanctuary.
23. Dedicate the day to introspection and inner reflection.
24. Embody leadership with courage and inner strength.
25. Engage in acts of kindness, guided by compassion.
26. Celebrate originality; express your true self authentically.
27. Offer heartfelt support and empathy to a friend.
28. Let your self-expression flow freely and authentically.
29. Contemplate the strength of your foundational beliefs.
30. Explore new experiences with an adventurous spirit.

May
3 Personal Month

May unfolds a 3 vibration, bringing together two distinct yet complementary energies. The introspective nature of 7 seeks solitude and reflection, valuing rest and relaxation as you reevaluate the trajectory of your life. In contrast, the vibrant energy of the 3 encourages social engagement and outward expression.

Balancing these contrasting vibrations is essential; this is your year to delve inward while also embracing the world around you. Use this opportunity to explore life's significant questions, meditating and communing with nature along the way. May invites you to harmonize the inward focus you've maintained throughout the year thus far. Celebrate the arrival of spring with friends and revel in the joy of life.

Make a point to reach out to others and accept any invitations that resonate with you. This is a creative month; channel your imaginative energy to bring your ideas to fruition. After several months of introspection, now is the moment to merge your spiritual and material worlds.

Embrace this time to play, create, and fully enjoy life. Keep things simple, allowing abundance to flow freely into your experience. Engage in writing, singing, dancing, or any other form of self-expression that speaks to your heart.

May is indeed a 3 month; when your creative juices flow abundantly, leading to fresh ideas that can cultivate prosperity. This playful time encourages you to keep things uncomplicated while maintaining your focus. Whether you choose to redecorate, redesign a project, write a story, or dance, allow yourself to thrive in this vibrant energy.

Personal Day
(May)

1. Create an agenda and complete it with mindful intent.
2. Stay open to today's opportunities; reflect on their significance.
3. Engage in heartfelt dialogue with your partner; listen deeply.
4. Carve out "me" time in a tranquil space for reflection.
5. Audit your accounts thoughtfully for your financial well-being.
6. Cherish forgiveness and love; they lead to inner peace.
7. Start a creative endeavor with others for an enriching collaboration.
8. Follow your intuition to deepen your self-understanding.
9. Express yourself through singing, dancing, or writing today.
10. Focus to accomplish personal and professional goals.
11. Welcome distractions for unexpected insights or new paths.
12. Enhance your space with mindful improvements reflecting you.
13. Enroll in an online course to expand your self-knowledge.
14. Balance material concerns with your spiritual essence.
15. Cultivate compassion and understanding in your relationships.
16. Acknowledge your independence and individuality in your growth.
17. Take still moments to listen to your intuition for decisions.
18. Attend social gatherings; immerse in enriching connections.
19. Visualize a solid foundation for your future aspirations.
20. Ignite your adventurous spirit; let your heart lead you.
21. Cherish family gatherings while honoring your boundaries.
22. Reflect on your spiritual journey; align with your true path.
23. Focus on your aspirations; elevate your goals now.
24. Honor the greater good with kindness, spreading positivity.
25. Open up to new experiences that foster growth.
26. Maintain balance, harmony, and peace in daily tasks.
27. Dedicate time to your gratitude journal; reflect on abundance.
28. Complete tasks and check items off your list for satisfaction.
29. Explore the unknown with an open heart and mind.
30. Be bold in your pursuits; seek adventures that inspire you.
31. Treat yourself and a companion to a delightful night out.

PERSONAL YEAR 7

June
4 Personal Month

This inward-focused year is a time for deep reflection, and you will reap the rewards by integrating meditation into your routine. If you have yet to establish a schedule that allows for a journey into your inner self, now is the time to do so. Engage with the profound questions that can shape your life: What do I truly desire? What is my life purpose? Am I living a fulfilled life? The energy of 7 invites you to explore these significant inquiries, while the 4 energy emphasizes the need for structure and discipline.

Develop a new schedule that aligns with your deepest aspirations, for this month calls for diligence and offers little room for deviation from your plans. Both the 7 and 4 energies resonate with health, so it is important to be attentive to your diet and exercise regimens; this month is an excellent opportunity to incorporate these practices into your daily life.

Be aware that legal matters may surface during this time, and you have the supportive energy of the 4 vibration to assist you in finding resolutions. Strengthen your foundation now as you prepare for the expansive and dynamic energy of 5 that awaits you in July.

June embodies the essence of a 4 month, focusing on organization, discipline, and diligence. Prioritize your health by committing to a balanced diet and a consistent exercise routine. Bring your creative endeavors from last month into tangible form and take the time to complete any lingering projects. Use this as an opportunity to reset your foundation in anticipation of the exciting developments that the 5 month will bring.

Personal Day
(June)

1. Prepare for change; embrace it as an opportunity for growth.
2. Dedicate energy to mindful work in the comfort of home.
3. Incorporate gentle exercise to rejuvenate your spirit.
4. Reflect on your finances and achieve balance within.
5. Complete the project needing your attention; embrace release.
6. Compose a thoughtful to-do list for the month ahead.
7. Address unfinished matters with care and attention.
8. Savor the moment; enjoy today fully without reservation.
9. Recognize diligence nurtures your endeavors for fulfillment.
10. Stay open; change invites new experiences on the horizon.
11. Cultivate relationships; pay attention to those around you.
12. Engage in quiet contemplation; explore your thoughts deeply.
13. Be open to changes at work; adapt with grace as needed.
14. Release what no longer serves you to lighten your load.
15. Reflect on fresh insights, allowing them to guide you.
16. Focus on details; they hold the key to deeper understanding.
17. Identify what brings you joy and pursue those passions.
18. Stand on solid ground, both literally and metaphorically.
19. Level up your workload; view challenges as growth opportunities.
20. Enhance your home to create a peaceful environment.
21. Mind your diet; choose fresh foods that support well-being.
22. Honor your knowledge; let it inform your decisions.
23. Complete your to-do list; celebrate each accomplishment.
24. Welcome a new chapter in your life with openness & excitement.
25. Read between the lines for deeper truths in experiences.
26. Hold yourself accountable for your choices and impacts.
27. Avoid overthinking; trust the process and let clarity emerge.
28. Prepare for a fast-paced month; greet all that comes your way.
29. Brighten your space with new decor for a beautiful environment.
30. Commit to personal growth and nurture your evolving self.

July
5 Personal Month

This is a period of unexpected change that may lead to surprising outcomes. After a year defined by introspection, you may find that your life's direction has evolved significantly. The 7 energy offers you the space to contemplate profound life questions and reassess your path.

With the invigorating influence of 5, it is now time to shift your focus outward. July presents a pinnacle of opportunities for transformation after months of reflection. Embrace as many opportunities as possible and have the courage to take risks. This is your year for personal growth, making July an ideal time for a vision quest or a personal development seminar; any endeavor that enhances your self-awareness will be met with rewards.

The changes you adapt to this month will undoubtedly contribute to your overall well-being. Cultivating adaptability and allowing the energy to flow will serve you well, even as you remain mindful of the potential for chaos. Avoid retreating into hiding; instead, embrace the fast-paced environment of July, filled with possibilities.

In summary, July is a 5 month, a time of unexpected change that invites travel and adventure. You may find yourself altering your direction entirely. Promote yourself and leverage your communication skills confidently. Step up, take risks, and welcome the transformations that this month brings, as they are ultimately designed for your greater good. Allow the energy to flow freely and savor the excitement that accompanies this new chapter.

Personal Day
(July)

1. Recognize opportunities; choose with mindful intention.
2. Delve into a self-improvement book for your spiritual journey.
3. Strive for balance in your lifestyle amid daily chaos.
4. Express your spirit through uplifting kind gestures.
5. Write down your dreams; manifesting starts with clarity.
6. Embark on cooperative endeavors to enhance growth.
7. Dance freely, letting your spirit express joyful energy.
8. Follow clear paths as you navigate your purposeful journey.
9. Savor a spontaneous adventure; enjoy new experiences.
10. Cherish moments with a friend during your evening together.
11. Take a day trip to explore new territories; be curious.
12. Check in on your business; infuse innovation into practices.
13. Trust your inner guidance; it will illuminate your path.
14. Try something new; let curiosity lead your brave exploration.
15. Listen to your intuition; it guides your spiritual journey.
16. Live and love authentically; connect beyond comfort zones.
17. Focus on success while aligning efforts with your values.
18. Let each day lead you to limitless new horizons.
19. Engage in meaningful conversations to deepen connections.
20. Meditate in nature; feel tranquility and hug a tree.
21. Organize your life intentionally; respect supporting structures.
22. Uplift strangers with warmth and kindness; every act matters.
23. Explore new dimensions; let your spirit wander and grow.
24. Silence your inner critic; foster self-acceptance & compassion.
25. Encourage creativity to wander & discover; inspiration awaits.
26. Adjust foundational beliefs to align with your true self.
27. Pursue your wildest desires for joy and fulfillment.
28. Offer full attention to those close; this bond is sacred.
29. Embark on a vision quest for insights into your aspirations.
30. Confidently express your authority; champion your beliefs.
31. Commit to balance and harmony in your endeavors for enrichment.

PERSONAL YEAR 7

August
6 Personal Month

While this year has been marked by introspection and self-improvement, the vibrational energy shifts in August, turning your focus toward family and relationships. As the energy of 6 emphasizes home and connection, it is important to step beyond your comfort zone and engage deeply with your loved ones, who will likely need your support now more than ever.

Consider planning a family holiday or a long weekend getaway, taking advantage of this time to foster closer bonds. Additionally, this month presents a perfect opportunity to enhance the intimacy of your romantic relationship; organize a special event that celebrates your connection.

Invest time in home improvement projects to create a nurturing environment. Strive to find harmony in all your relationships, including those in your career, as your priority is to nurture and elevate your connections with the ones you love.

While being of service to others brings benefit to all, it is equally important to set aside moments for your own well-being. Engage in meditation and take peaceful walks in nature to restore your energy and clarity.

August is indeed a 6 month; your time dedicated to home and family. Embrace your responsibilities by attending to your home life and nurturing your relationships. Make the most of this time with family; consider scheduling a vacation or tackling those home improvement projects you've been wanting to undertake. Seek harmony both in your career and at home, and take this opportunity to realign your priorities for a fulfilling experience.

Personal Day
(August)

1. Carve out quiet time in a sacred space for tranquility.
2. Reflect on achieving balance; harmony nurtures heart & mind.
3. Embody love & forgiveness; let these energies permeate you.
4. Approach responsibilities with grace & kindness; comfort others.
5. Express gratitude for your family; it strengthens relationships.
6. Emanate joy and spread warmth and positivity to everyone.
7. Establish boundaries; honor them for peace of mind.
8. Embark on a delightful adventure with a loved one; try new things.
9. Engage in heartfelt conversations to deepen emotional connections.
10. Make peace with your inner critic; offer kindness, not judgment.
11. Invest time in your career; nurture aspirations patiently.
12. Cultivate kindness through good deeds; share compassion widely.
13. Nurture relationships by spending quality time with loved ones.
14. Use diplomacy to resolve lingering issues with a gentle approach.
15. Channel creativity into home improvements for beauty and comfort.
16. Develop a clear project plan; thoughtful action empowers you.
17. Dedicate a day for activities that nourish your soul and joy.
18. Create lasting memories with loved ones; savor shared moments.
19. Meditate and connect with your intuition; trust its wisdom.
20. Find your center to maintain balance amid life's challenges.
21. Let go of what doesn't serve you; surrender to guidance.
22. Set new goals with your partner, aligning visions for growth.
23. Be willing to compromise for harmony in relationships.
24. Enjoy an entertaining evening out; relish joy and connection.

25. Honor structure & discipline; they are cornerstones of peace.
26. Acknowledge amazing events today; welcome life's offerings.
27. Step up and fulfill responsibilities; nurture your caring spirit.
28. Retreat to your happy place with a captivating book.
29. Honor yourself and your wisdom; trust your authority.
30. Practice forgiveness and let love fill your heart.
31. Stay attentive to new ideas; each insight fosters growth.

September
7 Personal Month

Note: Because September is the ninth month, it is always the same number as your personal year. This means you have double the energy of your personal year for thirty days. If the current year calculates to the same value as your personal year, then you receive triple that number's energy in September.

September invites you to turn your focus inward. This is an opportune time to revisit life's profound questions: Am I aligned with my true self? What is my purpose? What do I genuinely desire in life? Take this moment to fortify the foundation of your inner self.

Explore the depths of your being, connect with your intuition, and, most importantly, heed the guidance that arises. Trust that you will be led precisely where you need to be.

September encourages self-awareness, introspection, and reflection, allowing you to pause and regenerate after a month spent in service to your family in August. Reflect on your journey thus far and reassess the direction in which you are heading. Consider whether your path aligns with who you are at this moment. Now is the time to initiate change, be it through a spiritual quest or, at the very least, a retreat into nature. You deserve this solitude to gain clarity and truly ground yourself in your current identity.

September is defined as a 7 month, a time for rest, relaxation, and rejuvenation. Solitude is essential for inward focus, providing the space you need to evaluate your past experiences and the trajectory of your future. Engage in the study of metaphysics, take a retreat, and immerse yourself in the healing embrace of nature.

Personal Day
(September)

1. Analyze emerging opportunities carefully before proceeding.
2. Conclude outstanding projects; completion brings clarity.
3. Honor individuality to convey your ideas authentically.
4. Collaboration is essential; nurture relationships with colleagues.
5. Take frequent breaks to enjoy the day's quiet moments.
6. Maintain a balanced diet and exercise for your well-being.
7. Embrace spontaneity for unexpected inspiration in research.
8. Stay diligent with responsibilities; advance your work continuously.
9. Create a sanctuary for solitude and focused concentration.
10. Abundance may come in unconventional forms; stay open.
11. Develop patience and understanding in today's interactions.
12. Today is favorable for negotiating collaborative efforts.
13. Acknowledge and reciprocate contributions from others.
14. Step out of your cocoon; engage socially, even briefly.
15. Check in on your health; self-care supports your pursuits.
16. Introduce new elements to ignite creativity and innovation.
17. Enhance your workspace with organization or decor.
18. Reflect on your journey; are you progressing toward goals?
19. Review finances; clear records ensure stability.
20. Release control over outcomes; let go of unproductive thoughts.
21. Reassess objectives; align efforts with your aspirations.
22. Let others lead today; collaboration yields new insights.
23. Reconnect with acquaintances; a letter or call revives connections.
24. Choose practicality; find order amidst research complexities.
25. Share findings to promote your work in the community.
26. Respect boundaries for yourself and others to boost productivity.
27. Walk in nature to gather thoughts and observations.
28. Trust your expertise; present ideas with confidence.
29. Extend kindness; consider volunteering your time or skills.
30. Ground yourself in ambition and achievement; build your journey.

October
8 Personal Month

Note: October is always the same number as your personal year next year, making it a brief preview of the coming year.

The energy of 8 brings a focus on business, management, and organization. This month serves as a reminder to embrace your role as an authority figure. The energy is expansive and empowering; too vibrant to squander in introversion.

With business and finances taking center stage, you are likely to be propelled into a leadership position. Now is not the time for timidity; face your fears, step beyond your comfort zone, and take charge of your circumstances. Manage all aspects of your life diligently, keeping a watchful eye on your finances, as money is likely to flow more readily this month.

You may encounter challenges from those who oppose your authority, but rest assured, the energy is on your side, equipping you to stand firm in your power. The efforts you commit to now will lay the groundwork for the empowering experiences awaiting you next year, which will be devoted entirely to your growth.

As you navigate this spiritually enriching year, relish the navigation of a material-focused month. Strive to maintain balance between these two realms, for your dedication and hard work will be rewarded.

Ultimately, October represents an 8 month; an engaging time that emphasizes power and authority. Business becomes a primary focus, demanding that you embrace your leadership role. Organize and manage every aspect of your life thoughtfully, ensuring a harmonious balance between your material and spiritual worlds. Step into your authority and make the most of this transformative month.

Personal Day
(October)

1. Contribute to a cause that aligns with your values and skills.
2. Initiate a new research project or read to fuel your spirit.
3. Center yourself and trust your intuition for business decisions.
4. Let creativity flow; uncover innovative ideas for your enterprise.
5. Structure your workday for maximum productivity & creativity.
6. Create variety in your pursuits; stay open to new opportunities.
7. Be ready to assist those in need; offer your skills & support.
8. Use imagination to revisit familiar approaches with fresh insights.
9. Focus on advancing your material goals in your entrepreneurial journey.
10. Shepherd ideas to fruition; add finishing touches to projects.
11. Maintain independence; showcase individuality in ventures.
12. Pay attention to details; thoroughness leads to success.
13. Reconnect with an old friend to rejuvenate your network.
14. Activate practical skills to tackle challenges & drive progress.
15. Subtly promote your brand for a strong market entry.
16. Define boundaries to protect your focus and creativity.
17. Rest and recharge to maintain energy for entrepreneurship.
18. Keep finances balanced; invest wisely for sustainable growth.
19. Share talents and successes to contribute to the community.
20. Collaborate with others to enhance your ventures.
21. Allow projects to develop naturally; avoid forced efforts.
22. Take time for enjoyment and play; rediscover your joy.
23. Ensure foundational systems are solid for business stability.
24. Engage in networking to meet new allies for your business.
25. Nurture key relationships; they are essential for support.
26. Create a workspace that supports energy flow and inspiration.
27. Stay alert to financial opportunities for strategic growth.
28. Seek solutions to obstacles, resolve them efficiently.
29. Share knowledge selectively to foster collaboration.
30. Use diplomacy to resolve conflicts and ensure harmony.
31. Optimize communication to enhance collaboration and influence.

November
9 Personal Month

This month signifies the conclusion of a significant cycle in your life. It is an opportune time to eliminate anything unwanted, unnecessary, or redundant, both physically and metaphorically. Take the time to sift through your closets, desks, and offices, while also letting go of unproductive habits and negative thought patterns. Now is the moment to create space for what you truly wish to carry into your future.

Interestingly, January of the next year will also present itself as a 9 month, offering you another chance to clear away any remaining clutter. For now, however, direct your focus towards compassion, forgiveness, and unconditional love. Engage in service to humanity by volunteering during this holiday season, allowing your actions to reflect the larger vision of what you aspire to create.

As you prepare for December, recognize that it, along with February of next year, is imbued with the energy of new beginnings, marked by the vibration of 1.

November is indeed a 9 month; the conclusion of a nine-month cycle. Embrace this time to clean out, finish up, and release anything that does not serve you. Take the opportunity to reap the rewards of your hard work from the preceding eight months, making way for the new beginnings that await you in the coming month. Trust your intuition as you contemplate what you wish to manifest next; allow your creativity to flourish and always strive to serve the greater good.

Personal Day
(November)

1. Honor self-governance; lead projects that reflect your values.
2. Collaborate virtually to achieve common humanitarian goals.
3. Share insights on digital platforms; stay open to new ideas.
4. Organize solitary days with a structured schedule for productivity.
5. Stay attentive to synchronicities guiding your path today.
6. Send a thoughtful message or virtual gift to brighten someone's day.
7. Rejuvenate in your personal sanctuary, finding peace and inspiration.
8. Meet tech opportunities and take calculated bold steps.
9. Organize physical and digital spaces; clear what's unnecessary.
10. Assess options carefully; make well-reasoned decisions.
11. Trust instincts to creatively resolve tech and personal challenges.
12. Allow spontaneity in solitude for moments of joy and innovation.
13. Apply practical reasoning to enhance productivity in all endeavors.
14. Welcome unpredictability; let it inspire creativity and flexibility.
15. Enhance your living space for beauty and conducive thought.
16. Flow with life's rhythms, adapting to changes as they come.
17. Manage finances wisely to support your humanitarian efforts.
18. Wrap up tasks that no longer align with your vision.
19. Focus on future aspirations, building on your skills and knowledge.
20. Extend apologies as needed to foster healing and connection.
21. Find joy in solo activities that invigorate your spirit.
22. Address legal or financial matters needing resolution for growth.
23. Anticipate success in digital endeavors; promote effectively.
24. Make your expertise accessible, offering guidance online.

KNOW YOUR FUTURE

25. Reflect on your path to ensure alignment with your goals.
26. Lead initiatives with quiet authority; show leadership through actions.
27. Release what no longer serves you; prepare for advancements.
28. Use your intelligence to inspire others in virtual groups.
29. Attend to the details in your projects for success.
30. Engage in online discussions; share your views and learn.

December
1 Personal Month

You are presented with a clean slate as the year comes to a close, heralding new beginnings. Now is the time to reflect on what you wish to manifest over the next nine months. This has been a year of introspection, prompting you to ask yourself significant questions: Am I pursuing my passion? Am I aligned with the dreams I set at the beginning of the year? Do the goals established during my 1 year in 2017 still resonate with me?

The energy of 7 invites you to delve inward and reassess your true aspirations. Establishing a consistent meditation practice will prove beneficial as you prepare for the bustling 8 year ahead. Keep in mind that both February and November next year are 1 months, granting you further opportunities to redefine your intentions.

Take the time to sit in quiet reflection and follow your inner guidance. It is crucial to understand what matters most to you as you transition into the powerful 8 energy.

December embodies the essence of a 1 month, signifying new beginnings. Plant the seeds of your intentions, and set your goals for the upcoming nine months. With the promise of numerous new projects on the horizon, summon the courage to embrace a leadership role and confidently navigate this exciting chapter.

Personal Day
(December)

1. Cultivate a peaceful atmosphere, fostering love and connection.
2. Let your joyful spirit uplift those around you.
3. Organize thoughts and actions with intention.
4. View changes as opportunities for personal growth.
5. Contribute your gifts to enhance community well-being.
6. Explore topics that resonate with your spirit for knowledge.
7. Honor action and ambition; let them guide your path.
8. Release attachments that hinder your spiritual journey.
9. Today is ideal for establishing agreements; show integrity.
10. Practice patience; let situations unfold naturally.
11. Nurture optimism; it fosters growth and opportunity.
12. Align your moral compass with truth and compassion.
13. Exercise discernment; curb impulsive decisions wisely.
14. Approach conflicts with love and understanding for healing.
15. Prioritize health; start a new exercise routine for self-care.
16. Foster gratitude and welcome abundance as a blessing.
17. True success lies in serving humanity with compassion.
18. Use leadership to forge new paths for yourself and others.
19. Cherish friendships; inspire love and companionship.
20. Quiet self-doubt; focus on the abundant gifts around you.
21. Pay attention to details; clarity aligns with your values.
22. Stay open to new ideas; maintain clarity to avoid overwhelm.
23. Engage in actions that resonate with your responsibilities.
24. Honor your need for rest; reflection and rejuvenation matter.
25. Focus on the greater good; embrace collective rewards.
26. Clear what no longer serves your spiritual journey.
27. Seek improvements; today is for growth, not complacency.
28. Extend a helping hand, embodying service and compassion.
29. Invest in self-improvement through enriching seminars.
30. Honor your work ethic; it shows commitment to your vision.
31. Embrace individuality and courage to inspire adventures.

Personal Year 8

In Personal Year 8, you're presented with abundant opportunities to explore and harness your personal power across all facets of life. This transformative cycle emphasizes a pragmatic approach, particularly in your career, where growth in professional roles, social networks, and financial prosperity is within reach. Leverage the insights gained from the past year to actively pursue and manifest your aspirations.

Expect to challenge authority more frequently as you navigate this year, inviting you to look beyond traditional hierarchies for wisdom. Financial issues take center stage, presenting a prime time to confront prosperity challenges head-on. Engage in ventures such as real estate and smart investments, where rewards stem from your ambition and efforts.

This cycle highlights personal empowerment and calls for leadership, encouraging you to embrace management roles. Your mental acuity and intuition are heightened, enabling you to take calculated risks and address past disempowerment with assertiveness.

Financial gains are a focal point, reflecting the hard work of previous years. However, balance your financial pursuits with ethical intentions to achieve true prosperity. Maintain a positive mindset and prioritize actions that serve the greater good, understanding that wealth is an energy flow rather than the sole measure of success.

This year serves as a pivotal turning point, rich with opportunities for personal and professional advancement. By integrating past lessons, intuition, and a focus on the bigger picture, you align your life with your values and aspirations. Embrace these opportunities, allowing them to guide you toward a future where personal power and financial prosperity are intertwined with ethical living and compassionate service.

Adopt a positive attitude and align your actions with the greater good, transcending ego-driven pursuits. Honor strong morals and ethics, recognizing that life encompasses more than a financial report. Money is merely energy, fluctuating in its presence. If your sole focus is on amassing wealth, then that becomes your life's center. However, by serving the greater good, you establish a sustainable and fulfilling relationship with prosperity.

PERSONAL YEAR 8

January
9 Personal Month

Entering a personal year that aligns with the universal year signifies that you are immersed in the powerful vibrations of 8 for the current year, which will bring an intensified focus on business, career advancement, and self-empowerment. With the duplication of this energy, anticipate a busier year filled with new opportunities for prosperity and the expansion of your authority.

As you navigate this transformative year, pay attention to all facets of your life, as they may require reorganization. You may find yourself thrust into a leadership role, with others looking to you as a figure of authority. This year is the perfect time to learn how to balance your material aspirations with your spiritual growth.

Beginning the year with a 9 month invites you to engage in a process of decluttering; eliminating and releasing anything that no longer serves you. This act of cleaning is an ideal way to kick off your 8 year. Approach this task with efficiency and a mindset of 'lightness,' using your intuition to guide the release of unwanted items and thoughts. Some things may fade away regardless of your readiness, so embrace this change and make space for new blessings.

Remain creative and strive to maintain balance amidst these transformations. Serving the greater good during this time will undoubtedly yield rewards in the future.

January is indeed a 9 month, marking the conclusion of a nine-month cycle. Now is the time to clean out, finish tasks, and release anything that does not enhance your life. Take stock of the benefits of your hard work from the past eight months and prepare for the new beginnings that await you next month. Utilize your intuition to determine what you wish to create next, and allow your creativity to flourish as you dedicate yourself to serving the greater good.

Personal Day
(January)

1. Take charge of your journey; lead with vision & impact others.
2. Collaborate with diverse stakeholders to uplift communities globally.
3. Communicate openly and welcome diverse viewpoints.
4. Organize your day intentionally to meet commitments.
5. Stay attuned to synchronicities that guide your path forward.
6. Brighten someone's day by delivering flowers personally.
7. Rejuvenate in inspiring spaces to maintain your well-being.
8. Be bold; take calculated risks to drive progress.
9. Declutter your space and mind for new possibilities.
10. Weigh options carefully today; align choices with your mission.
11. Trust your intuition to make informed decisions.
12. Host an impromptu gathering to celebrate teamwork.
13. Use practical wisdom to enhance productivity and execution.
14. Choose unpredictability to drive innovation and creativity.
15. Beautify your workspace to reflect your values and aspirations.
16. Go with the flow; adapt to business rhythms without resistance.
17. Focus on financial sustainability; manage budgets with care.
18. Conclude ventures that no longer serve your mission.
19. Maintain clear focus on your aspirations and goals.
20. Extend apologies to foster healing in relationships.
21. Engage in enjoyable activities that promote camaraderie.
22. Address outstanding legal matters for clear pathways.
23. Anticipate success in sales and promotions; approach enthusiastically.
24. Be available to those seeking guidance; share your expertise.
25. Reflect on your trajectory; ensure alignment with goals.
26. Lead with confidence to inspire trust and respect.
27. Release what doesn't align with your mission; move forward.
28. Use your insight to lead discussions & encourage collaboration.
29. Complete projects by addressing details and finalizing outlines.

30. Participate actively, sharing perspectives while respecting others.
31. Wrap up today's tasks and map out plans for tomorrow.

February
1 Personal Month

February emerges as a transformative 1 month, presenting you with the opportunity to organize, manage, and expand the business aspects of your life. This month serves as a platform for you to manifest your desires for this year. Reflecting on January as a 9 month, you were encouraged to release what was unnecessary, thereby making space for new manifestations to take root now.

Take the time to list your desires; identify what you must have, what would be nice to include, and what your wildest dreams are for the year ahead. Clarity is essential in articulating what you wish to attract into your life. This year is all about uncovering your personal power and embracing your role as your own authority. It is a year brimming with expansion and opportunities.

As new beginnings unfold this month, seize the moment to actively cultivate your desires. Do not remain in the background; take the wheel and drive your own life forward. You are the leader now, equipped with the courage to take risks and think outside the box. Harness this powerful energy to lay the groundwork for your legacy this year.

Pay attention to your intuition, which will be particularly strong now. In this month focused on outward expression during an equally outwardly focused year, remember to carve out moments for introspection and listen to your inner guidance.

February is, indeed, a 1 month, symbolizing new beginnings. This is the time to plant seeds, set your goals, and establish your intentions for the next nine months. With a busy month ahead filled with new projects, gather the courage to embrace your leadership role wholeheartedly.

Personal Day
(February)

1. Cultivate a peaceful workplace; foster collaboration & creativity.
2. Let your cheerful spirit shine, motivating your team to excel.
3. Be an effective manager by organizing tasks with purpose.
4. See changes as opportunities for growth and innovation.
5. Connect with your community to drive meaningful impact.
6. Dedicate time to research topics that spark your interest.
7. Harness action, ambition, and achievement to drive initiatives.
8. Let go of past methods for a higher purpose aligned with your vision.
9. Today is great for solid business deals; uphold your integrity.
10. Practice patience; allow processes to unfold naturally.
11. Maintain optimism; it can inspire your team & boost productivity.
12. Align your moral compass with ethical principles in leadership.
13. Exercise self-discipline; make well-thought-out decisions.
14. Approach conflicts with love to foster a supportive culture.
15. Prioritize your health with a new exercise regimen for energy.
16. Hold gratitude and welcome abundance; recognize your team's contributions.
17. True success comes from serving humanity; guide your vision.
18. Use leadership skills to forge new paths and strategies.
19. Value friendships; inspire love & companionship in your network.
20. Quiet your inner critic; focus on the positives of your journey.
21. Read the fine print; attention to detail protects your interests.
22. Stay open to new ideas while keeping your focus sharp.
23. Act on your responsibilities with diligence and integrity.
24. If you need rest, honor that need; rejuvenation is vital.
25. Focus on the greater good; collective success leads to fulfillment.
26. Remove obstacles to prepare for shifts and new opportunities.
27. Seek continuous improvement; avoid complacency in projects.
28. Extend support to others; reinforce teamwork & collaboration.
29. Invest in self-improvement seminars or enriching books.

March
2 Personal Month

March invites you to pay close attention to your intuition. Following the fast-paced energy of February, life will take a moment to slow down. This is the perfect time to nurture the seeds you planted last month. The energy of 2 emphasizes cooperation and partnership, making it essential for you to actively listen to others.

While last month was focused on your individual pursuits, this month encourages collaboration and mediation. You may find yourself feeling more sensitive; however, strive to maintain a sense of detachment and observe from a distance. This month is an opportunity for inward reflection, allowing you to strengthen your relationship with your intuition and trust its guidance.

The 2 energy fosters a deeper connection with the Divine, while the 8 energy focuses on organization and prosperity. Attend to the details of your previous manifestations, taking the time to fill in any gaps. This introspective phase will be invaluable in planning for the year ahead.

Both energies stress the importance of balance, so aim to keep your equilibrium intact. Expect a more pronounced flow of money this year; however, remain vigilant regarding your bank balance. Note that the authoritative nature of 8 may also bring someone who challenges your authority this month; thus, exercising diplomacy will be crucial.

March is recognized as a 2 month, emphasizing the need for attention to detail. Focus on the little things that matter, nurturing the seeds you planted last month. Cooperation within your relationships is essential, especially after the egocentric energy of the previous month. This may prove to be an emotional time, requiring the application of your diplomacy skills to navigate effectively.

PERSONAL YEAR 8

Personal Day
(March)

1. Use creativity to develop a marketable, innovative product.
2. Organize and prioritize tasks to enhance productivity.
3. Release control and let strategic plans unfold naturally.
4. Strengthen partnerships through quality time and dialogue.
5. Engage with literature to enhance your business acumen.
6. Make informed investment decisions to maximize resources.
7. Volunteer in sectors aligned with your ethical principles.
8. Assemble a team to initiate a promising business venture.
9. Evaluate real estate for potential investment opportunities.
10. Harness imagination to drive innovation and solutions.
11. Conduct thorough due diligence; build a disciplined work ethic.
12. Stay alert and adaptable to seize unexpected opportunities.
13. Undertake home projects that increase property value.
14. Recharge in nature to boost mental acuity & decision-making.
15. Regularly assess your portfolio to align with your goals.
16. Adopt a broad perspective to benefit the community.
17. Draft a comprehensive to-do list and execute tasks.
18. Practice diplomacy to mediate conflicts and enhance teamwork.
19. Design a productive day with activities that bring you joy.
20. Focus on completing key projects and achieving objectives.
21. Prepare for market changes to maintain competitiveness.
22. Find solace in a well-organized home for strategic planning.
23. Dedicate time for introspection to refine strategies.
24. Demonstrate leadership; assert your authority with confidence.
25. Engage in corporate social responsibility by supporting causes.
26. Value originality; express your unique ideas in business.
27. Offer support and guidance to foster collaboration.
28. Communicate effectively across platforms to share ideas.
29. Reflect on the stability and resilience of your business.
30. Take on new ventures with an adventurous mindset.
31. Respect boundaries; provide advice only when solicited.

April
3 Personal Month

April is your month to fully embrace and utilize all of your creative talents across various artistic endeavors. The vibrant energy of 3 supports your imagination, encouraging you to expand upon the manifestations you set in motion back in February. This is your year for business and organization, and with the infusion of the creative energy of 3, the time has come for you to explore your creations and broaden your horizons.

Aim to reach new heights with the aspirations you have already initiated earlier this year. Delve deeper into your true desires, focusing intently on abundance. The number 3 also emphasizes communication, so if you have a speech to present, April is the ideal month to share your voice. However, be mindful of negative self-talk; your words hold power, so maintain a positive outlook.

Take the opportunity to connect with your emotions and learn to express them openly. Address any unresolved issues within your relationships, as this is not only a time for creation but also for connection, Make the most of this month socially; dance, enjoy leisure activities, and have fun before the diligent energy of the 4 arrives in May.

April is a 3 month, where your creative juices will flow abundantly, offering you fresh ideas to cultivate abundance. This is a playful time, but remember to keep things simple and focused. Engage in activities such as redecorating, redesigning a project, writing a story, or dancing—all wonderful ways to express your creativity and enjoy the season.

Personal Day
(April)

1. Create a detailed agenda and commit to completing it.
2. Be poised to seize any opportunity that comes your way today.
3. Have a heartfelt conversation with your partner; listen closely.
4. Carve out 'me' time in a serene space to recharge your spirit.
5. Conduct a thorough audit of your bank accounts; knowledge is power.
6. Embrace forgiveness and love; they lead to inner peace.
7. Launch a creative venture with others, harnessing collaboration.
8. Allow intuition to flow freely; follow its guidance unwaveringly.
9. Dance, sing, or write; today is for joyful self-expression.
10. Maintain focus; your dedication will yield results.
11. Welcome distractions; they may lead to new possibilities.
12. Enhance your space with decor that reflects your energy.
13. Enroll in an online course; invest in your growth.
14. Ensure your material and spiritual accounts are in harmony.
15. Cultivate compassion and understanding for lasting success.
16. Honor your independence and individuality with pride.
17. Sit quietly and listen to your intuition's valuable insights.
18. Attend gatherings joyfully and enjoy your new connections.
19. Envision a solid foundation for your aspirations; stand firm.
20. Ignite your adventurous spirit; follow your heart's lead.
21. Relish time with family while respecting your boundaries.
22. Reflect on your spiritual path; seek alignment with your true self.
23. Focus on aspirations and aim to elevate yourself.
24. Honor the greater good; perform kind acts to brighten the world.
25. Invite new experiences into your life; feel the excitement.
26. Maintain balance, harmony & peace in all your pursuits today.
27. Write in your gratitude journal; acknowledge your abundance.
28. Complete tasks on your checklist with purpose & satisfaction.
29. Explore the unknown with an open heart; welcome growth.
30. Be bold and seek new adventures; unleash your spirit.

May
4 Personal Month

This month, you embark on a journey to discover your personal power. Address any authority issues and embrace your role as your own authority figure. Business, management, and organization will take precedence, and you may find yourself stepping into a leadership position.

Balance is essential in all aspects of your life as you navigate these two even numbers together. The energy of 4 is one of diligent work, providing you with the necessary foundation to move forward with confidence. This month, keep your focus on your responsibilities and maintain a strong work ethic.

While you may have experienced a surge of creative ideas last month, now is the time to bring those concepts to fruition and finalize any ongoing projects. Prioritize your health through a balanced diet and regular exercise, as discipline, structure, and diligence will be your faithful allies during this period.

Utilize this working energy to establish a solid platform that will support you throughout the rest of the year. June promises to be an expansive month, and having a firm footing will be crucial for your growth.

For the next few weeks, remain in your safe space and dedicate yourself to hard work. Keep a positive mindset, and the rewards of your efforts will surely come to you.

May is characterized as a 4 month, emphasizing the importance of organization, discipline, and diligence. Attend to your health by focusing on diet and exercise, and ensure you bring your creative endeavors from last month into tangible form. Complete ongoing projects and reset your foundation in preparation for the expansive energy of the upcoming 5 month.

PERSONAL YEAR 8

Personal Day
(May)

1. Prepare for an upcoming shift; approach with confidence.
2. Dedicate efforts to productive work from home today.
3. Incorporate exercise into your routine to boost efficiency.
4. Balance your finances thoroughly to ensure accountability.
5. Focus on completing your project; time management is vital.
6. Create a detailed to-do list to stay organized this month.
7. Address incomplete tasks by filling in necessary details.
8. Allocate time to enjoy life; balance among responsibilities is key.
9. Diligence yields results; persistence is essential.
10. Change is imminent; anticipate and adapt accordingly.
11. Nurture relationships; they are pivotal to your success.
12. Engage in contemplation to reflect on your goals and dreams.
13. Stay receptive to work shifts; heed them as they arise.
14. Release items or habits that no longer contribute to progress.
15. Reflect on new ideas that can inform your decisions.
16. Keep sharp focus on details; they're crucial for success.
17. Identify what brings you joy; incorporate those activities.
18. Ensure your foundations are solid, both personally and professionally.
19. Rise to the challenge and level up your responsibilities.
20. Improve your home environment to foster productivity.
21. Be mindful of your diet; prioritize nutritious foods for health.
22. Honor your knowledge; trust in your capabilities.
23. Conclude your to-do list diligently; mark your achievements.
24. Value the chance to begin a new chapter in your journey.
25. Read between the lines for deeper understanding.
26. Hold yourself accountable for actions and commitments.
27. Avoid overthinking; trust instincts and make decisive choices.
28. Prepare for a fast-paced month; stay organized and proactive.
29. Bring home flowers to brighten your space and well-being.
30. Commit to self-improvement and professional growth.
31. Strive to maintain balance and harmony in all aspects of life.

June
5 Personal Month

Balance, organization, management, and the quest for your personal power emerge as the foremost priorities this year. Achieving balance is especially crucial during this dynamic 5 month. Prepare yourself for life lessons and opportunities that will foster your growth in personal empowerment.

Direct your efforts towards enhancing your career, while remaining vigilant as money may flow more freely in both directions this month; exercise caution in your spending. Your authority may be tested as well, and the combined energies of 8 and 5 signify a period filled with dynamic change, transition, and abundant growth opportunities.

Unexpected changes may lead to travel and adventure, and you may find yourself wanting to shift the trajectory of your career. Be mindful that alterations may also arise in your home life and relationships. Embrace the unpredictability of this month, as it is sure to bring surprises. The energy of 5 is associated with promotion, making this an ideal time to put yourself forward.

Step up and take risks; you will undoubtedly emerge as a transformed individual by the end of the month as the lessons of life unfold before you. The themes of freedom and expansion will form the foundation for June, so remain curious and seize every opportunity that arises.

June is indeed a 5 month; a time characterized by unexpected changes that usher in travel and adventure. You may find yourself altering your path entirely, so take this opportunity to promote yourself and leverage your communication skills effectively. Embrace the chance to take risks, as the transformations of this month are destined to enhance your life. Allow the energy to flow freely and welcome the exciting possibilities that await you.

Personal Day
(June)

1. Seize opportunities before you; make choices decisively.
2. Read a self-improvement book to enhance leadership skills.
3. Maintain a balanced lifestyle amid turbulent chaos.
4. Express your presence with kind gestures to those around you.
5. Draft a list of your wildest dreams; set the stage for manifestation.
6. Choose collaboration to achieve powerful outcomes together.
7. Dance joyfully; let your energy uplift your surroundings.
8. Follow clear paths that lead directly to your goals.
9. Appreciate an adventurous day; indulge in spontaneity.
10. Plan an engaging evening out with a friend; foster connections.
11. Take a day trip to explore new horizons and experiences.
12. Check in on business operations; think creatively for solutions.
13. Trust your inner guidance; it's essential for leadership.
14. Embrace challenges of trying something new; grow beyond comfort.
15. Follow your insights; they will guide you to success.
16. Live boldly; step outside traditional boundaries for new opportunities.
17. Focus intently on success; your concentration leads to accomplishment.
18. Let today guide you to new horizons filled with potential.
19. Engage in meaningful talks with loved ones to strengthen bonds.
20. Meditate in nature; honor tranquility and ground yourself.
21. Stay organized and follow rules that support productivity.
22. Uplift a stranger with kindness; create a ripple of positivity.
23. Venture into new understanding; curiosity fuels innovation.
24. Quiet the inner critic; create space for optimism and acceptance.
25. Inspire creativity to explore uncharted territories & passions.
26. Adjust your foundation to align with your goals.

27. Act on something from your desires list; make dreams real.
28. Give undivided attention to someone close; enrich that bond.
29. Embark on a vision quest for insights and clarity.
30. Confidently express your authority; lead with intention.

PERSONAL YEAR 8

July
6 Personal Month

The energy of 8 emphasizes organization, management, and financial matters, bringing these themes to the forefront in your life this year. It is likely that this has been a busy year for you thus far, with money flowing more freely; ideally bringing in more than it is going out. Regardless of the flow of currency, it is crucial to remain vigilant about your finances.

With the arrival of the 6 vibration, now is the time to redirect your energy toward the domestic realm. It is an opportune moment to realign your priorities in your home life. Engage in productive tasks such as cleaning out the garage, reorganizing your desk, or completing a home improvement project; these activities are excellent outlets for your energy.

For the next few weeks, family, home, and responsibility will take center stage. Focus on enhancing your closest relationships, as your loved ones may need your support more than usual. Make time to relax and plan a vacation to enjoy moments with those who matter most. While honoring your responsibilities, remember to prioritize self-care.

Rest assured, you will have the opportunity to rejuvenate next month as your focus shifts inward.

July is characterized as a 6 month, a time dedicated to home and family. Embrace your responsibilities by attending to your household and relationships. Use this time to connect with family; consider scheduling a vacation or focusing on home improvement projects. Strive to find harmony in both your career and domestic life, and take this opportunity to realign your priorities for a more fulfilling experience.

Personal Day
(July)

1. Allocate time for yourself in a space that fosters focus.
2. Balance is essential for effective leadership in all aspects.
3. Cultivate unconditional love and forgiveness in interactions.
4. Address responsibilities with grace; strong leaders inspire compassion.
5. Express gratitude for family support; their contributions are vital.
6. Radiate joy and positivity; your demeanor uplifts your team.
7. Reinforce your boundaries while maintaining professionalism.
8. Plan an adventurous outing with a loved one; explore together.
9. Engage in heartfelt conversations to deepen your connection.
10. Transform your inner critic into a constructive ally.
11. Invest time in your career; seek growth opportunities aligned with goals.
12. Demonstrate kindness with good deeds; lift others as a leader.
13. Nurture relationships by spending time to foster collaboration.
14. Use diplomacy to resolve issues with tact and understanding.
15. Choose a creative home project that enhances your space.
16. Develop a plan to ensure the success of your initiatives.
17. Designate a day for self-care and nurturing your spirit.
18. Create memories with loved ones to reinforce your network.
19. Meditate to connect inwardly; trust your intuition for guidance.
20. Identify your center; maintain balance through life's challenges.
21. Let go and surrender to wisdom; it fosters resilience & growth.
22. Collaborate with your partner to align new goals for success.
23. Be willing to compromise to maintain equilibrium in relationships.
24. Make time for an evening out; nurture joy and connection.
25. Emphasize structure and discipline in achieving your objectives.
26. Stay open to today's amazing events; leverage them for direction.

27. Step up and fulfill responsibilities with accountability.
28. Retreat to your happy place with a good book for inspiration.
29. Honor your wisdom; exercise your authority with confidence.
30. Practice forgiveness; let unconditional love uplift you.
31. Stay open to new ideas; welcome each as a pathway to innovation.

August
7 Personal Month

PERSONAL YEAR 8

August unfolds as a reflective 7 month. This year has defined itself through themes of organization, management, and mastering your world. It has been a busy time, brimming with new opportunities. You may have noticed an increase in financial flow, both incoming and outgoing, requiring you to maintain balance across various aspects of your life.

August is your time to rejuvenate, relax, and replenish your energy. The energy of 7 invites you to turn inward and reevaluate your life's direction. Take this precious opportunity for introspection and connect with your intuition. Consider participating in a personal growth class or immersing yourself in a self-help book; engage in activities that promote your improvement and well-being.

As you focus on inner balance this month, realign your priorities to cultivate inner peace. Pay attention to your health; enhance your diet and exercise regimen, and consider undertaking a body cleanse. This month is dedicated to nurturing your internal self, as next month you will return to the demanding pace of your business life, supported by a double 8 vibration.

August is indeed a 7 month, a period for rest, relaxation, and rejuvenation. Solitude is essential for fostering inward focus; take the time to reevaluate where you have been and the path you wish to pursue. Dive into the study of metaphysics, contemplate taking a retreat, and cherish moments spent in nature as you navigate this transformative phase of your journey.

269

Personal Day
(August)

1. Opportunities are coming; analyze actions meticulously before acting.
2. Tie up loose ends; finalize projects and move on decisively.
3. Assert your individuality; let your true self guide your leadership.
4. Collaboration is essential; ensure team members recognize this.
5. Carve out time for solitude; it enhances clarity and focus.
6. Prioritize health with proper nutrition and regular exercise.
7. Be open to spontaneity; allow unexpected insights to enhance productivity.
8. Take charge of your responsibilities; they are non-negotiable.
9. Create a reflection space; value alone time for strategic thinking.
10. Expect abundance in various forms; success extends beyond money.
11. Cultivate patience; it's vital for effective team management.
12. It's an opportune time for negotiating crucial agreements.
13. Recognize others' contributions; it fosters loyalty.
14. Balance solitude with social engagement for broader perspective.
15. Schedule a health check; your well-being is integral to leadership.
16. Introduce diversity in projects; explore uncharted ideas.
17. Invest in your environment; a tidy space boosts productivity.
18. Reflect on your journey; assess progress toward your vision.
19. Keep meticulous records; balance accounts for financial propriety.
20. Release control over what you can't influence; focus on the possible.
21. Align actions with goals; regularly assess your progress.
22. Let capable team members lead initiatives; collaboration is key.

23. Reconnect with old contacts; thoughtful outreach benefits your network.
24. Stay pragmatic; create order from complexity in operations.
25. Advocate for your vision; make your contributions known.
26. Uphold your boundaries while respecting others' limits.
27. Walk in nature to clear your mind for strategic contemplation.
28. Exercise authority confidently; present ideas clearly.
29. Contribute to the community; support those in need.
30. Let ambition and success form your leadership foundation.
31. Use diplomacy to navigate challenges; strive for balance.

PERSONAL YEAR 8

September
8 Personal Month

Note: Because September is the ninth month, it is always the same number as your personal year. This means you have double the energy of your personal year for thirty days. If the current year calculates to the same value as your personal year, then you receive triple that number's energy in September.

The 8 vibration amplifies the energies of business, money, organization, authority, and balance. When the current year calculates to the same value as your personal year, then you receive triple that number's energy. This is a prime opportunity to uncover your personal power and assert yourself as an authority in your field.

Focus on expanding your career and establishing your expertise, as the energy of 8 is synonymous with empowerment. Embrace this potent energy, as it presents a unique chance you won't encounter again for another nine years. You possess heightened mental acuity and clarity of focus, so summon the courage to step outside the confines of convention and pursue your greatness.

Expect a significant flow of money this month, both incoming and outgoing. Make prudent investments and be open to reaping the rewards of a profitable year. The reciprocal nature of 8 energy encourages you to uphold a strong moral compass while serving the greater good.

Maintain your focus on the positive, and you will find that those good vibrations are returned to you.

September is indeed an 8 month, a dedicated time for hard work, with a strong emphasis on power and authority. Business takes precedence, and you are called to embrace a leadership role. Organize and manage all aspects of your life while diligently balancing your material ambitions with your spiritual aspirations. Step confidently into your authority and make the most of this transformative month.

Personal Day
(September)

1. Invest in meaningful causes globally; support them or use your skills.
2. Launch a new research project or read to spark innovative ideas.
3. Center yourself and trust your intuition in financial navigation.
4. Encourage creativity to generate bold ideas for finance.
5. Structure your workday precisely to optimize productivity.
6. Embrace various experiences; stay open to unexpected growth.
7. Stand ready to assist those in need with your resources.
8. Use imagination to reshape traditional approaches for success.
9. Focus on expanding your reach; push boundaries of possibility.
10. Refine & complete projects; realize every idea with excellence.
11. Celebrate individuality and express it boldly in your ventures.
12. Pay attention to detail; thoroughness ensures your success.
13. Reconnect with friends to rekindle inspiring networks.
14. Activate practical skills to solve challenges efficiently.
15. Promote your ventures assertively; showcase your impact.
16. Define and uphold boundaries to protect your vision.
17. Prioritize rest to sustain energy and drive as an entrepreneur.
18. Maintain balanced accounts; invest strategically for growth.
19. Apply talents to support global betterment through success.
20. Collaborate with others, combining strengths for success.
21. Let endeavors unfold naturally; embrace organic growth.
22. Allocate time for joy; rediscover creativity and enthusiasm.
23. Ensure a stable foundation for your entrepreneurial pursuits.
24. Engage with new people to expand your global network.
25. Nurture important relationships; they are key to success.
26. Create a space that inspires positive energy and innovation.
27. Stay alert to financial developments for strategic growth.
28. Address problems with effective solutions; move forward.
29. Share insights openly; contribute to discussions and inspire.
30. Use diplomacy to resolve conflicts and preserve harmony.

October
9 Personal Month

Note: October is always the same number as your personal year next year, making it a brief preview of the coming year.

This is a time of completion amid your busy year. This month offers a unique opportunity to address unresolved issues, finalize contracts, and complete ongoing projects. The energy of 9 centers around resolution and the art of letting go, inviting you to release anything that no longer serves a purpose in your current life.

After a year bustling with business and authority matters, October allows you the chance to tidy up and lighten your load as you prepare to finish the year gracefully. Clear off your desk, organize your office, or clean out the garage. Take the necessary steps to create space for what you wish to manifest in the coming months.

This month serves as a preview of the year ahead, giving you a brief window for early preparation for the opportunities that the next year will present. Trust in the Divine and be attentive to your intuition, which may become more pronounced at this time. Embrace compassion and forgiveness, wearing these qualities openly as you seek to resolve any lingering differences.

October is indeed a 9 month, the culmination of a nine-month cycle. Clean out, finalize, and let go of anything that does not enrich your life. Reap the rewards of your hard work from the past eight months and make room for the new beginnings that await you next month. Allow your creativity to flourish as you dedicate yourself to serving the greater good.

Personal Day
(October)

1. Take charge of your journey; lead with purpose and inspire change.
2. Collaborate with partners committed to humanitarian goals.
3. Express ideas through diverse platforms; stay open to viewpoints.
4. Plan your day strategically; be adaptable to challenges.
5. Stay attuned to synchronicities that guide your efforts today.
6. Spread joy by gifting flowers; small kindnesses make big impacts.
7. Rejuvenate your spirit in places that inspire happiness.
8. Embrace opportunities; take calculated risks to advance your mission.
9. Clear physical and mental clutter for new ideas and projects.
10. Today is decision day; weigh options to align with your values.
11. Trust your intuition to navigate challenges confidently.
12. Celebrate spontaneity with an impromptu gathering for connection.
13. Approach work practically to ensure productive outcomes.
14. Let unpredictability fuel creativity and adaptability.
15. Beautify your workspace to create an inspiring atmosphere.
16. Flow with your projects; adapt to obstacles instead of resisting.
17. Focus on financial sustainability; align resources with goals.
18. Conclude activities that don't serve your mission; make space.
19. Keep your gaze on future aspirations; build on your vision.
20. Extend apologies as needed to foster healing in relationships.
21. Engage in joyful activities to inspire and energize you.
22. Address lingering legal or financial matters for clarity.
23. Anticipate a productive day focused on sales and promotion.
24. Be available to offer guidance and support to others.
25. Reflect on your thoughts and journey; align with your aspirations.
26. Lead with authority and confidence to inspire trust.

27. Let go of burdens that no longer serve your purpose.
28. Use intelligence to guide your team, fostering collaboration.
29. Complete projects by addressing missing components and refining.
30. Actively participate in discussions; share insights respectfully.
31. Wrap up today's tasks and create a plan for tomorrow's efforts.

PERSONAL YEAR 8

November
1 Personal Month

This month offers you the opportunity to revisit the desires you articulated at the beginning of the year. February also carried the energy of 1, prompting you to consider whether you have manifested the goals you set for yourself months ago. Are you still aligned with your aspirations, or have your dreams evolved as you have?

You are not the same person you were earlier in the year, and it's natural for your ambitions to shift accordingly. Throughout this year, you have dedicated considerable effort toward your career and business endeavors. As part of that process, organizing your workspace and home has become essential.

You have likely confronted your fears and embraced your role as your own authority. The lessons learned along the way have contributed significantly to your personal evolution, giving rise to new and exciting dreams. Take a moment to reflect on what you truly desire for the coming year. This is a crucial time to engage in preliminary thoughts about what you wish to create in the year ahead.

November represents a 1 month; a time for new beginnings. Now is the moment to plant the seeds of your intentions, setting clear goals for the next nine months. Expect this to be a busy month filled with fresh projects and opportunities. Have the courage to step into a leadership role and navigate this exciting chapter with confidence and clarity.

PERSONAL YEAR 8

Personal Day
(November)

1. Cultivate a peaceful atmosphere for innovation and collaboration.
2. Let your cheerful demeanor shine, motivating your team.
3. Be an effective manager; organization is key to your vision.
4. View changes as stepping stones to growth and new ventures.
5. Connect with your community; your impact fosters relationships.
6. Dedicate time to research topics that spark your interest.
7. Choose action, ambition, and achievement for your journey.
8. Let go of outdated practices to pursue higher purposes.
9. Today is great for business deals; let integrity shine.
10. Exercise patience; allow ideas to develop organically.
11. Cultivate optimism; it's a powerful tool for overcoming challenges.
12. Align your moral compass with your core values for trust.
13. Be mindful of impulses; make decisions reflecting your vision.
14. Address conflicts with empathy & understanding for positivity.
15. Prioritize health with a new exercise regimen for well-being.
16. Focus on gratitude; welcome abundance from your hard work.
17. True success comes from serving others and the greater good.
18. Use independent leadership skills to forge new paths.
19. Celebrate friendships and inspire camaraderie at work.
20. Quiet your inner critic; focus on the bright side.
21. Pay attention to fine print; diligence protects your interests.
22. Stay open to new ideas while maintaining clear focus.
23. Prioritize responsibility; trust & accountability drive business.
24. If you need rest, take time to recharge and refresh.
25. Focus on the greater good; collective rewards lead to success.
26. Clear distractions and clutter for upcoming changes.
27. Continuously seek to improve; complacency has no place here.
28. Offer support to others, fostering collaboration and success.
29. Engage in self-improvement through seminars or books.
30. Honor your work ethic; it sets a standard and inspires.

December
2 Personal Month

After being characterized by your individual pursuits, November ushers in a shift toward cooperation and partnership as the year draws to a close. This is a time to focus on the details and to complete the remaining aspects of what you have manifested during this bustling 8 year. Trust your intuition as you connect with your Divine guidance.

Emphasizing cooperation and diplomacy is essential now; nurturing harmonious relationships will greatly benefit you. The energy of 2 encourages you to align yourself with those who can offer support, fostering sensitivity and understanding in your interactions. You may find yourself deferring to others as you work toward your own aspirations.

As the holiday season approaches, you may encounter a range of emotions; therefore, strive to maintain a positive outlook. Ground yourself and practice patience as you seek reciprocity within all your relationships. Focus on creating harmony and balance in every endeavor.

December embodies the essence of a 2 month, directing attention to the finer details. Take the time to attend to the little things and nurture the seeds that you planted last month. Cooperation in relationships becomes paramount, especially following the preceding month's emphasis on self. This emotional month may require you to employ your diplomatic skills as you navigate the complexities of connection and support during this time.

PERSONAL YEAR 8

Personal Day
(December)

1. Tap into your creativity to craft something that reflects you.
2. Harmonize your tasks by organizing and prioritizing mindfully.
3. Enjoy life's flow; let insights and plans guide you.
4. Cherish your partner with a nourishing meal and deep conversation.
5. Engage with literature that broadens your horizons.
6. Invest resources wisely for gain and spiritual fulfillment.
7. Volunteer where your heart finds joy, connecting with the world.
8. Gather like-minded individuals for a purposeful project.
9. Explore real estate for enjoyment and potential growth.
10. Let your imagination innovate creations that serve your goals.
11. Maintain due diligence while infusing work with integrity.
12. Stay open to unexpected blessings that nurture your journey.
13. Enhance your space with improvements reflecting your beauty.
14. Find joy in nature; connect your inner peace with the world.
15. Review your finances wisely, aligning with your vision.
16. Look at the bigger picture; uplift and serve your community.
17. Create a balanced to-do list with tasks and spiritual practices.
18. Exercise diplomacy to resolve conflicts; find common ground.
19. Design a day that harmonizes joy and productivity.
20. Dedicate energy to responsibilities, weaving purpose into work.
21. Embrace life's changes; consider their lessons & implications.
22. Find balance at home, creating a sanctuary for mind and soul.
23. Reflect inwardly while staying aware of your connection.
24. Lead with confidence, drawing from strength and authority.
25. Engage in kindness, enriching yourself and those you help.
26. Celebrate your uniqueness; balance individuality with connection.
27. Offer empathy and support to friends, nurturing growth.
28. Take every chance to express yourself authentically.
29. Build stability in both physical and spiritual foundations.
30. Approach adventures with enthusiasm; balance thrill & insight.
31. Respect boundaries; communicate with sensitivity and care.

Personal Year 9

Personal Year 9 marks a period of introspection and transition, contrasting the ambitious drive of the previous year. This year invites you to pause, embrace your intuition, and reflect deeply on your journey. It's a time to balance life's facets, resolve past issues, and cherish compassion towards yourself and others.

Use this year to release what no longer serves you, both emotionally and materially. Let go of burdens and attachments, paving the way for new beginnings. This period encourages shedding negative patterns, refining intentions for the future, and expanding beyond self-centered desires to contribute positively to the world.

Your intuition will guide you through resolving past matters and preparing for fresh starts. Detach from negative influences and embrace new opportunities. Although this year may bring emotional challenges, it's about opening to better experiences. Completing the nine-year cycle in numerology, it offers a chance to finish unfinished business and begin anew.

Reflect on past achievements, declutter your life, and enjoy the fruits of your labor. Focus on meditation and forgiveness to clarify your path. Embrace the changes in relationships, careers, and lifestyles, viewing them as necessary steps toward transformation. Engage in humanitarian efforts, and let your creativity flourish.

Recognize that Year 9, while associated with loss, also heralds new beginnings. Trust in life's flow, understanding that challenges can lead to rewards. Express yourself creatively, fostering compassion and forgiveness. This year culminates in growth and lessons, preparing you for the new journey ahead. Engage with your community, uplift others, and contribute to causes that ignite your passion.

As you move forward, reflect, release, and renew, maintaining hope and inspiration. Let the energy of completion propel you toward the expansive new beginnings that await in the next cycle. Welcome the transformative possibilities of Personal Year 9 with an open heart and a clear vision.

PERSONAL YEAR 9

January
1 Personal Month

The 1 month marks a significant turning point as you enter the final year of the nine-year numerology cycle. This month offers you the opportunity to reap the rewards of the hard work you have invested in previous years. It is also a time of release, as you will find yourself letting go of anything unnecessary. Be prepared, as many items from your life may fade away whether you feel ready to release them or not.

Now is the moment to declutter and create space for the aspirations you wish to nurture in the coming year. Beginning your nine-year cycle with a 1 month invites you to concentrate on what you want to manifest over the next nine months. Take the time to list what you want to retain in your life and what you wish to cultivate. Both aspects are essential to your journey this year.

In a 1 month, you are at the center of your world; your desires matter deeply. Embracing a spirit of service will yield rewards, so focus on contributing to the greater good. Trust your heightened intuition, as it is stronger this year, and heed the guidance you receive. Embrace the role of humanitarian and allow your creativity to flourish. If you have committed to personal growth and are open to receiving, this year promises to be wonderfully rewarding.

January is indeed a 1 month, a time for new beginnings. Plant the seeds of your intentions, set your goals for the upcoming nine months, and prepare for a busy month filled with new projects. Have the courage to step into a leadership role and guide your journey toward success.

PERSONAL YEAR 9

283

Personal Day
(January)

1. Cultivate a peaceful atmosphere to foster collaboration.
2. Let your cheerful nature shine, uplifting others around you.
3. Organize resources wisely in your management role.
4. Prepare for changes; view them as growth opportunities.
5. Connect with your community to impact those in need.
6. Allocate time to research topics that spark your passion.
7. Action, ambition, and achievement drive your efforts today.
8. Let go of outdated practices for a higher purpose.
9. Engage in business with integrity and transparency.
10. Practice patience; let processes unfold naturally.
11. Maintain optimism; it inspires resilience in others.
12. Allow compassion and integrity to guide your decisions.
13. Curb impulsive choices; take time to think carefully.
14. Address conflicts with love, promoting healing.
15. Prioritize health with a new exercise routine.
16. Focus on gratitude; welcome abundance from service.
17. True success comes from serving humanity; let that guide you.
18. Use leadership skills to explore new paths and innovate.
19. Dedicate time to nurture friendships and foster connections.
20. Silence your inner critic; focus on the positives.
21. Read the fine print; diligence is key to leadership.
22. Stay open to new ideas while keeping your focus sharp.
23. Act responsibly; align actions with the greater good.
24. Rest when needed; self-care is vital for leadership.
25. Focus on the greater good; collective rewards enhance well-being.
26. Remove distractions to prepare for transformative changes.
27. Seek improvement; embrace today's growth opportunities.
28. Prioritize helping others; embody a spirit of service.
29. Engage in self-improvement through inspiring books.
30. Honor your work ethic; it sets a motivating example.
31. Embrace individuality and courage; seek uplifting adventures.

February
2 Personal Month

The 2 energy invites you to embrace the completion of the numerology cycle. Now is the time to release what no longer serves you, creating space for new beginnings in the next year. In this month marked by heightened intuition, pay close attention to the guidance you receive, as it will ease the process of letting go, helping you gain insight into what is departing from your life.

Focus on the details and attend to the small matters that require your attention. This month will be more inward-focused and slower-paced compared to the dynamic energy of January. Allow yourself to go with the flow, embodying the spirit of diplomacy as you cooperate with those around you. This is not a time for leading, but rather for allowing others to guide you.

The energy of 2 is conducive to nurturing relationships, so remain open to the possibility of forming new connections. Be mindful, as this can also be a sensitive and emotional time; it is crucial to address any issues as they arise. Expect a period of gradual growth over the coming weeks, allowing yourself the time to nurture the aspirations you set in motion in January.

Practice cooperation and compromise, using your personal power to navigate situations subtly and indirectly. Focus on your inner development, fostering a spirit of harmony within yourself and in your interactions with others.

February is indeed a 2 month, an opportunity to emphasize attention to detail. Take care of the little things and nurture the seeds you planted last month. Cooperation in your relationships takes precedence, especially following the preceding month's focus on personal pursuits. This emotional period may call for you to employ your diplomatic skills as you navigate the complexities of your connections.

PERSONAL YEAR 9

285

Personal Day
(February)

1. Channel creativity to bring something beautiful to completion.
2. Organize tasks mindfully; embrace the flow of life.
3. Let go gracefully; allow life to unfold naturally.
4. Cherish your partner with a meal and meaningful talk.
5. Dive into a book that enriches your mind and soul.
6. Make investments that align with your values for peace.
7. Volunteer where compassion guides you; offer your heart.
8. Gather visionaries to create something meaningful together.
9. Explore real estate joyfully; pursue fun and opportunity.
10. Dream boldly; craft new and wondrous creations.
11. Infuse your work with love and purpose as you tackle tasks.
12. Welcome surprises with an open heart; trust your journey.
13. Beautify your home with projects that reflect harmony.
14. Reconnect with nature; embrace its calming serenity.
15. Evaluate your portfolio to ensure it supports your goals.
16. Envision contributions to humanity; see the bigger picture.
17. Craft a to-do list that balances tasks with self-compassion.
18. Mediate with kindness; guide disagreements toward understanding.
19. Design a joyful day filled with uplifting activities.
20. Direct efforts with focus and passion to achieve goals.
21. Accept change gracefully; trust the journey of life.
22. Find comfort in the sanctuary of your home.
23. Dedicate time for reflection; explore your heart's desires.
24. Lead with confidence; embody your true authority.
25. Offer kindness to those in need; enrich your community.
26. Celebrate individuality; express your unique essence.
27. Extend compassion to a friend; nurture your connection.
28. Share your truth openly; let your authentic self shine.
29. Ground yourself in thoughts of stability and enduring love.

PERSONAL YEAR 9

March
3 Personal Month

Both the 3 and 9 energies are inherently creative, and this is an ideal moment to channel that energy into any artistic endeavors. Allow your imagination to expand and revel in the joy that this month brings. The energy of 3 embodies happiness, luck, and even the potential for prosperity.

Expect March to be a social and bustling month. While it is a prime time for connection and enjoyment, you can still maintain productivity; just ensure that you don't become distracted and lose your focus. A touch of discipline will help you maximize the benefits of both the 3 and 9 energies.

Be aware that emotions may run high this month. It's important to address any issues as they arise, embracing the theme of letting go that is central to a 9 year. With your creative mind, you may glean insights into what is necessary and what is unnecessary in your life.

Your intuition is heightened this year, so don't hesitate to express yourself openly and listen with an open heart. Connect with the Divine as you navigate this creative period, and maintain a positive mindset; it will help ensure that everything falls into place.

March is indeed a 3 month, where your creative juices flow abundantly, bringing forth fresh ideas that can lead to abundance. This playful time encourages you to keep things simple and remain focused. Engage in activities such as redecorating, redesigning a project, writing a story, or dancing; each is a wonderful means to express your creativity and celebrate the energy of the moment.

PERSONAL YEAR 9

Personal Day
(March)

1. Create an agenda; let your guidance help you complete it.
2. Be open to opportunities the Universe presents today.
3. Engage in a heart-to-heart with your partner; listen deeply.
4. Take 'me' time in a tranquil space to nurture your spirit.
5. Reflect on your financial health; audit your accounts clearly.
6. Know forgiveness and love bring you peace.
7. Start a creative venture with others; collaboration amplifies joy.
8. Let intuition flow freely; the Universe whispers guidance.
9. Express yourself through singing, dancing, or writing today.
10. Concentration and focus help manifest your goals.
11. Accept distractions; they may lead to enriching paths.
12. Enhance your home to reflect your spirit; redecorate with love.
13. Take an online course for personal growth and enlightenment.
14. Balance your material and spiritual accounts for harmony.
15. Practice compassion to elevate your interactions with others.
16. Celebrate your independence; let your individuality shine.
17. Contemplate quietly; listen to your intuition's guidance.
18. Attend gatherings with an open heart; enjoy new connections.
19. Envision a sturdy foundation for your dreams' strong base.
20. Ignite your adventurous spirit; follow your heart's whispers.
21. Savor family time but maintain boundaries for peace.
22. Reflect on your spiritual path; align with your true purpose.
23. Focus on aspirations and embrace the growth that awaits.
24. Honor the greater good with acts of kindness; let blessings flow.
25. Invite new experiences; stay open to possibilities ahead.
26. Strive for balance, harmony, and peace in all you do.
27. Write in your gratitude journal; reflect on your abundance.
28. Complete tasks with intention; enjoy checking them off.
29. Venture into the unknown; remain open to growth.
30. Be bold; seek new adventures with courage.
31. Treat yourself and someone special to a joyous night out.

PERSONAL YEAR 9

April
4 Personal Month

The 4 vibration offers you the opportunity for completion, harvest, and rebirth. This month invites you to continue the process of letting go that you've already begun this year. It is time to release any unnecessary energy in your life, regardless of the realm it occupies. Take the initiative to clean out your closets and eliminate anything that no longer serves a purpose.

Forgiveness is essential during this period, as it will help lighten your spiritual burden. Embrace the conclusions and endings that are present now, making way for new beginnings next year. The energy of 4 is one of diligence, focus, and determination. Utilize this vibration to physically declutter your life, ensuring that you maintain a disciplined approach as you bring your creations from last month to fruition.

Make it a priority to finish any incomplete projects and address unresolved family issues. This is not the month for taking risks; opportunities for that will arise next month. Instead, pour your energy into hard work and see your commitments through to completion.

Get organized, prioritize your health through proper diet and exercise, and resolve any legal matters that may be pending. Use this time to lay a strong foundation for the remainder of the year, as May will serve as a launching pad for many new opportunities.

April is indeed a 4 month, one that emphasizes organization, discipline, and diligence. Take stock of your health and ensure that you are nourishing both your body and mind. Bring your creative aspirations from last month into tangible form by completing projects and resetting your foundation in preparation for the expansive energy that awaits you in the 5 month ahead.

PERSONAL YEAR 9

Personal Day
(April)

1. Prepare for an impending shift.
2. Dedicate efforts to working from home today.
3. Make time for exercise to boost energy and focus.
4. Balance your finances with careful planning.
5. Complete the ongoing project you've been focused on.
6. Draft a comprehensive to-do list for the month.
7. Fill in gaps and finalize any outstanding tasks.
8. Carve out moments to enjoy the day amid productivity.
9. Diligence pays off in the long run.
10. Accept that change is on the horizon.
11. Give extra attention to nurturing your relationships.
12. Engage in quiet contemplation to reflect on goals.
13. Stay open to potential shifts in your work environment.
14. Release possessions or habits that no longer serve you.
15. Reflect on new insights and ideas that emerge.
16. Focus keenly on the details of your tasks.
17. Identify what brings you joy; make time for it.
18. Ensure you're on solid ground personally and professionally.
19. Level up in your career by embracing new challenges.
20. Improve your home environment for enhanced comfort.
21. Watch your diet; prioritize fresh, nourishing foods.
22. Honor your knowledge and trust your abilities.
23. Complete your monthly to-do list diligently.
24. Embrace opportunities for a new chapter in life.
25. Read between the lines for deeper meanings.
26. Hold yourself accountable for your actions.
27. Avoid overthinking; trust your instincts and proceed.
28. Prepare for a fast-paced month; stay organized.
29. Bring home flowers to brighten your space.
30. Focus on self-improvement; dedicate time to growth.

PERSONAL YEAR 9

May
5 Personal Month

Now is the time of completion and harvest. This month invites you to embrace endings as you make room for new beginnings. Themes of forgiveness, letting go, and compassion come to the forefront, encouraging you to remove any unnecessary burdens from your life in order to lighten your load.

The energy of 5 embodies expansion and change, promising growth opportunities throughout this month. Prepare yourself to seize these opportunities, as travel and adventure may lie ahead. Now is the perfect moment to blaze new trails in every aspect of your life. Step into the spotlight and take the risks necessary to elevate yourself; this is your time for self-promotion.

The 5 energy actively supports your endeavors to expand not only in your career but also within your home and relationships. Do not succumb to timidity or fear; instead, let expansion be your mantra and embrace the liberty that comes with it. Remain curious and strive to reach new heights, for what you open yourself to this month will flow abundantly into your life. Remember, these changes are all aimed at enhancing your well-being, but be mindful of attracting unnecessary drama.

May is characterized as a 5 month, a period marked by unexpected change that brings forth opportunities for travel and adventure. You may find yourself altering your path entirely. Embrace this time to promote yourself and tap into your communication skills effectively. Step forward and take risks, as the transformations experienced this month are destined to enrich your life. Allow the energy to flow freely and welcome the exciting possibilities that await.

PERSONAL YEAR 9

Personal Day
(May)

1. Honor opportunities presented; choose with love and intent.
2. Immerse in a self-improvement book that nurtures your growth.
3. Maintain balance, even amid life's delightful chaos.
4. Express love through kind gestures that inspire others.
5. Dream boldly; write down aspirations for manifestation.
6. Collaborate with others to create meaningful connections.
7. Dance joyfully and let your spirit shine with positivity.
8. Follow clear paths that bring direction to your journey.
9. Savor an adventurous day; appreciate life's wonders.
10. Plan an enjoyable evening out with a friend.
11. Take a day trip to explore new destinations and experiences.
12. Stay connected to your business; think creatively.
13. Trust your inner guidance; your heart knows the way.
14. Step outside your comfort zone; try something new.
15. Heed intuitive prompts; they guide you forward.
16. Live fully; embrace experiences that enrich your spirit.
17. Focus on success while radiating love and light.
18. Let today lead you to new horizons of hope.
19. Engage in deep conversations with loved ones for connection.
20. Meditate in nature; find tranquility and wisdom.
21. Organize your surroundings; follow rules for clarity.
22. Lift a stranger's spirits; your kindness can brighten their day.
23. Explore new dimensions; embrace curiosity and wonder.
24. Calm your inner critic; practice self-compassion.
25. Encourage creativity to flourish; explore new expressions.
26. Adjust your foundation to align with your values.
27. Act on desires; let your dreams become reality.
28. Offer full attention to someone close; nurture that bond.
29. Embark on a vision quest for deeper insights about your path.
30. Express your authority confidently, leading with love.
31. Commit to balance and harmony in all your activities.

June
6 Personal Month

This year is marked by completions, endings, and the process of letting go. It is essential that you engage in the act of clearing out what no longer serves you, all the while keeping in mind that you are creating space for what the Universe will send your way next year. Embrace the process of surrender, and focus on concluding any unfinished projects.

The energy of 6 casts a spotlight on your relationships, revealing that some associations may come to an end while others may undergo transformation. Embrace these changes, trusting that what concludes now is ultimately for your greater good. This is a month dedicated to nurturing the connections closest to you, but remember that self-care is equally important; you cannot pour from an empty cup.

Take responsibility for your environment by completing any home improvement projects; you will undoubtedly feel more at ease once these tasks are accomplished. Allow yourself to release what clearly seeks to depart from your life, thereby making room for new beginnings. Consider taking a vacation to enjoy quality time with your family and rejuvenate your spirit in nature.

Commit to serving others, realigning your priorities as you strive to find harmony and balance in your life.

June is a 6 month, emphasizing the themes of home and family. It's vital to address your responsibilities, attending to both your home and relationships with diligence. Use this month to devote valuable time to family, whether it be through planning a vacation or engaging in home improvement projects. Seek harmony within both your career and your domestic space, taking this opportunity to realign your priorities for a more fulfilled existence.

PERSONAL YEAR 9

293

Personal Day
(June)

1. Set aside time in a sacred space to nurture your well-being.
2. Reflect on the importance of balance to ensure harmony.
3. Radiate unconditional love and forgiveness for inner peace.
4. Approach responsibilities with grace and kindness.
5. Express gratitude for your family's contributions; deepen bonds.
6. Let joy & happiness create a positive atmosphere around you.
7. Reinforce your boundaries while showing love and compassion.
8. Embark on a fun adventure with a loved one; try something new.
9. Engage in heartfelt conversations for openness and understanding.
10. Build a positive rapport with your inner critic as an ally.
11. Allocate time to expand your career; align with shared values.
12. Perform acts of kindness to express your compassionate nature.
13. Nurture relationships by spending quality time together.
14. Use diplomacy to resolve lingering issues and foster harmony.
15. Initiate a home project that reflects your creative vision.
16. Create a detailed plan to complete your projects collaboratively.
17. Dedicate a day to yourself for activities that recharge you.
18. Create lasting memories with loved ones; cherish every moment.
19. Spend time meditating to connect with your intuition.
20. Find your center and maintain balance amid life's challenges.
21. Let go of what no longer serves you; surrender for guidance.
22. Collaborate with your partner to set shared future goals.
23. Be willing to compromise for equilibrium in your relationship.
24. Enjoy an evening out; relish the joy of shared experiences.
25. Emphasize structure as essential in your partnership.
26. Stay open to events today; they may lead to new opportunities.

27. Step up and fulfill responsibilities; demonstrate accountability.
28. Retreat to your happy place with a good book for escape.
29. Honor yourself and your wisdom; be a trusted guide.
30. Practice forgiveness and let go of grievances for love.

PERSONAL YEAR 9

July
7 Personal Month

This marks a period of reflection and inward exploration. As you navigate the final year of the numerology cycle, this time signifies completion and harvest. It's essential to wrap up any unfinished projects and release everything that no longer serves you. With the promise of new beginnings on the horizon next year, create the necessary space for the opportunities that await you. Embrace letting go as your guiding mantra, recognizing that closure is achievable across every dimension of your life, including your lifestyle, career, habits, and behaviors.

Incorporating the energy of 7 grants you the freedom to relax and rejuvenate after a month devoted to serving others. Now is the moment to redirect your energy inward, reevaluating your past experiences and considering the direction in which your life is headed. The synergy of the 9 and 7 energies provides a unique opportunity for profound self-examination.

Time spent in introspection will yield generous rewards. Engage in meditation, take leisurely walks in nature, or embark on a weekend retreat to nourish your sense of well-being. Prioritize what serves you best, and seek inner peace as you move through this transformative month.

July is indeed a 7 month, a time for rest, relaxation, and rejuvenation. Solitude is essential for focused reflection, so allow yourself to reassess your life's journey and contemplate the path you wish to pursue. Consider delving into the study of metaphysics or spending time amidst nature as you embrace this opportunity for renewal.

Personal Day
(July)

1. New opportunities are emerging; reflect on decisions thoughtfully.
2. Attend to unfinished tasks; completing them brings peace.
3. Honor your unique identity; let it shine in all you do.
4. Cultivate cooperation; foster kindness and understanding.
5. Slow down; savor the beauty of each day.
6. Prioritize your well-being; nourish your body and move.
7. Be open to spontaneity; let synchronicities guide you.
8. Take responsibilities seriously; fulfill your commitments.
9. Create a sacred space for refuge and cherish solitude.
10. Abundance is coming; it comes in many forms, not just money.
11. Nurture patience and understanding within yourself today.
12. Today is great for engaging in meaningful negotiations.
13. Acknowledge others' contributions; reciprocity strengthens bonds.
14. Step out of reflection; connect with others for enrichment.
15. Schedule a wellness check; self-care is an act of kindness.
16. Introduce variety into your routine; try something new.
17. Beautify your surroundings to reflect your inner self.
18. Reflect on your journey; assess alignment with your values.
19. Keep finances in order; balance accounts for security.
20. Release control of what you can't influence; find peace.
21. Align actions with cherished goals; track your progress.
22. Allow others to lead; support their initiatives for growth.
23. Reach out to an old friend with a heartfelt message.
24. Stay grounded; find order amid chaos for clarity.
25. Promote yourself gently; share your work to inspire others.
26. Maintain boundaries while respecting others' limits.
27. Take a nature walk to center your thoughts in tranquility.
28. Trust your instincts; express yourself authentically.
29. Serve humanity by offering your time or skills; small acts matter.
30. Let ambition for goodness and success guide your efforts.
31. Approach challenges with diplomacy; seek balanced resolutions.

PERSONAL YEAR 9

August
8 Personal Month

A year defined by completion and the act of letting go characterizes the 9 cycle, where clearing out and finishing up becomes essential in order to simplify your life. This month offers you the opportunity to balance your releasing efforts; whether you choose to intensify your decluttering or take time to relax and enjoy the rewards of your diligent work thus far.

A 9 year can be relatively easy if you have previously invested in your personal growth. However, if you have not already done so, you may find yourself burdened by obligations accumulated from the previous years. Your focus this month centers on financial matters, management, and the empowerment that comes from assuming your own authority. You may be called upon to step forward and assert yourself, or you may find yourself on the receiving end of a promotion at work. Whatever transpires, rest assured that these developments aim to bring harmony and balance into your life.

August is indeed an 8 month, emphasizing work, power, and authority. This month will require you to embrace a leadership role, focusing intently on your business and personal life. Organize and manage every aspect of your existence, ensuring that you maintain a balance between your material pursuits and spiritual well-being. Step confidently into your authority and navigate this month with purpose and clarity.

PERSONAL YEAR 9

Personal Day
(August)

1. Give generously to causes close to your heart; support them.
2. Embark on discovery by starting a new research project or book.
3. Center yourself in love; trust your intuition in business.
4. Let creativity blossom; use love and inspiration for ideas.
5. Structure your workday with care and flexibility for passions.
6. Choose a variety of experiences; welcome joyous surprises.
7. Offer love and support to those in need; uplift others.
8. Use imagination to breathe new life into established paths.
9. Aim for growth; pursue new horizons to make an impact.
10. Complete projects with love, ensuring every idea shines.
11. Be true to yourself; express your spirit with warmth.
12. Attend to details with love; they form the foundation of success.
13. Reconnect with old friends; reinforce nurturing bonds.
14. Use practical skills to address challenges and drive progress.
15. Share ventures with joy; step into the spotlight confidently.
16. Maintain boundaries with love; direct energy to your passions.
17. Prioritize rest; nurture your spirit to stay vibrant.
18. Manage finances carefully; invest in line with your values.
19. Use your talents to make a positive impact in the world.
20. Collaborate in love and unity; maximize combined efforts.
21. Let endeavors unfold naturally, guided by love.
22. Dedicate time to play; rediscover joy that fuels your spirit.
23. Ensure a solid foundation supports your loving ventures.
24. Engage with new people and build transformative friendships.
25. Treasure relationships; give them love and attention.
26. Create a space for positive energy and inspiration to flow.
27. Stay mindful of finances; focus on opportunities aligned with values.
28. Address challenges with love; release them peacefully.
29. Share knowledge generously; enrich others with insights.
30. Use diplomacy to resolve conflicts; promote harmony.
31. Communicate with love; enhance connections in your community.

PERSONAL YEAR 9

September
9 Personal Month

Note: Because September is the ninth month, it is always the same number as your personal year. This means you have double the energy of your personal year for thirty days. If the current year calculates to the same value as your personal year, then you receive triple that number's energy in September.

As the final number in the numerology cycle, 9 signifies completion and embodies a time of significant endings. Trust that the things that leave your life are ultimately for your highest good. This is the moment to address any unfinished business and release anything that is unnecessary. Excess baggage is not worth carrying into the next year.

Rather than dwell on what you must let go, focus on what you wish to take with you. Consider the emotional and tangible burdens that you want to retain. Now is the opportunity to lighten your load and embrace the rewards that life has to offer. If you have dedicated yourself to personal growth, you will likely see many benefits during this time.

Practice forgiveness and strive to forget past grievances. Approach every situation with unconditional love and compassion, recognizing the Divine presence in all things. Embracing love and empathy will serve you well, especially during this transitional time.

This month may present challenges if you find yourself clinging to the past. Instead, direct your energy toward serving humanity, maintaining a positive mindset as you prepare for the new beginnings that await you in the upcoming 1 year.

September is indeed a 9 month, the conclusion of a nine-month cycle. Take this time to clean out, finish up, and let go of anything that does not enrich your life. Reap the rewards of your hard work from the previous eight months, and create space for the exciting new opportunities that lie ahead. Trust your intuition as you consider what you wish to manifest next; be creative and always strive to serve the greater good.

PERSONAL YEAR 9

Personal Day
(September)

1. Take charge of your life; lead by example to impact others.
2. Collaborate with others to achieve shared humanitarian goals.
3. Express thoughts openly through various channels; embrace diversity.
4. Structure your day to follow through on commitments.
5. Stay attuned to synchronicities that guide your actions today.
6. Brighten someone's day with flowers; spread kindness and warmth.
7. Rejuvenate in joyful spaces; allow time for reflection.
8. Welcome opportunities; take courageous risks for the greater good.
9. Clear physical and emotional spaces for new growth.
10. Make informed decisions by weighing options against values.
11. Trust your intuition to navigate challenges and find harmony.
12. Celebrate spontaneity; organize an impromptu gathering.
13. Approach tasks practically; enhance productivity with common sense.
14. Embrace unpredictability to enrich experiences and innovate.
15. Beautify your spaces to reflect your commitment to service.
16. Go with the flow; adapt to changes gracefully.
17. Focus on sustainability; manage resources and balance accounts.
18. Conclude activities that no longer serve your mission.
19. Keep your focus forward, supported by your aspirations.
20. Extend apologies to create space for healing connections.
21. Engage in joyful activities that uplift your spirit.
22. Address unresolved matters for clarity in future endeavors.
23. Prepare for a productive day in sales and promotion.
24. Offer guidance to those who can benefit from your expertise.
25. Reflect on your path; ensure alignment with your goals.
26. Demonstrate authority confidently, leading with integrity.
27. Release burdens that no longer serve your journey.
28. Use your intelligence to inspire your team for success.

PERSONAL YEAR 9

29. Attend to project details; ensure completeness in your plans.
30. Participate in discussions, sharing opinions while staying respectful.

PERSONAL YEAR 9

October
1 Personal Month

Note: October is always the same number as your personal year next year. This means it is a brief preview of the coming year.

Now is a time for new beginnings as you transition out of your nine-year cycle. You began this year with the same energy you experience now, but the intervening eight months have been marked by expansive growth. Reflect on what is on your manifestation list for the next nine years; this month offers you the opportunity to outline your aspirations in preparation for the coming January.

Consider what you have released this year. Who have you forgiven, and what further items on your list are ready to be let go? While this year has been about cleaning up and letting go, your current focus shifts to creating space for the future. It is crucial to identify what you wish to carry forward.

Embrace this time to make room for new beginnings and relish the rewards of your hard work throughout the year. With your intuition heightened, trust and follow the guidance you receive. Allow your creativity to flourish as you contemplate what you wish to manifest. By focusing on the positive aspects of this year, you will attract the rewards that follow.

October represents a 1 month, symbolizing fresh starts. Use this time to plant seeds, set your goals, and establish your intentions for the next nine months. This month is likely to be bustling with new projects, so summon the courage to embrace a leadership role and guide your journey with confidence.

PERSONAL YEAR 9

Personal Day
(October)

1. Create a peaceful atmosphere that fosters collaboration and well-being.
2. Let your cheerful spirit shine, uplifting those around you.
3. Be an effective manager by organizing tasks for collective impact.
4. View changes as opportunities for growth benefiting the community.
5. Engage with your community to make a meaningful difference.
6. Dedicate time to research topics that spark your interest.
7. Channel action and ambition to drive initiatives for the greater good.
8. Let go of attachments for higher purposes that benefit the community.
9. Today's great for sound business deals; let integrity guide you.
10. Practice patience; allow processes to unfold naturally.
11. Cultivate optimism; it inspires resilience and collaboration.
12. Align your moral compass with principles serving the common good.
13. Exercise self-control; consider the long-term impact of choices.
14. Approach disagreements with love to foster support at home.
15. Prioritize well-being with a new exercise regimen; stay healthy.
16. Focus on gratitude; welcome abundance from helping others.
17. True success arises from serving humanity; let this guide you.
18. Use leadership skills to forge paths that inspire others.
19. Celebrate friendships; foster love and support in your network.
20. Quiet your inner critic; focus on positives for progress.
21. Pay attention to fine print; clarity protects everyone's interests.
22. Stay open to new ideas for the greater good; keep focus clear.
23. Commit to actions that align with your community's well-being.
24. If you need rest, take the chance; self-care is essential.
25. Focus on the greater good; contribute to collective progress.

26. Clear unnecessary items; make space for new opportunities.
27. Strive to improve projects; there's always potential for growth.
28. Offer support first; embody a spirit of community service.
29. Engage in self-improvement through seminars or inspiring books.
30. Honor your work ethic; it inspires others and builds accountability.
31. Embrace individuality and courage; pursue paths of growth.
32.

PERSONAL YEAR 9

November
2 Personal Month

November unfolds as a 2 month, inviting you to deepen your connection with your intuition and heed its guidance. As you approach the conclusion of your nine-year cycle, this time signifies resolution, completion, and a thorough review of the previous years.

The rewards for your diligence and achievements are now on the horizon. Recognize that life operates in cycles, with an ebb and flow that brings various experiences into and out of your life. Remain open to what transpires and surrender to the gifts the Universe bestows upon you. Trust in the Divine presence that guides all things.

Utilize your diplomatic skills and strive for cooperation with those around you. This month is about listening and receiving, allowing space for new beginnings while practicing compassion and forgiveness for those in need. Commit to serving humanity in ways that contribute to the greater good.

November is indeed a 2 month, a time to focus on the details and attend to the small, yet important aspects of life. Nurture the seeds you planted last month, as cooperation within your relationships is paramount following the previous month's emphasis on self. Prepare for an emotional journey this month, as it may require the application of your diplomatic skills.

PERSONAL YEAR 9

Personal Day
(November)

1. Channel creativity to craft something that reflects your spirit.
2. Organize tasks clearly, prioritizing your spiritual path.
3. Practice forgiveness; release what no longer serves you.
4. Nurture your relationship with a heartfelt meal and talk.
5. Engage with literature that enriches your mind and spirit.
6. Invest wisely; consider both material and spiritual growth.
7. Volunteer where your heart feels called; serve with compassion.
8. Gather kindred spirits to collaborate on meaningful projects.
9. Explore real estate dreams without attachment to outcomes.
10. Use imagination to create new ideas inspired by a calling.
11. Approach work with diligence and integrity; follow principles.
12. Welcome the unexpected with an open heart; trust timing.
13. Beautify your space with projects reflecting peace & harmony.
14. Reconnect with nature; find solace in its tranquility.
15. Reflect on your finances; ensure alignment with your values.
16. Envision how to contribute positively to humanity's purpose.
17. Craft a mindful to-do list, balancing action with reflection.
18. Moderate conflicts with empathy for understanding and harmony.
19. Design a day that uplifts your soul with genuine joy.
20. Devote energy to meaningful work with focus and intention.
21. Accept change as a constant part of your journey.
22. Find comfort in your home; nurture your soul there.
23. Dedicate a day to self-reflection on your spiritual landscape.
24. Step forward with courage, serving as a beacon of light.
25. Perform acts of kindness; extend love and support to others.
26. Express your individuality authentically, honoring your spirit.
27. Offer compassion to a friend; deepen your connection.
28. Share your truth openly; engage in heartfelt communication.
29. Ground yourself in thoughts of stability and spiritual wisdom.
30. Embark on adventures with an open heart and inner truth.

PERSONAL YEAR 9

December
3 Personal Month

December is a 3 month, the conclusion of the year, and the finale of your nine-year cycle. This final month is characterized by its abundant creativity, inviting you to harness your imagination and contemplate what you wish to cultivate and welcome into your life over the next nine years. Remain open to receiving guidance and allow the wisdom that emerges to expand your horizons.

As you celebrate the close of this cycle, take a moment to cherish this gift of time. Embrace the festive spirit of the holiday season: socialize, enjoy the company of friends, and make new connections. Utilize your creative talents to express yourself, be it through singing, dancing, writing, drawing, or any other passion that inspires you. Fully immerse yourself in the joy of life and all that it has to offer.

Feel the blessings of this season and deepen your connection to the Divine. The number 3 is considered lucky, so take delight in the joyous atmosphere that surrounds you. Share your creative gifts as a means of serving humanity, and endeavor to end this nine-year cycle on a high note, maintaining a positive outlook for the years to come.

As December unfolds, allow your creative juices to overflow, sparking new ideas that can lead to abundance. This is a playful time, so keep things simple while remaining focused. Engage in activities such as redecorating, redesigning a project, writing a story, or dancing; each an opportunity to celebrate the creativity that defines this transformative month.

PERSONAL YEAR 9

Personal Day
(December)

1. Craft an agenda for your endeavors; complete it with passion.
2. Stay open to accepting opportunities that arise today.
3. Have a heart-to-heart with your partner; listen with compassion.
4. Take time for yourself in a peaceful space to nurture creativity.
5. Review your bank account for clarity on your finances.
6. Forgiveness and love foster inner peace and healing.
7. Start a creative project with others to combine talents.
8. Let intuition guide you; trust your instincts on new paths.
9. Sing, dance, paint, or write; express yourself today.
10. Use focus to bring your artistic vision to life.
11. Embrace distractions; they can inspire creative directions.
12. Revitalize your space by redecorating and enhancing it.
13. Engage in self-development to nurture artistic growth.
14. Balance your material and spiritual accounts for harmony.
15. Extend compassion & understanding; they foster connection.
16. Honor your independence; let your individuality shine.
17. Sit quietly and listen to your inner voice; trust it.
18. Attend social gatherings; immerse in joy and connections.
19. Visualize a strong foundation supporting your creative journey.
20. Ignite your adventurous spirit; follow your heart's path.
21. Enjoy family gatherings while honoring your boundaries.
22. Reflect on your spiritual path; ensure it aligns with your essence.
23. Focus on aspirations; elevate your creative practice.
24. Honor the greater good by blessing someone with your talents.
25. Invite fresh experiences as you grow.
26. Strive for balance, harmony, and peace in all endeavors.
27. Write in your gratitude journal, acknowledging life's beauty.
28. Complete an item on your creative to-do list; celebrate progress.
29. Explore the unknown with an open heart for expansion.
30. Use your creativity to make a gift for your partner.
31. Find your creative space and let your imagination flow.

PERSONAL YEAR 9

Personal Year 11

In a master year defined by the number 11, your thoughts and aspirations expand cosmically, reaching into the boundless realms of spirituality, metaphysics, and inspirational pursuits. This year encourages you to transcend ordinary limits and delve into heightened spiritual vibrations, elevating your experience to new heights reflective of an 11 year.

Honor your intuition with confidence as you bravely confront the unknown, preparing yourself to achieve unprecedented levels of spiritual growth and expanded consciousness. This transformative journey opens doors to profound insights and wisdom.

By grounding yourself in a strong moral code, you create a solid foundation from which to serve the greater good. This period calls upon you to dispel fears and self-doubt, fully embracing your purpose to inspire and uplift humanity. As you align with this calling, you become an integral part of a larger tapestry of enlightenment and service, contributing positively to the world around you.

Personal Year 22

The 22 presents an extraordinary opportunity to serve humanity on a grand scale. Your heightened personal power is now palpable and within reach, enhanced by intuitive skills that bolster your elevated work ethic. This is a pivotal moment to begin constructing your legacy, using your visionary talents and dedication to bring your grandest dreams to fruition.

Your managerial prowess is at its zenith, complemented by profound spiritual insights. This year beckons you to learn new skills that will enable you to accomplish your desires and execute your master plans. While the energy of this year infuses all aspects of your life with intensity, bringing the potential for great achievements, it also introduces significant challenges.

Summon the courage and strength needed to confront these challenges and persist. This period is ripe with potential and offers the promise of enormous accomplishments. Seize the opportunity to look back on this chapter with pride and the satisfaction of having pursued your endeavors with excellence.

To navigate this pinnacle effectively, perseverance, commitment, and a balanced lifestyle are essential. Harness your boundless imagination to craft a legacy that serves the greater good, reflecting the profound impact you are capable of achieving.

About the Author

Suzan Owens is a renowned Numerologist known for her ability to connect with individuals and organizations, unlocking potential through the power of Numerology. With a diverse clientele, including celebrities and executives, Suzan guides people and teams toward peak performance using personalized insights.

Author of the award-winning Wisdom of Numerology, Suzan provides practical tools for harnessing one's true power. Her second book, Know Your Superpowers, Know Your Future, further empowers readers to embrace their potential Superpowers for success.

Suzan's expertise extends to real-world applications, such as deciding when to launch your new business and creating mind maps for success. Her strategic use of Numerology enhances decision-making, leadership, and personal growth personally and professionally for clients.

A sought-after keynote speaker, Suzan captivates audiences with empathy and actionable advice. Her insights help both individuals and organizations turn ideas into achievable plans. Suzan is available for podcasts and TV talk shows, where she can offer viewers valuable tools for personal and professional empowerment.

www.ingramcontent.com/pod-product-compliance
Lightning Source LLC
Chambersburg PA
CBHW071949040426
42447CB00009B/1288